MONA LISA'S PAJAMAS

Also by A. Craig Copetas

Metal Men: Marc Rich and the 10-Billion-Dollar Scam

Bear Hunting with the Politburo:
American Adventures in Russian Capitalism

MONA LISA'S PAJAMAS

DIVERTING DISPATCHES
FROM A ROVING REPORTER

A. CRAIG COPETAS

UNION SQUARE PRESS
An imprint of Sterling Publishing Co., Inc.

New York / London
www.sterlingpublishing.com

Mona Lisa's Pajamas would not have been possible without the joyful inspiration of the late Leda Liounis of Sterling Publishing, Co., Inc. Leda was sunlight, held together by laughter that will never cease to echo.

Portions of articles contained herein have been previously published:
© 2008 Bloomberg L.P. All rights reserved. Reprinted with permission. (Articles 1, 2, 3, 5, 6, 9, 11, 13, 14, 15, 16, 19, 25, 26, 27, 28, 29, 37, 38, 40, 41, 42, 43, 47, 48, 49, 50, 51)
© 2008 Dow Jones & Company. All rights reserved. Reprinted with permission. (Articles 4, 7, 8, 10, 12, 17, 18, 20, 21, 22, 23, 24, 30, 31, 32, 33, 34, 35, 36, 39, 44, 45, 46)

Library of Congress Cataloging-in-Publication Data

Copetas, A. Craig, 1951–
  Mona Lisa's pajamas : diverting dispatches from a roving reporter / A. Craig Copetas.
    p. cm.
  Includes bibliographical references and index.
  ISBN 978-1-4027-5764-8 (hc-trade cloth : alk. paper)
1. Voyages and travels—Anecdotes. 2. Travelers' writings, American. 3. Travel writing.
4. Travelers—Anecdotes. I. Title.
  G465.C6465 2009
  910.4—dc22

                                                          2008028667

10   9   8   7   6   5   4   3   2   1

Published by Sterling Publishing Co., Inc.
387 Park Avenue South, New York, NY 10016
© 2009 by A. Craig Copetas
Endpapers and part opener maps © 2009 by Ben Gibson
Distributed in Canada by Sterling Publishing
c/o Canadian Manda Group, 165 Dufferin Street
Toronto, Ontario, Canada M6K 3H6
Distributed in the United Kingdom by GMC Distribution Services
Castle Place, 166 High Street, Lewes, East Sussex, England BN7 1XU
Distributed in Australia by Capricorn Link (Australia) Pty. Ltd.
P.O. Box 704, Windsor, NSW 2756, Australia

Manufactured in the United States of America
All rights reserved

Sterling ISBN 978-1-4027-5764-8

For information about custom editions, special sales, premium and corporate purchases, please contact Sterling Special Sales Department at 800-805-5489 or specialsales@sterlingpublishing.com.

For Matthew Winkler,
no buts about it

CONTENTS

Part Two: The Games Billionaires Play 72

Part Three: Beyond Caviar   178

NOTES FROM
A FOREIGN DESK

Ragu Menon's office smells of boiling lentils. His desk is a piece of plywood lashed to a lopsided fire hydrant alongside a splintered yellow hut on the northeast corner of Jamnal al Rajaj Road and Nariman Boulevard in Mumbai.

In the filthy shanties of India's financial capital, where everyone has a story to tell and a problem to be solved, Menon is one of the more important men in town. He's also one of the finest reporters I've met in my nearly forty years as a foreign correspondent. He writes around twenty pieces each day for his clients, people who can't read or write themselves. His handwritten missives range from love notes to letters home to mundane correspondence. On a dilapidated Godrej Prime typewriter he fills out forms. Housing applications. Legal documents. Today it's an accident report that involves a watermelon, and Menon is letting me question the victim.

"Find out more about the scar," Menon scolds me, pointing to the infected slash on the old man's right cheek. "The ministry wants to know about the wound and cares nothing about the blood on his feet."

Menon's chestnut brown eyes bore into stories that need to be told. His clients can't afford to have his accounts of their dramas be anything less than utterly absorbing.

"I was a newspaper journalist for years, but couldn't take it any longer," Menon says. "Too many rules. Always being told what to write and how to write it made me physically and spiritually ill." He walked out of the newsroom in 1996. He also left his family and friends behind. "I essentially vanished into the streets to write about this," he explains, gesturing toward the long line of customers who pay around twenty-five cents each for their stories to be chronicled on government forms and dusty sheets of wrinkled paper.

A few moments after the old man with the scar—and now a smile—walks away, clutching my description of how a carving knife landed in his face after he slipped on a pile of watermelon seeds, Menon pours two glasses of sweet lime soda and explains why we're here. "Their stories still captivate us, don't they?" he says. "Curiosity, you know what I mean?"

***

Mona Lisa's Pajamas is an assortment of my captivations and curiosities: an accidental report on a high-heeled Italian detective I heard about over coffee in the Piazza Navona in Rome; a tale about bored billionaires who find nothing remarkable in diving beneath the Straits of Hormuz to purchase a luxury submarine; a yarn about the special love between a Russian golf pro and a set of clubs built from the scrapped leftovers of a Soviet nuclear missile aimed at the United States.

"There is no fortress so strong that money cannot take it," Marcus Tullius Cicero reminded the citizens of Rome during his tenure as *quaestor*, a member of the empire's Federal Reserve Board. A good portion of the comedies and tragedies in *Mona Lisa's Pajamas* are monetary dramas reflected through Cicero's trenchant observation. My method is what T. S. Eliot called the "objective correlative," a set of characters and objects contained in a narrative chain of events that terminates in a sensory experience.

In other words, I am a storyteller. I work and live in faraway places that most folks will never have the opportunity to visit. My job is to tell you what I see. You won't catch these sights and sounds on television.

I am your eyes and ears, and that's really all you need to know about me.

The stories in *Mona Lisa's Pajamas* were originally written for delivery to your mailbox or perhaps to your front door, landing with a thud after being hurled by a kid riding a bicycle. Many of these stories, which first appeared in *The Wall Street Journal* and *Bloomberg News,* were further fleshed out and updated for this book. Returning to those past scenes was at times more bitter than sweet.

One of the characters I wrote about, Rick Massagee, was the world's greatest air racing pilot, a man who took me on a harrowing flight to the edge of space so I could experience what he could not explain. He was killed when his plane crashed a few months after we had landed safely in a cow pasture outside Vienna.

After the story ran, I received a phone call from a reader who said Massagee's exploits "carried me from one place to another." The caller did not know that what he had just described was the original meaning of the word "metaphor." In English, this word has come to represent a literary device by which one thing is described in terms of another; but in its Ancient Greek context, it meant "to carry over" or "transport." Today, there are very few American newspaper editors with the patience to grasp that distinction, and they welcome metaphors and allegories on the news pages about as much as they would soggy ink. However, as a foreign correspondent, I've been fortunate enough to work with editors who do understand the difference and realize that each of my stories serves as a ticket for readers to join me on that journey from one place to another.

A great editor is one with the magic to make a reporter believe he's smarter than he thinks he is. The relationship between the irresistible force of a writer and the immovable object of an editor is actually quite simple: a writer is only as good as his editor. And an editor is only as good as his writer.

Ghastly editors want to slap the chip off a writer's shoulder and are quite toxic about it. Great editors slyly reposition the chip and then disappear for cocktails. The coteries of press critics who nowadays monitor America's newsrooms on the Internet and elsewhere pretty much just focus on the noxious ones. So here's a sentence in celebration of the truly great editors at *Bloomberg News* and *The Wall Street Journal* who punched this ticket for your journey: Jim Ruane and James Pressley in Brussels, Jeff Burke and Phil Revzin in New York, Anne Swardson in Paris, David Henry in Frankfurt, and William Ahearn, the leader of the pack.

"Just go there and tell me what you see," says Ahearn, a former executive editor at the Associated Press, who often reads his writers' stories aloud, like lyrics to a song, while walking his dog down a country lane.

"Somebody will always talk to you," Ahearn says, revealing the frustrating paradox about a profession created for the sole purpose of asking people questions they don't want to answer.

At the same time, it's also hard to get folks to shut up. Especially now, in a cyberspace age clogged with blogs, choreographed press events, and celebrities delighted to spin themselves on glossy magazine pages in return for cash payments and story-approval rights. What the moguls and the mighty don't like is being observed in unscripted motion. Once that happens, they become characters on my stage, with no opportunity to change costume.

The dueling demands of editors occasionally provide the intellectual slapstick. Consider the gifted book editors Philip Turner and Leyla Aker, whose combined wit and pencils have greatly helped fine-tune *Mona Lisa's*

Pajamas. In an early version of this introduction, I correctly wrote that Honoré de Balzac was a French writer. "This sounds affected; people are going to know who Balzac was without prompting," Turner replied in the manuscript. Turner is correct, but I've never met a newspaper editor who would assume that all readers know that Balzac was a French writer whose first book was actually a hilarious libretto for a comic opera based on (the English poet and playboy) Lord Byron's yarn about Conrad, The Butt Pirate. The big difference between a newspaper and a book-publishing house is the latter's belief that you already know Balzac is as French as my wife. Ordinarily, I can't afford to take that chance.

In the halcyon days of the newspaper business, before the arrival of Drudge and the dot.coms, the pieces I write were commonly called "Hey, Martha" stories: foreign dispatches that prompted the typical American husband reading the morning paper over a percolated cup of Chase & Sanborn coffee to shout, "Hey, Martha, you gotta read this," across the formica breakfast table as she was pouring syrup over a high-cholesterol hillock of bacon, eggs, and Aunt Jemima pancakes. Although those times, tastes, and technologies are long gone, the thing that fuels my love affair with Martha remains: curiosity about characters distinctive enough to remain evergreen on paper or flashing off a computer screen.

The tools required to chronicle the human comedy in the Internet Age remain low-tech: a Moleskine notebook and a disposable pen. A durable notebook is indispensable. And I'm wary of reporters who use expensive pens; it's been my experience that those wielding snazzy *stylos* believe they're more important than the characters they're writing about. Besides, fountain pens leak at high altitudes and, in a war zone, are the only thing harder to refill than an ice bucket.

On the streets of Old Bombay, Menon mostly uses a pencil.

PART ONE:
MONEY, POWER, GREED, AND A VISIT TO THE TIBETAN PLATEAU

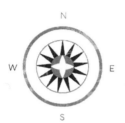

BHUTAN'S GROSS

NATIONAL HAPPINESS

TSHERING JAMTSHO UNCOILS the burgundy robe from around his chin and smiles as the first light of a Himalayan dawn streams through the casement chiseled into a cold stone cell at the Pangrizampa Monastery. Twigs crunch outside, a voice calls out from the dark, and an apprentice enters the chamber gripping the *Mopai*. The ancient 250-page goatskin volume provides trained human calculators, called *tsips*, with intricate mathematical and astronomical formulas to compute a client's fate and fortune before birth, during life, and in the afterlife.

"I am one of the forty calculators," Jamtsho says over cups of the pungent yak-butter tea his predecessors began serving clients here in the Kingdom of Bhutan more than 1,500 years ago. "What is your investment question?" the 25-year-old financial analyst and Buddhist lama asks. "Large numbers of Western businessmen come for our guidance."

Jamtsho says some three hundred American and European bankers and businessmen each year make the grueling journey to Bhutan—a country about the geographical size of Switzerland, with 180 broadband subscribers, five elevators, and seven hundred thousand inhabitants—to have the calculators of Pangrizampa use the hand-scripted *Mopai* as a financial forecasting tool.

"There's nothing extraordinary about this," says Tashi Yezer. He should know. Yezer is the chief executive officer of the Royal Securities Exchange of Bhutan, the country's stock market, where the trading bell rings only on

Tuesdays and Fridays at eleven A.M. "The exchange closes when our four stockbrokers are done," he notes.

Clients' questions for Jamtsho must be specific. Discretion is guaranteed. Fees are modest. Some give food; others offer household goods. Western businessmen mostly pay cash, placing humble handfuls of foreign currency in a glass next to a statue of Buddha and a copper incense burner in the temple's prayer room. It has been enough to help fund construction of the monastery's new annex and dormitory.

"The *Mopai* is a time machine," says Tshering Nidup, a 28-year-old *tsip* who began his studies at the age of six. "It's a portal into all aspects of a visitor's past, present, and future."

And on this day, far beyond the confines of the calculation chamber, another coterie of analysts at the Federal Reserve Board on Constitution Avenue in Washington contemplate the "Green Book," the forecast by the Fed's staff for the $14 trillion U.S. economy. They are watching crude oil surge to a record $110.70 a barrel, the MSCI World Index extend its eleven-percent drop for the year, and a Carlyle Group mortgage-bond fund moving closer to collapse after defaulting on about $16.6 billion of debt. Gold has surpassed $1,000 per ounce for the first time, and the dollar slides to a twelve-year low against all major currencies as the Fed fails to convince investors that emergency funding has the magic to stem $195 billion in subprime-mortgage writedowns and credit losses, and the wherewithal to prevent a recession.

"And you want to know why businessmen are curious about Bhutan?" Yezer says.

"I am not surprised," Jamtsho adds, as the sun illuminates the roaring thunder dragons that decorate the frosty white-and-turquoise calculation chamber. "If they did not come here to ask questions, they would go bankrupt."

Lily Bafandi, director of MB Investment Management AG, a privately held Zurich-based asset-management firm with sixty clients, says there's nothing flaky about asking a group of cheerfully puzzling lamas to help chart a sound investment strategy. "Wall Street market logic is narrow-band," Bafandi says, a few days before trekking back onto the Tibetan plateau with her client book, a laptop, and a satellite phone to stay in touch with global markets. "I do a lot of business from inside tents in the Himalayas. Buddhist mantras program my mind to vibrate in different dimensions, and all of it can drive clients crazy. Some understand what I'm doing; others would love to understand, but they never will."

Fingering a necklace of rudraksha beads, designed to pacify negative energy and provide wisdom, and with three Buddhist prayer mantras playing on her office stereo system, the money manager tries to untangle the perplexities of an investment strategy based on what she calls "Zen economics." "By applying what I learn in Bhutan, money is made beyond conventional market norms," is Bafandi's cryptic explanation. "It's a pilgrimage to discover the knowing and pass it on to clients."

Many institutional investors at first called it witchcraft when Adam Smith said that money made beyond conventional market norms was the work of an "invisible hand." Yet Bhutan prime minister Kinzang Dorji, sitting beneath an embroidered tapestry of Buddha in the country's capital city, Thimphu, says he wouldn't be surprised if Wall Street isn't ready to embrace a capital market that's mostly regulated by entrepreneurial spirits. "We call the economic model 'Gross National Happiness,' and, after thirty years of applying this ancient principle, we've discovered it's more important than Gross Domestic Product," says the prime minister, whose name means "thunderbolt" in the local language, Dzongkha. "GNH is a method of balancing sustainable growth against the often-damaging results of rampant wealth. Keeping that balance is the most difficult challenge facing any global leader."

Just how Western bankers can pull off the multibillion-dollar juggling act is spelled out in a 755-page government memorandum entitled *Gross National Happiness and Development*. "May this volume of papers contribute to the happiness of all sentient beings," runs its epigraph.

For Bank of Bhutan Ltd. chief executive officer Kinga Tshering, preserving the harmony between Bhutan's $1 billion GDP and GNH requires him to get the blessing of calculators before he triggers a major investment project. And that means more to him than ensuring that the local lamas sanctify the bank's new (and only) cash machine.

Similarly blessed are Bhutan's twenty thousand megawatts of clean and renewable hydropower; Tshering says he spends much of his time ensuring that neighboring India's and China's enormous appetites for energy don't end up cursing the national treasure of waterfalls and river basins. "Foreign governments throughout the region are extremely eager to broker deals that will permit them to tap our hydropower," observes Tshering, who prior to joining the bank was CEO of the Bhutan Electric Authority. "But we made a highly conscious decision to judge investments based on Buddhist philosophy and not on free-market materialism. Dumping our resources to the highest bidder for billions and billions of dollars is not our approach. Bhutan's approach to the inevitability and necessity of modernization is to follow a middle path. Intuitive economics. Western banks sacrificed intuition for wealth."

In a land where officials prefer to serve up smiles instead of statistics to prove a point, the prime minister says the best way to comprehend how Bhutan's economic model can be applied as a solution to the current global crisis is to watch a demonstration of archery. It's Bhutan's national sport, and the 57-year-old Dorji is locally renowned as the game's Tiger Woods.

As eleven people jeer "Rab-chay!" (an epithet meaning "one who is unable to father children") at me, the prime minister instructs me to shoot homemade wooden arrows from a bamboo bow at a ten-inch-wide circle from a distance of 164 yards. After the arrows flop to the ground far short of their target, Dorji calls archery a metaphor for GNH: "The distractions were there on purpose to hone intuition, to do what's right under any circumstances." In 1983, he set a world record by shooting thirty-three consecutive bull's-eyes under similar conditions.

"I have no doubt that Western banks consider us to be primitives," Tshering laughs. "By their standards, a profit mandate is more important than a social mandate. The subprime crisis occurred simply because lenders packaged irresponsibility and sold it off to the highest bidder." Amid the market turmoil, Tshering has initiated an ambitious five-year plan to turn his bank into a global player by showing institutional investors the wisdom of making GNH a priority. "I intend to ultimately export Bhutanese bankers to New York and London and have them carry the philosophy of GNH as the model for corporate governance. The last thing I want is Western bankers coming here to modernize us with anything other than technology."

Over at the stock exchange next door, the ground floor of a traditional Bhutanese timber building decorated with lotus flowers, clouds, and phalluses to ward off evil spirits, trading in the sixteen listed companies has stopped and the combined market value holds firm at $25 million.

"We take a holistic approach to capital markets that's missing in the West," Yezer says, focusing on a nearby mandala, a geometric pattern that represents the universe. "Buddhism isn't a religion or an excuse for how we do business, but it is based around a basic economic fact: what goes around, comes around. We call it karma."

TEST PILOTS

"GO **JURASSIC**"

Deep inside the cool labyrinth of a Bombardier, Inc. hangar, a squadron of corporate-jet test pilots has been assembled to study Giovanni Fusco's chickens. The four-pound birds are plucked, primed, and shot at three hundred miles per hour (483 km per hour) into the aluminum fuselage of a new $33.5 million corporate jet, product of the world's third-biggest commercial aircraft maker.

For Bombardier's thirteen test pilots—an unusual fraternity of professional aviators who can spend more than six years breaking in a prototype corporate jetliner before government authorities certify it for sale—understanding the fowl science of Giovanni Fusco is one of many safeguards against a calamity in the air.

"One chicken tells us nothing," explains Fusco, showing off the cannon that rapid-fired waves of defrosted roasters and the occasional Canada goose at the Global 5000, an eight-passenger plane that travels at subsonic speed. The birds are used on the ground because planes can encounter them in flight. "Stress-test specifications require a sustained burst," the aerospace engineer says. "My job is to show the pilots that I've done everything possible to break the plane on the ground before they take to the air."

It's the unthinkable catastrophes that are most worrisome.

"Defining the boundaries of aircraft performance is risky business," says Peter Edwards, president of Bombardier's Aerospace Business Aircraft Division. Sitting in the company's executive conference room in Montreal, he observes that annual profit-and-loss reports don't reflect the guts and grit required to test a jet before corporate clients such as Wal-Mart, DaimlerChrysler, and Microsoft founder Bill Gates decide on the type of bar they want installed in the cabin.

"We've lost pilots," Edwards says. Six Bombardier test pilots have died in two plane crashes over the past fifteen years. He sweeps a hand across the table and pushes aside a pile of analytics that show that his company's twenty-seven thousand aerospace workers make, sell, and maintain sixteen types of aircraft that annually generate more than $11.3 billion in revenue. "Test pilots must have a mind-set of disciplined thinking, because what they go through is the toughest job in the aircraft business. If our aircraft test program isn't the toughest in the world, well, then I'm not doing my job."

Chuck Ellis says the job description is what first attracted him to the experimental cockpit in 1989, because "somebody's got to fly one of these things for the first time." And "I also thought it was cool," he says as he flies a Bombardier Challenger 300 at forty-five thousand feet (13.7 km) above the prairie and the company's flight test center in Wichita, Kansas. A few of the fifteen Bombardier test aircraft are fitted with a ballast tank that holds a thousand pounds of water. Flip an in-flight switch, and the water sloshes around to change the aircraft's center of gravity. And one plane holds "ten thousand pounds of lead bricks, just to see how the aircraft will react to the load, and when the on-board computer fails, it's back to stick and rudder," Ellis says.

Test pilot Doug May points his gloved finger to twelve o'clock high. The light of Earth evaporates into the blackness of space. "Look," the aviator says, banking the Challenger 300 for a better view. "This is why we fly." It was in this sky above the wheat fields where the Learjet flew its maiden voyage on October 7, 1963.

"Oh, it's just nuts what we do," Ellis says. "But there's absolutely nothing on earth to compare with this. Every day, test pilots have new mysteries to solve. You must really love to fly when the on-board computer is switched off and not get upset that you can make more money shuttling business-men as a corporate or commercial airline pilot."

Bombardier says test-pilot salaries are proprietary information. Leo Knaapen, corporate communications director, puts them "in the six-figure range."

Ellis says one reward is membership in what's clearly one of the most exclusive clubs on earth, the Society of Experimental Test Pilots. Fewer than seventy-five of the hundreds of pilots who each year enroll in test-pilot schools manage to graduate with their wings to become SETP members—a few miles short of initiation into the Association of Space Explorers, the club for those who have ventured fifty miles (80 kilometers) or more beyond Earth.

Tuition for the program at such places as the U.S. Air Force Test Pilot School at Edwards Air Force Base in California is about $1 million. "We fly some real hot airplanes, but it's not fun and games," Ellis says. "It's a year of mainlining aspirin and drinking from a fire hose."

After the schooling, Bombardier test pilots meet Daniel Van Rijckevorsel.

"Go Jurassic," barks Bombardier's pilot instructor at twenty-five thousand feet (7.6 km) over Denver in a lacerating wind-sleet storm. The command has nothing to do with dinosaurs. Van Rijckevorsel has shut down most of the cockpit's multifunction display panel, turned off the automatic pilot, and ordered me to manually descend and land a $44 million Global Express.

"This is a very difficult test and many have failed it," Van Rijckevorsel calmly warns as the cockpit fills with sirens and what's left on the computer screen flashes "PULL UP" because the aircraft's "sink rate" is too steep.

"Come on, fly it without the computer, you can do it," encourages Van Rijckevorsel, who earned his wings in 1968 and since then has trained more than a hundred pilots and test pilots. "No automation. No outside help. It's all in the hands," he says as one of the engines flames out.

After narrowly avoiding the peaks of the Rocky Mountains, Van Rijckevorsel switches off the storm, the sirens, and the Rockies. They're all part of the Global Express simulator, a $12 million machine that the industry publication *Aviation Week & Space Technology* says can recreate more emergencies and engine failures in one arcade flight than most pilots will ever see in their careers.

The visual and sensory realism is remarkable, and Van Rijckevorsel says any pilot who can't handle one of his simulations isn't a test pilot. "Pilots need to immediately react to uncertainties, but these days most everything in a plane is predictable. Yet there are always problems between reality and computer calculation. I cause those problems."

H. T. Blasiak, Bombardier's general manager for customer training, calls solving them "playing the piccolo." Blasiak spent twenty-two years flying Voodoo jet fighters and logging twenty-six hours in the cockpit of a Soviet MiG-29 for the Canadian Air Force before joining the company in

1996 to teach some two thousand customers a year how to handle a corporate jet. "In my day it was all Jurassic, hands on stick at 1,200 miles per hour, controlling 16,700 pounds of thrust," he recalls. "You must be confident, coordinated, and technically sound. Life is safer in simulators."

Even with the safety of the simulator, Blasiak says, test-piloting the real thing remains a hands-on business. He flexes his fingers around an imaginary control stick. "You can have all the technology and computerized safety features in the world, but what any corporate jet can do is ultimately found in the feel of the controls," Blasiak says. "You don't fly software."

3

IRAQI BANKERS DODGE
BULLETS AND A
SMOLDERING WHALE

S AMIR AL-ABI, supervising manager of the Southern Region Iraqi Central Bank, trembles in the back seat of a Ford Excursion as outside the window the pop-pop-pop of AK-47 assault-rifle fire spills from one of the eighty-eight banks he has administered since 1995.

"Go! Go! Go!" al-Abi screams, wrapping his arms around his two young sons, pushing them to the floor. "If they see me, they will kill me," he says. "This is now my life."

The driver pulls a hard turn in front of the gutted Rasheed Bank on Revolution Street in Basra. Al-Abi's children are wailing. A gang of women, heads veiled in black scarves, runs past a donkey cart piled with countertops and emptied cash tills. They stumble across the concrete rubble to participate in the pillage of the nearby Rafidain Bank.

"God willing, don't let anyone see me," al-Abi moans. "They will kill us all," he says, over and over. "Their money is gone, and they think I have taken it."

Bankers in oil-rich southern Iraq dodge bullets, not irate creditors. Their flow charts and computer models have been plundered, along with the desks the accountants once sat behind. As politicians and companies elsewhere concoct projects for reconstructing the country, Iraqi business people are wearing flak jackets, and hostile takeovers can be blood-soaked adventures in combat capitalism. Their message: it will take longer than anyone in Washington thinks to rebuild Iraq.

Hurtling past a brace of Challenger tanks that churn up the sidewalk outside the destroyed Southern Central Bank headquarters, the car stops and al-Abi lifts his head to peek out the window at the crowd.

"They're all Ali Babas," al-Abi says, spitting out the expression Iraqis use to describe looters. The machine gunner atop one of the British Desert Rat tanks swivels his weapon toward the Ford, sights the vehicle for a moment, and then turns the barrel on the perhaps two hundred looters rushing in and out of al-Abi's office.

The Ford plows a slow path through the mob of Ali Babas. Some pound the windows with fists. Others hurl stones. They demand water, money, food, medicine, jobs, and telephones. Still on the floor, al-Abi's children nervously chew on Oreo cookies as the vehicle leaves the riot and stops safely behind the Natural History Museum. Thin columns of black smoke—the result of vandals setting fire to a stuffed whale—rise from the museum's shattered windows.

Al-Abi and his sons get out of the vehicle and stand in a puddle of slop. A dead dog floats on the surface. Nearby, children are hauling away buckets of fetid water. The banker gestures at the plundered ruin around him: the smoldering remains of the Sheraton Hotel, cartons of phones churned into plastic mush by tank treads, baking under the heat of the sun.

Three miles (five kilometers) away, black smoke fills the sky. The sprawling headquarters of the Southern Iraqi Oil Co. and its adjacent warehouse complex are in flames. All that's left is the burned-out shell of its tower office block and a few dozen looted heavy-equipment warehouses. The armed Ali Babas have stripped the place bare, right down to the toilets and the oil derricks.

Ten miles (16 kilometers) to the southeast, where more fires rage along the strips of oil pipes that snake across the Al Faw peninsula, anti-tank fragmentation mines and hockey-puck–sized antipersonnel mines encircle the pumping stations.

"So Wall Street wants to know how much it will cost to rebuild Iraq," al-Abi says. The banker doesn't answer the question. Instead, he instructs his sons to say "thank you" for the cookies, and then they walk away, toward the gunfire on Day 17 of the war in Iraq.

Businessmen in Basra say they have no clear idea of how much it will cost to rebuild Iraq's southern oil capital. Any discussion of joint venture and refinancing the oil industry is "premature and foolish," reckons Mustafa al-Badar, the chief engineer and manager in charge of the Iraqi Drilling Co. and the man once in charge of some thirty oil fields south of

Baghdad. He squats atop a sandbagged bunker in front of his office at an oil-field camp outside the nearby town of an-Nasiriyah.

Yet as U.S. troops plow across the Iraqi border, the economic cost of this war escalates on a daily, sometimes hourly, basis. For instance, former U.S. defense secretary James Schlesinger says it will cost the U.S. $27 billion annually for the next several years, and a further $17 billion a year to maintain seventy-five thousand troops in the country to keep order. The calculator at the independent Council on Foreign Relations totals up a minimum of $3 billion.

And as American tanks swarm into Baghdad, Congress is authorizing $2.5 billion in reconstruction funds, or $3.5 billion including ongoing Pentagon spending. The United Nations Development program figures reconstruction will cost a minimum of $10 billion. Yale university economist William Nordhaus says somewhere between $20 billion and $100 billion is required to begin rebuilding the country.

At the same time, al-Badar says, all foreign investment in Iraq is bound to be hobbled by the country's debt: $126 billion of official and commercial borrowing, $320 billion of war-reparation claims following the 1991 invasion of Kuwait, and as much as $100 billion in claims dating from the Iran–Iraq War of 1980–1988.

Central Command spokesman Brigadier General Vincent Brooks, speaking days after the invasion on the issue of reviving Iraq's economy, said, "The commerce can begin." The talk inflames al-Badar. "I can't find food, and America wants to do oil deals," he says.

Indeed, Iraqi businessmen from President Saddam Hussein's mostly Sunni Muslim regime, many of whom would not speak on the record for fear of being attacked by former clients, creditors, and enranged Shiite Muslims, say the country needs to build at least ten power plants to restore full electricity to twenty-five million people before any real commercial activity can begin. At the same time, banking and oil executives in southern Iraq say hospitals need to be constructed in twenty-one cities throughout the country, along with twenty-five thousand schools for some 4.2 million children.

Back in the bunker, Iraq Drilling's al-Badar watches armed looters, driving taxis, buses, and donkey carts, rage through the compound. "They stole my roof," al-Badar says as automatic-weapon fire is heard coming from his company's razed conference room. "Let's get out of here." Ten minutes later, al-Badar is in tears, holed up in the oil-camp home of his senior engineer, Mohammad Ahmed Batoosh. Outside the window, two armed men wrap a heavy chain used to hoist oil-drilling gear around a two-ton generator bolted to a concrete slab. They loop the chain around the hitch of a stolen $750,000 truck once used to haul derricks and drive off, pulling the generator from its moorings and dragging the power station down the road. Sparks fly.

"I heard on the radio the American government expects us to shortly start pumping 2.6 million barrels of oil a day," Batoosh says. "Where do they get these figures? Are they mad? We have three hundred wellheads here and the looters completely destroyed them. From where am I supposed to pump the oil? With what equipment? Who will do the work? Who will give us the money to pay them?"

On the battered coastal road heading south toward the port city of Um Qasr, flames rise from an abandoned oil tanker listing off one of the two plundered oil-terminal ports along the Shatt al-Arab waterway. Dozens of families along the route attempt to bore crowbars into oil pipelines in search of fuel. The ceramic tile billboards that once extolled the rule of Saddam Hussein have been torn down. In their place are coalition signs in English that read "Child Safety. Don't Throw Food and Drink from Vehicles to Children."

That's the least of the looming postwar headaches affecting Nicole Amoroso, a Canadian paid worker in Um Qasr with the charity organization Save the Children. "Rebuilding the economy is important, of course," Amoroso says, "but I don't want to hear about it. One in four children in Iraq are severely malnourished and there are a hundred thousand children in Basra now at risk of contracting cholera. These are the serious statistics that must be addressed before there can be any real economic activity."

"I have four million people in Basra who need water," adds Yousef al-Merag, a physician with the Kuwaiti Red Crescent now working in southern Iraq. "They can't drink oil."

Sean Furlong, an official with the media department at the U.S. government's Office of Reconstruction and Humanitarian Assistance, says the coalition is working to make Um Qasr the yardstick for the rest of the country to follow. "Um Qasr is the reconstruction model city for Iraq," he says.

Um Qasr, the largest of Iraq's six port facilities, is crucial to the reconstruction effort and to restarting oil exports. "The political pressure on us to get this port up and running at capacity is enormous," explains Fergus Moran, who heads Iraq operations for Stevedoring

Services of America, the Seattle-based company that won a $2.9 million contract to repair and manage Um Qasr's twenty-one docks. "The British soldiers who run this place now want to hand it over to me by the end of April. No way that's going to happen," he says. "There's no running water, no grid power, no place to live," Moran explains. "It's going to be six to eight months before we turn off the generators, and the equipment in the mills has been looted."

Looking for breakfast in a garbage dump in Um Qasr, Hasam Yasim, a thirty-eight-year-old economist, says he fails to understand how Western investors will be able to operate in Iraq.

"You cannot build an economy without first having food, health, education, and money," says Yasim, inspecting what's left inside a discarded U.S. military meal packet filled with flies and a portion of uneaten peanut butter. "We have none of that. It takes a great deal of time and money to pump and move oil," he says, putting the partially filled bag of peanut butter in a plastic bag. "What Saddam didn't steal from us has now been looted."

Even the new children's playground built days after the invasion by Leonard Abruzzese, a combat engineer with the U.S. Navy 124 Seabees, was ransacked by club-wielding locals. "There's simply not enough protection and humanitarian aid coming in," Abruzzese says. "The people ask, and the military can't give it to them."

Corporal Davey McReedy of the Royal Irish Guards slaps a fresh magazine into the breech of his rifle. Earlier that day, McReedy helped foil a Basra bank robbery that would have netted looters 700 million dinars, somewhere between $1 million and $2 million, depending on the black-market exchange rate for a currency that the U.S. says will soon be replaced with new notes.

"I don't understand why these people are looting their own future," McReedy says.

Yasim offers an answer. "We have nothing," he says. "This is what people who have nothing must do."

He says the armed Ali Babas have thrown him and hundreds of other people in this town of forty-five thousand inhabitants out of their homes because they have no money to bribe them with. His family now lives in a shanty behind the demolished police station.

Also in Iraq's southern oil patch and appraising the turmoil is Sara Akbar, manager of new business development at the Kuwait Foreign Petroleum Exploration Co. The rebuilding process, she says, will be a "volatile mix" of business, politics, and religion. "How quick the oil sector can be rebuilt depends totally on the will of the Iraqi people and how quick they want to restart production," Akbar says after a visit to the looted Rumaila oil field. "If they don't have the will, it will be a very long time."

Down on the coalition-controlled waterfront, local hired hand Mohammed Neamia Ismail waves an official letter embossed with two British flags and says the military has just cut his salary. Until D-Day plus twelve, U.S. and British forces employed around two hundred Iraqi dock-workers at $2 a day each. Now Ismail's monthly salary of $60 has been slashed to $20. Before the war, he says the Iraqi government paid him the equivalent of about $38 a month.

Ismail's reduced salary, the letter explains in English and Arabic, is "the after-hostility rate," though U.S. general Tommy Franks, U.S. Central Command chief, has yet to declare the war in Iraq over. "Now rates are more conductive to the Iraqi economy," the letter concludes.

"Is this fair?" Ismail asks as British soldiers walk past him carrying plastic lunch plates of hot cheese omelets, tubs of yogurt, and imported vegetables. "I made more money working for Saddam," he says.

Back near the garbage dump and sweating in a black robe, Sheik Mohammad Lazin, the imam of Um Qasr's Shiite mosque and the newly appointed minister of local general services, says he understands financial markets. "I know Wall Street, and all it thinks about is oil, oil, oil," Lazin says. "America freed Iraq from Saddam, but I warn you, all will be quickly forgotten if you continue to put your oil interests ahead of helping us."

Spinning his right forefinger in the steamy air, the cleric adds, "Let your Wall Street bankers and oil traders help the people of Iraq. Only then, when I am satisfied, will I tell the people to speak with you of oil."

HOW TO **SUCC**EED

IN BUS**INESS AND** AVOID

SERIOUS **HEAD TRAUMA**

"**A**LGERIA IS A REALLY NICE PLACE to do business," former British Special Air Service commando Paul Brown tells a study hall of businessmen in Agesta, Sweden. "The bad guys go around cutting executives' heads off with chain saws."

Brown, a trainer for the management consultant firm AKE Ltd., points to a gruesome photograph illustrating to what extent radical Muslims will go to topple the Algerian government. "Now, I can't teach you how to put your head back on," he says. "But I can show you how not to lose it in the first place."

What's going on here in the pastoral countryside outside Stockholm is called "adrenalin management," and the lessons for surviving while doing business in the high anxiety of the "hot zone" are often grisly. The aesthetic of Brown's management discipline is distinctly Omaha Beach, with study aids that include body armor, plasma bags, and Russian Makarov pistols. But the object of the exercise is all business: to turn me into the best-trained manager ever to have established a corporate beachhead.

Founded in 1991 by retired SAS staff sergeant Andy Kain, this U.K.-based company teaches executives how to handle themselves in regions such as the war-ravaged Democratic Republic of Congo or a Latin American jungle rife with terrorists looking to kidnap businessmen. Indeed, during the closing years of the twentieth century, armed guerrillas in the former Zaire killed two

French mining executives at their desks during the overthrow of President Mobutu Sese Seko. In natural-gas–rich Algeria, more than fifty thousand people have been killed during a five-year state of emergency. And along the Oringo River delta in Venezuela, Western oil-company officials are often harassed by bandits and revolutionaries.

"This is a growth business for the twenty-first century," says Kain, who charges more than $2,000 for AKE's intensive five-day course, including dodging simulated explosions from incoming mortar rounds and a bone-rattling seminar on off-road driving while under fire. "CNN can tell you how dangerous it is in the Congo," he explains. "I tell you how to survive the danger."

Another motive for taking the course is more, well, mercenary. Through a member of the Lloyds of London insurance pool, Cassidy Davis Syndicate Management Ltd., AKE graduates have been offered a thirty-percent reduction in hostile-region life and accident insurance coverage. "AKE-trained executives are better equipped to survive hostile environments," explains John van den Bosch, a Cassidy Davis underwriter who specializes in war-zone policies. "The risk is definitely on the increase," he warns. "Our company has paid out on all sorts of war-risk losses, from journalists getting killed to businessmen getting caught up in coups."

The insurance industry has no hard statistics on the number of executives injured or killed while doing business in war zones, but the U.S.-based Committee to Protect Journalists says that an increasing number of journalists are losing their lives covering armed conflicts around the globe.

AKE's corporate boot camp so far has groomed more than 250 combat-ready executives and three hundred journalists now stationed in Africa, Russia, Latin America, Southeast Asia, and the Middle East. Many of the journalists are women, but all of the executives are men, including mining engineers, geologists, lawyers, and accountants. And don't suggest to Kain that the idea of an AK-47–toting actuary sounds like the plot of a bad Hollywood action movie.

"The businessmen we train have to go into these areas to make deals during the worst conditions imaginable," he fires back. "You're usually shot because of what you wear when entering a situation that exists in various degrees of chaos. We teach you what to wear, the difference between artillery and shrapnel." But for the wandering global manager, does understanding the muzzle velocity of a howitzer contribute to tightening the bottom line? "Yes," Brown says. "Businessmen have been going into hostile regions for years, and our job is to enhance their awareness by translating SAS survival skills to the corporate population."

Although Kain says AKE's corporate client list must remain secret for security reasons, the deputy CEO of a large British industrial firm with substantial interests in Asia says the course provided him with "very useful, streetwise training that sharpened my skills in dangerous areas."

The course offers no gimmicks, and AKE's six former SAS trainers are clearly in a position to hone one's survival skills. Mustered in 1942 to operate deep behind German lines, the SAS still is one of the world's best-trained fighting units. Kain served with SAS teams in the Falkland Islands war, Northern Ireland, and "a lot of jungles I can't tell you about."

Adds the jovial but stern Brown, "Globalization is the buzzword in business these days, and the SAS has been into the globalization business since the beginning of World War II. You can't fight a war from a desk, and you can't get raw materials out of the Congo over a fax machine. Somebody has to go in. We make sure the ones tapped for the turmoil don't go in naked and helpless."

But don't arrive at an AKE management training seminar dressed for a shareholder's meeting. And don't expect to leave with a fancy book of diagrams or aphorisms. The only reading here is a sixteen-page pamphlet titled *Surviving Hostile Regions*. Printed on indestructible paper used by the military, the text explains booby traps, land mines—and how to ensure that a recoilless rifleman doesn't think your briefcase is a surface-to-air missile.

"It's not funny. *You* know what you are," Kain says. "But what do you look like from two hundred meters? Shape, shine, shadow, silhouette, movement. That gets you killed."

And should an executive end up on the wrong end of an artillery barrage, the field reference supplements a rigorous course-load on grave medical emergencies such as major bleeding, amputation, and compound fractures. "Our training is based on the assumption that a wounded businessman can be medevaced to a hospital within forty-eight hours," says Brown, who was an SAS combat medic for twenty years.

AKE says its training has saved the lives of businessmen and journalists working in Bosnia and Algeria. In 1996, near a Rwandan refugee camp in Goma, Zaire, one such incident was captured on video by a Swedish television crew. The tape shows TV Four cameraman Bengy Stenvak getting shot in the leg, and reporter Stefan Borg using the emergency medical techniques Brown taught him to save his colleague's life. "The film is an advertisement we'd rather not have," Kain says. "But it does prove a point."

Kain asks students to recall their own hot-zone experiences as part of the curriculum. At first blush, such discussions might come across like tall tales spun around a campfire. But the goal is to analyze individual encounters with chaos and to learn from them.

According to Kain, the typical danger-zone businessman is an adventurer who finds it rewarding to make deals under the worst conditions imaginable. "That's a big problem, too," he says. "They enjoy the risk, but really aren't prepared for it."

Kain will fail those students who he believes have not learned the basics. Although no one has ever flunked, he has expelled a few executives who approached the seminar as an "action school."

"I won't allow anyone to graduate this course without having learned it from top to bottom," Kain says. "Their lives and the lives of their co-workers depend on it. I don't guarantee this course will save your life. It will enhance your ability to survive."

STANDING GUARD WITH

CAMP HEIDI'S FINEST

THOMAS CADUFF HAS LOST HIS KNIFE. As a rule, that's not tantamount to crisis at ICN Group, the privately owned Swiss asset-management group he's run for more than two decades. However, for the Swiss Army, in which Caduff is a part-time captain, showing up at Camp Heidi without the regulation blade in his pocket could be viewed as a court-martial offense. The command center, named after the storybook goat girl, is charged with guarding the 2,100 global business and political leaders gathered a yodel away in Davos for the annual World Economic Forum.

"Red Swiss Army knives sold in shops are for tourists," says Caduff as an infantry platoon unleashes automatic-weapon fire on a hillside carpeted with cardboard targets. "Ours are silver, and they don't come with a corkscrew," he hollers over the barrage. "Can't drink wine while on duty." He must have left his knife at home, he says.

While the shopkeepers of Davos have stocked their shelves with the singular souvenir of a Swiss holiday, Caduff says the 1,500 soldiers the government has mobilized at a cost of $9.5 million would prefer WEF visitors to go home with the message that the Swiss Army is ready to roll in the war on terrorism. It is prepared to protect both the visiting moguls and the parka-clad protesters descending on the normally placid ski town of thirteen thousand inhabitants.

"Davos is an extremely rich terrorist target and a complex military operation," Caduff says, slinging an ammunition belt into one of the brigade's official command vehicles—the same black Audi Quattro he drives to the office in Zurich each day. "The WEF is the highest concentration of VIPs in the world, and right now we have more soldiers than trees encircling this town." For Switzerland's 346,500 part-time soldiers, the WEF's return to Davos is an opportunity. They can prove that an army primarily comprised of off-duty bankers, bureaucrats, and twenty-year-olds has what it takes to join the battle alongside the superpowers. "Protecting Davos is the absolute real thing for this army," explains Major Markus Ernst, an account controller at UBS AG, who is now patrolling a snow bank with a 9mm SIG Sauer pistol strapped to his hip.

Like all Swiss irregulars, Ernst each year must spend around twenty-one days away from his desk, shedding his suit for green fatigues. It's the law. Ernst estimates he spent nine hundred days during the 1990s as a soldier. "Fortunately I'm not an analyst, so I don't have to wear my gun to the office," the banker deadpans. Still, Ernst says Operation Minerva, the code name for the Davos deployment, is no stroll in the Alps. "It's vital we show the world that we can handle this mission," Ernst says. "It's the most important mission in the history of the Swiss Army."

Founded in 1291, the Swiss Army can trumpet itself as one of the world's oldest military forces, once famed for its prowess with pikes and the ability to use crossbows to shoot apples off the heads of children. Now, Caduff rues that WEF participants will mistakenly identify his troops with a line of Swiss Army brand "lifestyle tools" such as wristwatches, bicycles, briefcases, and the ubiquitous Swiss Army knife, which can cost up to $85 with a laser pointer. "The Army has no commercial relationship with those products," Caduff explains. "We don't sue those who use our name, because it's good public relations and because we are a very laid-back army."

And that's a problem for Sergeant Sandy Lucchia, one of Switzerland's 3,500 full-time professional soldiers involved in Operation Minerva. Lucchia's lumbering squad of weekend warriors is bunked down in an elegant chalet hotel in the middle of a snow-dusted vineyard. The door to the wine cellar is bolted shut and the only indication of a military presence is a green camouflage net draped over a hallway.

Outside, in a frosty parking lot, Lucchia rallies his youthful soldiers in a circle and brandishes what to the uninitiated appears to be a robusto-sized Cuban cigar. He describes it as *Gemeines Zwang-Hold*, "a mean wood stick," and says it's one of the Army's weapons against threats at the WEF. "This defensive weapon is applied on acupuncture points and immediately immobilizes an attacker," Lucchia says, using the stubby stick to take down a conscript, who is now whinnying in pain. "The soldiers mobilized for the WEF are kids who haven't seen any training for eleven months," Caduff says. "Every Swiss soldier takes his gun home, but until this week, they have been in the basement, leaning against the wine bottles." Still, Major Silvio Bianchi insists his men are "armed, loaded, and in the mountains" ready to thwart would-be saboteurs. "Our jets are flying to protect Davos air space from being entered by planes loaded with explosives," he explains.

On the ground, in a hamlet fortified to protect the power station that feeds electricity to Davos, snowmobile pilot Captain Boris Vollenweider blasts off with weapons and a passenger to patrol the peaks. He immediately fails to negotiate the first ridge in his path, sending the machine and all aboard tumbling down a ravine. "I'm so sorry," Vollenweider says, heaving the snowmobile off his passenger as a helicopter flutters in the distance. "We have very good doctors," the Swiss Army recruitment officer adds. "Would you like to see one?"

Back at the Army shooting gallery built into the foot of Mont Calanda (also known to locals as "Machine Gun Mountain" because errant gunfire over the years has wiped out the foliage that once grew above the bunkered range), Bianchi leans against his polished BMW station wagon. "There's violence in the air," he muses beneath the full moon. "We think there could be serious problems this weekend in Davos, and we are prepared for any action."

When it comes time for dinner, it's an army that resembles nothing less than a pot-luck gathering of corporate executives. During a meal for senior regimental officers attached to Operation Minerva, for instance, Captain Peter Oetil toted along a ream of paper mats sponsored by the Graubuendner Kantonalbank and festooned with the institution's logo. "We all try to bring something from work with us that everyone can use," says Oetil, the bank's senior compliance officer. "I brought the mats."

BMW brought the cars. At Camp Heidi, snuggled against an ammunition truck and surrounded by sentinels, a sport utility vehicle with military plates features a sticker on its rear window that reads: "Sponsored by BMW."

Regimental commander Major Juerg Kessler, the chief field officer in charge of Operation Minerva and the manager of the Zurich airport, bristles at the popular notion that his troops have thrown a *cordon sanitaire* around Davos just to guard the wealthy. "Our mission is not to protect rich and famous people," he explains over the regimental dinner of canned corn and spaghetti. "We intend to ensure that those coming to Davos to protest are protected and to defend their right to protest," Kessler says of the demonstrators who march through the village on an annual basis. "The task of the Swiss Army is not to protect globalization."

And as all trains to Davos must pass through the city of Chur, Swiss Army quartermasters are hoping both backpacking protesters and the corporate titans they are coming to rail against stop to shop at the genuine Swiss Army surplus store. "There are a number of interesting items on offer," Caduff says, walking through aisles of bins bulging with authentic Swiss Army horseshoes (2 francs per hoof), Swiss Army stew ladles (2 francs a spoon), and a Swiss Army hand-crank meat grinder (35 francs, and it's portable).

"I'm buying a set of Swiss Army bowls," says Maya Muzzarelli, a Swiss housewife here on vacation with her husband and two young daughters and who plans to march in Davos with the protesters. "They're a bargain at 5 francs. Perfect feeding bowls for our dogs."

Don't ask the clerk behind the register for a real Swiss Army knife, however. "You need to join the army to get one of those," Caduff says. All soldiers must pay nine francs for theirs. Cash only.

AN HONORABLE AND
ANCIENT SOLUTION TO
BOARDROOM DISPUTES

O N AN ICY ENGLISH MEADOW called Dead Man Heath, the fiery blasts of dueling pistols pierce the dawn fog, illuminating the crows that peck for their breakfast beneath the thorn bushes. The birds caw as David Spittles, a retired engineer, takes thirty seconds to reload and fire his $3,000 antique muzzle-loader while his opponent fumbles to stuff black powder and a lead ball into a similarly cumbersome nineteenth-century weapon.

"You lose," says the European Flintlock Dueling Pistol champion, calculating the non-lethal outcome from paper targets pocked with bullet holes.

"It's probably not wise to go back to live targets to conclude disagreements over women and gambling debts," Spittles reckons with a laugh. "But dueling was a legal means of settling business arguments and could possibly serve as a modern solution for boardroom disputes. It certainly would be cheaper and more effective than using lawyers."

Indeed, during the nineteenth century, the Paris newspaper *Le Figaro* ran a daily column on duels, recording more than 150 "important" shootouts between bickering businessmen.

At the Swiss headquarters of Poudrerie d'Aubonne SA, the world's largest maker of dueling-pistol powder, company officials say they're prepared for a return to dueling as a form of arbitration. The privately held Poudrerie already sells annually forty-five tons of black powder to 150,000 duelists in sixty countries.

"Business is booming," company President Claude Modoux says, walking past the cows grazing on the company's 861,000-square-foot (80,000-square-meter) site along the western shore of Lake Geneva. "I'm in the civil-explosives business," he explains amid the isolated wood huts and ten-ton iron rollers that since 1853 have been used to grind sulfur, charcoal, and potassium nitrite into dueling-pistol powder. "I also make dynamite, detonator cord, and nitroglycerin pills for people with heart ailments, but my love is black powder."

Modoux loved the product so much that he bought the factory from the Swiss government in 1996 and immediately filmed a corporate promotional video that features dueling footage. "The government wanted to close down the powder mill and spend four million francs to make the land environmentally friendly," Modoux says. "I paid them one franc and kept alive the tradition of Poudrerie d'Aubonne."

A handful of other companies in the U.S. and Europe, such as Goex Inc. of Doyline, Louisiana, continue to make black powder to fulfill annual global sales of some three hundred tons at about $9 million. But champion shooters say Modoux's powder is the "grand cru" of duel fuel, and competitively priced at $15 a pound.

"Modoux's product is quite economical," says Spittles, who each year ignites about six poounds of the stuff to fire six thousand homemade lead balls.

"Dueling is a rather dashing sport," muses John Miller, executive vice president of the U.S. National Muzzle Loading Rifle Association, the group that keeps the European sport of dueling alive in the New World. "Too bad it's such a politically incorrect pastime."

Technically, there may be little reason to believe dueling is on the cusp of a renaissance. According to Judge Robert Sack, who sits on the bench at the U.S. Second Circuit Court of Appeals in New York, the genesis of many modern laws grew out of the context of gentlemen preserving their honor with pistols. "That calls dueling to mind," Sack says. "Originally, some states codified their libel and slander laws as anti-dueling statutes."

"The last of the official real bullet duels were in the 1840s among insulted military officers and men of commercial means," said Alan Overton, an official at the Muzzle Loaders Association of Great Britain. "Gradually, the sport was overtaken by political correctness, but Modoux hasn't let that affect his production methods."

Modoux employs a 700-year-old recipe to cook up five grades of black powder that can fire anything from Napoleon's cannons to a $35,000 pair of eighteenth-century flintlocks made by English dueling-pistol master Robert Wogdon.

"Over half of our annual production of eighty tons is either 0-grade or 1-grade and goes to duelists," Modoux says. "The rest is for muzzle-loading rifles, shotguns, and artillery." Stroking his goatee, Modoux says his powder is so popular that plans are afoot to increase production capacity beyond a hundred tons a year. "You can shoot a gun a dozen times with my powder before having to clean it," he says, leaning against one of the wooden water mills that power the grinders. There's little metal about. Just one stray static burst, he says, could blow the factory across the border into France.

Modoux says his secret ingredient is the Serbian and Slovenian buckthorn alderwood his six *poudreries*, or powder specialists, transform into charcoal. "This wood is collected and stripped of bark by the Gypsies who live in Balkan forests," the powder purveyor says, slapping two hands against a 150-cubic-meter wall of wood that has been aged for two years and is now ready for the oven.

The formula is precise. Workers tightly wrap two-cubic-meter fagots and allow them to cook in furnaces heated to 572 degrees Fahrenheit. The bundles pop out eight hours later and look like enormous servings of burnt roast beef.

Master blender Michel Fiaux conducts a taste test. "A good dueling-pistol powder is like a fine cuisine," Fiaux says, letting his tongue savor the flavor of a charcoal nugget. "It's all in the ingredients," Modoux adds. "The relationship between our ingredients is intimate."

The charcoal is blended with sulfur and potassium nitrite, pulverized into the various grades beneath the creaking iron rollers, and then scattered on wood trays to mature for twenty-four hours. Inhaling the aroma of the final product, Fiaux wets his finger and takes a final taste. "There are three important things in life," Fiaux declares. "Wine, women, and black powder."

Modoux says the three tons of muzzle-loading cannon powder he sells each year contain from 470 to 520 grains per gram. "But achieving 0-grade dueling pistol powder is an art," he adds, sifting a hand through a mound of the explosive talc. "This contains a hundred thousand grains per gram and has absolutely no dust."

Dust often spelled death on the field of honor, according to British duelist Ken Hocking, an engineer at Unilever Ltd. in charge of building ice-cream factories. "Antique dueling-pistol collectors go to the auction houses looking for big brand names like Purdey, Wogdon, and the Manton brothers," Hocking says. "The cost of a dueling pistol has absolutely nothing to do with the accuracy of the shot. When the rich drop dead on the dirt, the most they can hope for is someone saying they had the good taste to use a Purdey pistol."

Two-time U.S. dueling-pistol champion Mike Yazel says it's a shame that most collectors are afraid to fire their pistols. "The old equipment is unique and lends to the mystique," says Yazel, proprietor of an orthopedic surgical-instrument workshop in Mentone, Indiana. "Muzzle-loading duelists are warmer and fuzzier than any other kind of shooters."

Leaning against the stuffed head of an Azerbaijani goat in the antique-gun department of the London auction house Bonhams, dueling-pistol specialist David Williams says most of his customers prefer to keep their "gentlemen's weapons" safely tucked in the original case. In 1996, Williams set a world record by selling a pair of matched dueling pistols made in 1765 by master gunsmith Henry Hadley for $309,207. The eighteenth-century price tag: £10 a pistol.

"The value of antique dueling pistols is greatly enhanced if there's provenance to prove they were once used in a duel," Williams says of a business that approaches $500,000 a year in sales. "Very few buyers actually fire the weapons. The investment could blow up in their face."

Even so, the British Code of Duel of 1824 is rather specific about how those injured in a "tradesman's duel" must act: "Treat the matter coolly and, if you die, go off with as good grace as possible."

According to an ad in an early-twentieth-century copy of *Olympic Review*, the official publication of the International Olympic Committee, duelists were encouraged to sharpen their aim with a blast of Benedictine liqueur before firing at human silhouettes. Between 1896 and 1912, the IOC included dueling pistols as a medal sport: five points for a thorax shot, three points for a head or groin shot, and two points for a knee.

"Olympic duelists wore shirts," grouses duelist Roy Ricketts, who's also treasurer of the Muzzle Loaders Association of Great Britain. "In a real duel, you kept reloading and shooting until someone went down. You shot bare-breasted because dirty shirts infected wounds and caused gangrene."

According to statistics published in the British Code of Duel, the odds were six to one against being wounded, and fourteen to one against being killed in a duel. Duelists pulled the trigger at the drop of a handkerchief. Anyone who fired before the signal was prosecuted for murder. In Britain and the U.S., the distance was twelve yards. French duelists paced off at twenty-five meters.

Hot-air balloon duels were the only exception, according to David Mayrall, a historian for the Muzzle Loaders Association. "French businessmen were fond of taking to the air and shooting at each other with blunderbusses," Mayrall says, recounting the story of two executives who settled a contract dispute while floating over Paris in 1870.

Back in the gun room at Bonhams, Williams cocks the trigger of a brass-barreled flintlock blunderbuss valued at £900. "Dueling from balloons with blunderbusses," Williams says. "That shows style."

FEARLESS FANS OF

FRENCH BERETS FIGHT

BASEBALL CAPS

HOLD ON TO YOUR HAT. That's precisely what Chrystel Baudorre did when Fidel Castro's office phoned her one frosty November morning back in 1997 as she was contemplating the dismal future of her company's 200-year-old beret business. "The Cubans wanted a hundred thousand Che Guevara berets to commemorate the anniversary of their revolution," recalls Baudorre, one of the two remaining beret-makers in France. But the Cuban government haberdasher had presented the newly appointed marketing director of Blancq-Olibet SA with a dilemma. "He wasn't sure if Che had worn a civilian beret with the squiggle on top or a military beret without the squiggle," Baudorre explains. "He wanted me to find out and to see if they might sell."

It was a daunting request, and an appeal Baudorre would leverage to declare war on the omnipresent U.S. baseball cap. Although John Wayne had sported the floppy wool hat without the so-called *cabillou* in the 1970s hit movie *The Green Berets,* and The Artist Formerly Known as Prince had pranced around the bandstand singing about the squiggled version in his popular music video on raspberry berets, Baudorre had the sales figures to prove that the world was no longer really hip to the once-jazzy shepherd's cap that the Maquis had turned into the symbol of the French Resistance.

"Can the beret ever again be cool is a tough question," muses jazzman Mike "the Doctor" Zwerin, who played trombone with Miles Davis's Birth of the Cool Band but always has taken the stage wearing his signature fedora. "I think the beret market went out with Dizzy Gillespie."

Indeed, back in the 1950s and 1960s, while Gillespie blew his horn and Guevara dashed around Africa and Latin America in his natty Bakarra Grande Luxe, France boasted twenty-two beret manufacturers selling millions of their pancake-shaped toppers to a diverse global market that included American beatniks and trendy Marxist revolutionaries. But since the demise of agitprop chic and an influx of cheap Asian and Eastern European knockoffs to fill Eiffel Tower tourist stalls, Baudorre and her staff in the hamlet of Nay have found it a tough task to target customers, outside of a few pricey French fashion houses such as Chanel and a rapidly decreasing number of army quartermasters.

Yet Baudorre remained intrigued by the Cuban offer, and her research suggested that Guevara's berets were French in origin and likely made by Blancq-Olibet. The Cubans were apparently ecstatic with her discovery that Guevara favored the company's looser-fitting model with the *cabillou* for a night on the town, and the smaller and tighter military beret for jungle fighting. So Baudorre directed her loomers to knit a thousand military and civilian berets embroidered with the gold star of the Cuban flag. "I gather Castro loved the samples," she says. But the Cuban government couldn't afford the $296,704 needed to purchase the hundred thousand berets. Stuck with a warehouse of authentic Che beret samples and facing a global market more interested in Red Man Chewing Tobacco baseball caps, Baudorre decided it was time to lift a few tactics from Guevara's *Fundamentals of Guerrilla War*. "The essence of guerrilla war against billions of baseball caps is to contradict the defeatist attitude of the beret," she says.

Armed with an MBA from the École Superieure de Commerce in Bordeaux and "something very deep in my French heart for the beret," Baudorre began wearing a Che beret on trips outside the Bearn region. Heads turned, word spread, and phone orders poured into the firm's Pyrenees Mountain mill house from all over the country. Blancq-Olibet president Jean Olibet says Baudorre prankishly sparked the "most unlikely corporate comeback in capitalist history" by rallying his firm's sixty employees into launching an assault on the ubiquitous American baseball cap.

"There's no question that Che Guevara and Fidel Castro saved the beret side of my company," says Olibet, whose firm in 1817 began making fezzes but diversified into Gore-Tex skiwear about fifty years after the bottom dropped out of the tarboosh market. "I was making only a few berets on the day the Cubans called. Now we make 1,500 berets each day, but we're trying to gear them toward a more pacifist market." Nonetheless, Olibet says he's just begun to fight. Though his current production of some five million berets annually is hardly an immediate threat to the baseball-cap industry, the blue-eyed beret boss says his company last year racked up over a million francs in beret sales and that his forces are on the move.

"There are no secrets to beret-making," says Bernard Fargues, the president of Olibet's only French competitor, Beatex SA. Though Fargues also comes to market with an impressive set of revolutionary credentials, like the circled A symbol of the anarchist movement some kids spray-painted on the walls around his factory in nearby Oloron, his strategy is to generate sales through cute catalog photos of babies wearing berets. However, "with all the baseball caps, the beret business isn't what it used to be," he says.

But Olibet's secret weapon in his struggle against the baseball cap is Lou, a new product line that Baudorre plans to take behind enemy lines in the U.S. Inspired by the Che beret, the Lou marketing campaign is based on festooning company logos on pure wool berets, and then persuading skeptical corporations to oust their nylon promotional caps in favor of berets. "At first, the corporate bosses thought a beret was too much a caricature and didn't dare buy it," Baudorre says. "I'm still convincing CEOs that berets create a happier atmosphere than baseball caps." In Europe, Operation Lou so far has mobilized some thousand corporations, including the Japanese auto maker Toyota and the French bank Caisse d'Épargne. Around 12,000 francs gets you three hundred logoed berets and free passes to the museum. The larger "alpine hunter" beret, the cut favored by Pablo Picasso, costs $50 a pop-top, with the high-end, silk-lined model with leather headband going for about $100 each.

"American corporations are the big enchiladas," says Billy Abrams, president of Tam-Beret Selections Inc., the South Carolina outfit that supplied Chi-Chi the Chihuahua with the berets he wore in television commercials for Taco Bell. Abrams's Internet hat company sells around 4,500 berets in the U.S. annually. Though all of them, including Chi-Chi's, were made in the Czech Republic, he says, that's only because the French embassy in New

York told him that France no longer made berets. "I don't know what's with those French guys," he says. Currently forging an alliance with Olibet's forces in the Pyrenees, Abrams vows to establish a fifth column on American soil "to eliminate corporate baseball caps once and for all."

Back at the induction center and smiling at a sexy pinup of Marlene Dietrich in a beret, Olibet says he's mystified by the French government's refusal to hoist the beret as another symbol of his country's stubborn defiance against global conformity to American culture, particularly since French historians claim the American game of Frisbee was stolen from the twelfth-century French children's pastime *beretolle,* or beret tossing. Olibet suspects there's a hidden discrimination against the hat because of the misconception that berets are Basque in origin and not really French at all. "We Bearnese were the only ones who made berets," he says proudly. "Though I believe the Basques had most of the sheep." But the politics of panache are a trifling matter for François Dupuis.

"Those interested in berets would be better off slapping a pork chop on their head," says Dupuis, the retired editor of the French newsweekly *Le Nouvel Observateur* and author of *Naguerre,* a beret-less bestseller on life in a French village on the eve of World War II. To be sure, Dupuis has good reason to grouse about his poster-boy status among the beret crowd. He's the main character in a popular *Le Nouvel Observateur* cartoon in which the illustrator Wiaz regularly depicts his pal wearing a beret and waving a baguette at political and cultural injustices.

Fingering his walrus moustache, the jovial Dupuis thunders, "I hate berets and none of my characters will ever wear one." And it's best not to mess with Dupuis, the only Frenchman ever to have been a member of the elite U.S. Army Special Forces Unit known as the Green Berets. "They needed someone who spoke French," says Dupuis, who holds dual French and American citizenship. "I wouldn't wear the beret then, and I won't wear one now." He pauses. "But let's not forget, the beret is certainly much smarter than those stupid American baseball hats."

***

Perhaps it will come as no surprise that beret boosters say the hat resurrected by Che Guevara is mired in a politically charged fashion dispute that stretches back to the Old Testament. Legends told here near the Grotto Massabielle, where in 1858 Bernadette Soubirous reportedly saw eighteen apparitions of the Virgin Mary, say that Noah emerged after forty days aboard the Ark wearing the world's first beret, which he apparently made from the felted wool of his ovine passengers. "Unfortunately, the writers of the Bible failed to include the story and the legend fails to tell us how the hat came about," says Olibet.

The first recorded beret sighting took place in 1461, shortly after a Bearnais stonemason accessorized the head of a statue with one on a thirteenth-century church in nearby Bellocq. According to the government documents of the time, France garnered valuable tax revenue from beret sales, specifying that "any beret-maker displaying his berets for sale at market shall pay one sol morlan for placement and table rights."

But regardless of historical stereotypes, Olibet says the days are long gone when beret sales were linked to the proverbial Frenchman sucking a maize-wrapped Gitane cigarette and throwing back a tumbler of calvados with his morning coffee. What remains essential, however, is manufacturing berets with the squiggle on the top, despite the fact that the *cabillou* is an absolutely meaningless appendage. "The *cabillou* is there because that's where the women started the process of knitting berets by hand," Olibet explains. "Mechanized looms eliminated the *cabillou* over a hundred years ago, but if we don't sew one on, the beret won't sell."

8

FORCING THE FRENCH

TO WALK

OVER HOT COALS

RIAN VAN DER HORST stands before a dozen French executives in a
sun-soaked classroom near the Bastille, fomenting a corporate revolution. "The global market wants results first and reasons second," the
American management consultant asserts, "and French managers still want
explanations first and results second." He chides his pupils, suggesting they
have been brainwashed into thinking a business theory must be "intellectually
complex." Nothing, he suggests, could be further from the truth.

Adjusting his glasses, Van der Horst pauses. He scans the men and
women seated around the horseshoe-shaped table, waiting for someone to
defend France's philosophical approach to problem-solving. No one does.
Van der Horst nods and continues. "The French tendency to fall in love
with abstractions makes them bad managers," he says. "It's why the entrepreneurial revolutions that took place in America and Britain during the
1980s passed France by."

Those are usually fighting words in France, where most of the levers of
corporate power are still pulled by an elite cadre of professionals who were
taught at top French schools to apply the same set of abstract management
principles to any enterprise, be it a computer company or a sewage system.

But instead of quarreling with Van der Horst, thousands of French executives have happily forked over more than $6,000 apiece to hear two weeks' worth of heresy at his management school, Repere SA.

The success of Repere says much about the state of French business today. Van der Horst is one of at least a dozen American management consultants who are suddenly in hot demand here, as the country struggles through massive economic problems and jarring restructuring. With their unemployment rate stuck at 12.8% and globalization putting their businesses under severe pressure, the French yearn for panaceas.

And the Americans are offering plenty of corporate cure-alls, from Total Quality Management to Situational Management, each with its own jargon. There are "motivational messages" and "benchmarks for products and personnel." There are even classes that aim to hone executives' awareness by training them to literally walk barefoot on hot coals.

Not all the American techniques border on the bizarre, of course. But they certainly are popular: U.S. firms control eighty-two percent of the $53 billion international management consulting market, according to a report issued by Alpha Publications U.K., a management-research group. "Their achievements are comparable to Hollywood's in its own sphere," it says.

The report is based largely on the stunning international growth of big U.S. consulting firms such as Andersen Consulting and McKinsey & Co., both of which have sizable operations here in Paris. But it took time for these Yankee notions, both mainstream and outré, to catch on in France, where Anglo-Saxon methods generally have been anathema to the management techniques expounded at the prestigious École Nationale d'Administration.

Charles de Gaulle established the ENA in the wake of World War II to revive the country's civil service after the Nazi occupation and the Vichy government had ravaged the French bureaucracy. Ever since, ENA and its older sister schools, the École Normale Superieure and the École Polytechnique, have selected and groomed the best and the brightest to manage French interests at home and abroad. Their training is rigorous, technocratic, and highly French.

The schools hand down principles that are at odds with the free-market theory Adam Smith set out in the eighteenth century—and can be traced back even further, to Jean-Baptiste Colbert, a seventeenth-century French minister whose name is still synonymous with state central planning. That schooling paid off handsomely in helping to rebuild the country after World War II. But along the way, many management consultants say, it created a high caste of leaders bent on control and unprepared for the rigors of a multicultural global marketplace that doesn't conform to French assumptions.

The French "management style is a factor for the high unemployment rate," argues Gerry Welker, an independent financial management consultant who works with large French brokerage houses such as Cecar SA. "It's very clear that inflexible, hierarchical systems don't allow companies or individuals the space needed for growth."

French managers these days talk like their Anglo-Saxon counterparts, calling for layoffs and restructurings that could unlock shareholder value. Some French companies over the past few years have recast their corporate hierarchies to accommodate the rapid-fire temperament of the global market. Restructuring at tire-maker Michelin SA and the car-parts giant Valeo SA, for example, has paid off with savvy new management teams and successful moves into fresh markets, including Asia and North America. And the French luxury business thrives on quirky personalities and quick decision-making: the sector today employs some 192,000 workers, is racking up average annual growth rates of at least twenty-five percent, and sells more than $21 billion worth of goods each year, rivaling the annual sales of the French aerospace industry, the Finance Ministry reports.

But silk ties and Dior dresses "do not an economy make," says Michel Castera, a former president of Pechiney Aluminum France SA. A polytechnician, Castera now serves as an adviser on French management issues at both Coopers & Lybrand and the Harvard Business School. "French managers are too monocultural in that they're unable to visualize what's happening outside of this country," he says. "France's success in the luxury-goods business is the icing on top of a cake that's not really there."

Besides, many French executives still tend to hand down decisions in fiats that alienate workers. These knee-jerk decisions, French executives say, are the result of French education, which has created a management corps that's unable to express itself. "The first thing you're taught at school in France is how to shut up," says Marie-Annick Flambard-Guy, a partner in the French executive-search firm Rossignol, Tod & Associates. "The second thing you're taught is how to deal with theories, when you should be taught how to speak your mind and deal with personalities."

Enter Van der Horst's specialty: Neuro Linguistic Programming. The French have taken to NLP, as it's called, the way they took to Jerry Lewis:

both fill a curious niche in the French psyche. NLP provides a handy bridge between the theoretical and the practical. "The structure of NLP is analytical," says NLP booster Linda Baker, training manager at Kodak-Pathé SA, the French marketing division of Eastman-Kodak Inc. "And the French are very enthusiastic about analysis. So NLP is by design a ready-made system that allows the French to clearly focus on an objective and what needs to be done to reach it."

Since 1985, some ten thousand executives from more than 330 companies—including Michelin, Sodexo SA, Castorama SA, and Glaxo Pharmaceutical SA—have signed up for Repere's intensive, two-week-long NLP training program. The goal, says Van der Horst, is to create a new generation of French managers with the skills to improve corporate communication, enhance productivity, and generate customer satisfaction.

NLP came out of southern California in the early 1970s, back when an upheaval in American society led to a breakdown in communications. The Vietnam War was winding down, psychedelic drugs were the thing, and computers were radically changing the workplace. Talk of a chasm-like "generation gap" filled the media. "People were unable to talk to each other because the radical change in culture prevented communication," Van der Horst says.

So along came two professors from the University of California at Santa Cruz, linguist John Grinder and psychologist Richard Bandler. Combining theories about human behavior and speech, they taught managers how to read body language and voice intonations to find out what their employees were really saying. They told corporate executives that they would get better results if they set clear, easy-to-verify targets written in plain, no-nonsense prose. They urged them to build a rapport with their workers, instead of handing down decisions through a chain of command. Over the years, NLP has evolved into a well-accepted management technique, with more than 250 books and four hundred Ph.D. dissertations devoted to it.

NLP studies indicate that people fall into one of two groups: those who thrive on making choices, and those who find comfort in day-to-day routines. The two groups are further subdivided into five categories based on how workers relate to their jobs, how long they are likely to remain with a company, and what portion of the population they represent.

In one such category, for instance, you find the "Similar" worker, who loves routine, accounts for five percent of the population, and will remain with the company for fifteen to twenty years. "Different" workers flourish with constant change and, if improperly handled, will remain only six to

eighteen months. They make up ten percent of the population. Most workers fall into the "Comparison" category, a mixture of Similar and Different
that accounts for sixty-five percent of the population.

These categories of workers will strike different chords in different corporate cultures. French managers, according to NLP studies, enjoy philosophy and abstraction, and therefore nurture a commercial culture that
demands standardized processes. U.S. managers, by contrast, prefer a stan-
dardization of results that encourages individual initiative, within limits.
And British companies, says Van der Horst, often go to the extreme: they
value non-conformist "different" types so much that it's difficult for managers to build successful teams.

The goal of NLP is to get people to understand these diverse personalities—
and to make them work together productively within a corporation. NLP
seeks a corporate balance between the grind of process and the spark of originality. "The international nature of business demands that companies seek
workers whose personalities don't fit into the classic definition of institutional
culture," Van der Horst says. "At the same time, no company wants to hire
someone who is anti-institutional. So how do you blend what appear to be two
different character types into traditional European corporate cultures?"

That, NLP advocates say, is the key to corporate prosperity and worker
contentment in France and elsewhere on the Continent. "This is really the
reason French companies keep coming back to NLP," says Van der Horst.
But does NLP really boost productivity and shore up the bottom line? That
depends, it seems, on whether you're hiring a young recruit or trying to
teach an old manager new tricks.

According to Van der Horst, NLP's most visible effect on productivity
occurs during the recruitment process. Repere claims that French compa-
nics that have used NLP models during the interview process have reduced
the turnover of new employees anywhere from ten to thirty-seven percent.

That was certainly the case for French hardware chain Castorama,
which has sent more than fifty of its managers to courses at Repere. René
Dupré, a Castorama store manager in Éragny, outside Paris, says NLP
methods have helped Castorama to "keep the shooting stars who would
otherwise want to leave the company after a few years."

Just as important, he says, the management technique has helped the
company to avoid hiring managers who lack the skills needed in modern
commercial situations: "NLP helps eliminate the sheep with five feet."

9

BUYING NOBLE TITLES
LETS BANKERS
BE DUKES OR EARLS

HAROLD BROOKS-BAKER is in the business of turning rabble into royalty. Seated at a table cluttered with heraldic emblems in a London carriage house lined with manuscripts that trace imperial pedigrees, the genealogist from Maryland has spent the past thirty years making deals in the nobility market.

The ancient trade in aristocratic titles, like the egos of clients who secretly negotiate with Brooks-Baker and other title brokers for the right to dub themselves noble, is still thriving. Brooks-Baker says Scottish baronies that in 1945 sold for around $15,000 fetch $200,000 on the open market today.

"No one can prevent you from purchasing a noble title and attaching it to your name," explains Brooks-Baker, publishing director of *Burke's Peerage*, the *Michelin Guide* of the blue-blood set since 1826. Nowadays, Brooks-Baker sells a noble title a week to customers who he says have included American media moguls, British bankers, and the owner of a Hollywood movie-stunt company.

After all, there's no monopoly on nobility.

"Did anyone ever try to stop Count Basie from calling himself 'count?'" Brooks-Baker says of a Cinderella industry in which $400 buys a dukedom in Devonshire and a fee of $200,000 festoons your name with the title Baron of Schleswig-Holstein. "Because of the confidentiality clauses in our contracts, nobody knows how you actually obtained nobility," he adds. According to the fine print, Brooks-Baker is forbidden from revealing the names of either buyers or sellers.

Title salesman Andrew Bulpin, the untitled proprietor of Elite Titles Ltd. in the Devonshire village of Newton Abbot, says his company over the past five years has sold more than a hundred noble British designations over the Internet to Japanese businessmen, U.S. entrepreneurs, and British expatriates. Clients want a title to embellish their newly acquired posh accents, Bulpin says. "The baronetage market booms whenever American television broadcasts reruns of shows like *Upstairs Downstairs*. A title still makes a difference in today's business environment. A title looks good on a business card, and it's legal."

Elite Titles charges neonobles around $500 to become a baron. "We're the low end of the market. I just go down to the local registry office and change the name of our client to Baron Somesuch," Bulpin says. Seated titles, those attached to a piece of land, are trickier and cost $2,000. "We sell you a 20-centimeter-by-20-centimeter piece of farmland that has absolutely no use," he clowns. "You give yourself any title you want and we enter it on the land registry. Most people become lords; you could make yourself a king, but who would believe it?"

The hundreds of monikers Brooks-Baker brings to market are no caprice. His dukes and counts are the real thing, titles originally bestowed on the hoi polloi by since-beheaded monarchs such as King Louis XVI of France and converted into blue-chip trade among deep-pocketed businesspeople seeking a personality boost or an extra edge in moving up a corporate hierarchy.

"It's a business that plays on the vanity of wealthy executives who have all the toys money can buy," he says, describing his practice as cosmetic surgery for the psyche. "A noble title is the final toy." Not just anyone can buy himself a title, however. "Buyers must have a correct and honorable manner."

German royals appear to have cornered the princeling market. "Under German law, commoners can be made princes if an existing prince legally adopts our client," Brooks-Baker says. "We are the middleman in the transaction. The cost is $500,000, and a German prince can technically adopt as many children as he wants. We sell two a year."

Over at Elite Titles, Bulpin says he's thankful the nobility trade is a niche market that offers no discounts for viscounts. "If our volume was huge, it would dilute the effect of having a title," he explains. "Our clients almost always get car rental upgrades and VIP service at hotels."

Commerce in what Italian Renaissance royals called the *frodi onorevoli* (honorable frauds) and *scelleratezze gloriose* (glorious rascals) ruffles the noble hackles administered by Patrick Dickinson, Richmond Herald at the College of All Arms in London. The 524-year-old college created by King Richard III is to the baronetage market what the Securities and Exchange Commission is to the New York Stock Exchange. However, it has never been able to close the loophole that says a proven ancestry is not a prerequisite to the official grant of arms that comes with all recognized titles.

"I don't approve of selling titles," Dickinson huffs. "The discrepancy between these bought-and-sold manorial titles and titles of honor has caused us quite a lot of concern. Such territorial titles are not titles of honor bestowed by the sovereign and are obviously confusing and misleading."

The desire for personal aggrandizement is ancient. Charles Darwin observed that all animals share a "universal passion for adornment." Andrew Carnegie named a university and museum after himself. John D. Rockefeller built a business center in the heart of Manhattan. Richard Scrushy, the founder and ousted chief executive of Health South Inc., had a full-size statue cast of himself for display near the Scrushy-endowed library of the American Sports Medicine Institute in Birmingham, Alabama.

For Brooks-Baker, the ultimate executive accoutrement is a noble title, a luxury business that took off in seventeenth-century England. Seeking revenue to pay soldiers to fight the Irish, King James I created the title of baronet and sold off scores of them for about $3,000 each (in seventeenth-century dollars). The trade left Britain and other European countries awash in noble titles. "Hundreds of legitimate titles become extinct every year," Brooks-Baker says. "It takes a tremendous amount of effort and research to find and verify the titles and create the coats of arms."

On the title trading floor at Burke's Peerage, baronetagers sit at three desks and operate much like arbitragers, seeking dukes and earls in one market for immediate resale elsewhere in order to profit from price-and-supply discrepancies. Brooks-Baker says the ultimate titles are emperor and king. "But you can't buy an empire or a kingdom," he explains. "Emperors and kings are royalty of the blood, and they are the ones with the ability to confer noble titles that can be resold."

That's where the baronetager comes in, picking up and selling the bestowed titles of prince, duke, marquis, earl, count, viscount, baron, and baronet to the highest bidder. Burke's Peerage ads in glossy magazines say customers can "acquire with confidence" a Scottish baronial title, approved by Lord Lyon, Queen Elizabeth II's representative in Scotland, for between

$140,000 and $180,000. Irish baronages go for $65,000 to $80,000 and come with the authorization of the Chief Herald of Ireland. "We also do French marquises for between $60,000 and $160,000," Brooks-Baker says.

Most titles come from impoverished nobles looking to raise cash. "For them it's like selling the family silver," Brooks-Baker says of the thousands of titles his company has sold over the past 180 years. "All legitimate titles come from families that usually have scores of various noble titles attached to their name, so they sell those titles they're no longer using."

A registration fee of $1,300 gets the deal rolling. The money is returned if Burke's Peerage fails to discover a "suitable title" within nine months. One title currently up for grabs is the Comte de Coussey. The price of becoming an officially registered French count with a cotton swab of farmland in Lorraine is $100,000.

But is buying a French title in today's market a sound investment strategy? "I would find it hard to believe," says Baronet Charles Elton, who received his nobility the old-fashioned way and doesn't use his hereditary title in his work as a television producer at Carlton Communications Plc.

Lord William Waldegrave, chairman of the financial-institutions group at UBS Investment Bank, says his title, awarded for political work, "may help in some more traditional societies, such as Japan, but otherwise I think it's entirely neutral." The title occasionally stirs bewilderment among his clients. "People sometimes think there are two people," Waldegrave explains, "one named Lord and one named William."

Count Riccardo Pavoncelli of Morgan Stanley eschews his ancestral family title at work as the head of the company's Italian investment-banking unit. Still, the glossy gossip magazines that carry photographs of Pavoncelli attending gala events identify him as a count who hails from a nineteenth-century Italian wheat-trading family of noble ancestry. "Pavoncelli is an extremely important count," Brooks-Baker says. "It's a title that opens doors. The name is associated with money and has social cachet."

Brooks-Baker says today's upwardly mobile noble often wants a title with more bite than a label that assures invitations to fancy parties. Some of his executive clients over the years have been seeking to purchase a title traceable to the fifteenth-century Florentine assassin and merchant Prince Rodrigo Borgia. "Businessmen have asked us to find titles connected to the Borgias," Brooks-Baker says. "If people are willing to pay, we can do it."

Bulpin of Elite says he wouldn't dream of asking the College of All Arms to approve his ennobled customers. "They wouldn't let our lords and ladies into the place," he snickers. Brooks-Baker says the college has never refused a noble application from Burke's Peerage. "I don't really know," Dickinson huffs.

"Royal families view what we do as a completely acceptable practice," Brooks-Baker says. "They've been doing the same thing for hundreds of years." Still, he figures it's likely a good thing that baronetage is a niche business. "If this market grew into a really big business, I'm sure the government regulators would step in."

10

THE PSYCHOLOGY OF
THE TUMMY-TUCKED TYCOON

FEAR AND ANXIETY WERE MUCH ON DISPLAY in Dr. Dev Basra's blue underground operating room up the street from Oxford Circus in London. The patient, a 27-year-old real estate tycoon, had arrived shortly after sunrise for the first of a series of facial procedures designed to renovate what he believed to be his unsightly looks. The pre-op went smoothly enough; but fifteen minutes and a change of heart later, the tycoon was gone.

"It was a case of aesthetics over anesthetics," Dr. Basra explains. "He didn't want to be overdone. He was so upset and embarrassed that he wanted to pay me anyway for the procedure. I've directed him to a counseling group of other patients preparing for the same procedure. He will be back."

Spring is the most popular time for businessmen and politicians experiencing the sags and bags of high-stress jobs to call on the skills of a plastic surgeon, according to a survey by the American Academy of Facial Plastic and Reconstructive Surgery.

"To do this job you need the hands of a lady, the eyes of a hawk, and the heart of a lion," says Dr. Basra, who for the past twenty years has been one of the top "face men" in Europe. "You also need to be a priest," he adds. "A lot of businessmen wanting plastic surgery have a guilt complex, and they look at the surgeon as a holy man who can accept their confession. I'm surrounded by these businessmen."

Dr. Basra remains on the cutting edge as European executives of all ages have recourse to the scalpel as a means of securing their power in an increasingly youthful-looking corporate world. And for such businessmen, Dr. Basra says every aging feature can become magnified: ruddy temples, limp eyelids, and baggy chins stare out from the mirror. The psychological pain is private and acute.

"Every businessman I have declined to operate on leaves with the greatest sense of disappointment one can ever imagine," Dr. Basra explains coolly. "Over five percent of the businessmen who come here don't need the procedure they want, but they all believe plastic surgery will change their life and will look elsewhere."

But publicly, at least, there is no "Top Ten List" of plastic surgeons to call on for the executive seeking nips and tucks. Advertising, though acceptable in the medical profession, is not the preferred route to finding a qualified plastic surgeon in the corporate environment. Dr. Basra says marketing is considered a more appropriate way to trumpet business among catwalk models and film stars. In the boardrooms of large corporations, say executives who have undergone "age-induced" surgical procedures, businessmen find their architects of the flesh by word of mouth, most often in hushed tones on a golf course or in whispers over whiskeys.

Sitting in his office near the bronze bust he cast of former British prime minister John Major, Dr. Basra rightly—and quietly—suggests that his name is one of those most often mentioned when the talk among businessmen turns to tummy tucks. Though Dr. Basra's roll call of plastic-surgery patients over the past thirty-five years must remain private, he asserts that the list of bankers, politicians, financiers, and top industrialists is so widespread that he finds it nearly impossible to dine at some exclusive restaurants without spotting one of his former patients at a neighboring table.

"I run into them all the time," Dr. Basra says with a smile. "Of course none of them would ever dream of coming to say hello to me in that environment. If they did, then everyone else in the restaurant would think they had had surgery with me," he adds. "Executives never own up to having had a procedure, and men have much more vanity than women."

The silence surrounding the power brokers who have requested the services of Dr. Basra and the handful of his equally discreet colleagues on the Continent has generated a shortage of numbers on precisely how many male executives have gone under the knife in hopes of salvaging their careers. But Dr. Basra suggests that U.S. statistics provide an accurate glimpse of the phenomenal growth of plastic surgery among European movers and shakers.

"The number-one executive procedure of choice is a blepharoplasty, or eyelid surgery," says Dr. Basra, whose pink pinstripe suit and silk tie woven with yellow birds make him indistinguishable from the property executive fidgeting in the waiting room of his Harley Street townhouse. Dr. Basra says nose jobs and face and forehead lifts also are popular.

"Businessmen who don't have power believe power is the biggest aphrodisiac in the world," Dr. Basra says. "But every powerful business-man who's been on my operating table says how they look is the most powerful aphrodisiac."

At the same time, Dr. Basra says, European business culture has yet to fully embrace the importance physical attributes can play in making deals.

"Americans are more aware of the role a plastic surgeon can have in business affairs, but European attitudes are changing quite fast," says Dr. Basra, who performs two operations a day and often travels around Europe to consult with other plastic surgeons and their patients. "Well over ten percent of my patients are executives, and during the next five years I sus-pect over thirty percent of them will be executives."

In the U.S., he says, the largest category of men who have undergone plas-tic surgery since 1997 fall into the fifty- to fifty-nine-year-old age group, with over thirty-six percent of them citing job-related reasons for their surgery. Yet Dr. Basra says physical danger is a very real threat for older executives, who are usually the most eager to maintain their youth and remain competitive. "I just had a sixty-five-year-old businessman who wanted a youthful nose," Dr. Basra explains. "But he was also obese and had a coronary bypass and high blood pressure. We're seeing more patients like that."

But regardless of a businessman's age, Dr. Basra says wives, mirrors, and corporate politics awaken his clients to the prospect of plastic surgery.

"He tugs at this chin, looks at the bags under his eyes, and says it must be done," says Dr. Basra, who once declined a businessman's plea to implant a ball bearing above his navel ("I couldn't bring myself to ask why," he says). Another patient, the chief executive of a European hotel chain, was so pleased with the outcome that he sent ten of his staff to have simi-lar procedures done, at the company's expense.

"Psychologically, something stops the high-powered executive in his career. If they don't meet with continued success, they blame it on a phys-ical feature and nothing else," Dr. Basra says. "A bit of vanity is okay, but sometimes it's difficult to tell a businessman he's a nut case and shouldn't have plastic surgery."

As for what it takes to locate a sensitive cosmetic surgeon, perhaps Dr. Basra's most remarkable suggestion is to find a surgeon with the ability to place a piece of carbon paper between two pieces of stationery and then write a love letter without making a copy. "Plastic surgery is the art of gentleness," Dr. Basra says. But no matter the soft touches he has carved into the hundreds of businessmen who have stretched out on his table, Dr. Basra cautions, "They all have one game face and there's always great apprehension on how the operation will turn out."

The young real-estate executive must have suddenly felt apprehensive that morning as Dr. Basra, dressed in his light-blue surgical gown and with a pair of red bifocal glasses perched on the tip of his nose, helped him lie down on the stainless-steel plateau and wheeled the anesthetic cart into place. Dr. Basra's partner, Dr. Alex Alexandrides, similarly dressed and precisely studying the tattoos he had etched onto the patient's face, picked up the "eye toolkit," the plastic-wrapped packet containing the eight sterilized implements required to perform a blepharoplasty.

The operation takes two hours. Additional elective procedures, which may include a one-hour operation to redecorate the patient's nose and a four-hour session to lift his flabby chin, cost £3,500 and £6,500 respectively. Dr. Alexandrides described the businessman as a dismorphaphobe—an individual who doesn't like his human form.

But the patient is now shaking. He sits up, puffing, and tells Dr. Basra he wants to talk in his office. Fifteen minutes later, the tycoon is dressed in his suit and gone.

Dr. Alexandrides glances at the businessman's medical chart and agrees that the fleeing patient will return for the operation. "He's what we call a SIMAN—single individual male narcissistic," Dr. Alexandrides says. "We had six meetings with him over the past few weeks and sent him to a clinical psychologist before agreeing to the operation. He's a very successful businessman, but with an anxiety level that makes him the highest-risk patient of all."

In his office, leaning against the life-size metal statue he made of a woman running, Dr. Basra says the constant battle of his profession is deciding if a patient's desire for plastic surgery is psychological or pathological. Gauging those reasons, he adds, is an exceptionally difficult task with affluent and respected businessmen, all of whom want to preserve their high-power status and walk away from surgery with the misconception that it will change their lives.

"Today, vanity progresses for economic reasons," Dr. Basra says sadly. "All of my executive patients have the bread; they come to me looking for the fruit," he adds, stroking his beard. "I've had successful seventy-two-year-old men in this office wanting me to tell them if they had come here to change their looks or because they were a failure in their lives."

EXECUTIVE **TESTOSTERONE**

IN SEARCH OF

ETERNAL **YOUTH**

STRETCHED OUT ON ONE of the black leather barber's chairs in his office beneath Mount Vesuvius, Michele Boellis tosses a bottle of liquid seaweed soap between his hands and offers a bittersweet observation on the profit center for male narcissism that has been in his family for nearly a century. "There was no food in Naples after World War II and all the men were emaciated," he says. They also needed a shave. "So my grandfather put small balls in their mouths to expand the cheeks and give a shave without cutting them," Boellis says. "Then they'd go out looking for women."

Some sixty years later, the Boellis Barbershop Spa for Men in Naples continues to fully exploit the male vanity of its twenty thousand customers.

"We take care of Wall Street businessmen who fly in from New York, European politicians, and jet-setters who arrive by yacht from Capri," Boellis says. "They want privacy." He adds, "Two types of men use spas: the old who want to look young, and the young who want to play around. All of them are willing to pay a lot of money for the opportunity."

Which is why the International Spa Association sees identifying and embracing the grooming rituals of modern male executives as the fuel to double the twenty thousand spas currently operating in North America, with similar growth forecasts in Europe and Asia.

"But they never talk about the experience," says Lynne Walker McNees, executive director of the ISpa industry group. "Guys have always gone to spas," she says of the forty-two million men she says her research shows visited spas last year. "They're just shy about it."

McNees is no casual observer of the anthropology of powerful men. Before joining ISpa in 1992, she spent four years working for President George H. W. Bush as the educational director of the White House Fellows Program. Her Lexington, Kentucky–based industry group has 2,400 members who monitor the grooming routines of male executives in sixty-four countries. McNees travels the globe and, with the help of PricewaterhouseCoopers, studies the habits of the 160 million people her organization reckons annually spent some $11 billion on everything from "rainshower massages" in Thailand to having their bodies slathered in Mexican chili pepper sauce.

"I'm probably having a massage right now, so please leave a message," says the recorded voice of *Spa Finder* magazine editor in chief Malcolm Abrams, whose most recent advertisment-packed issue is a 216-page homage to traveling executives with "jet lag, scaly skin, and a deep desire to take a long nap." Abrams says the days of spas billing themselves as elite decompression chambers for the thin-and-rich crowd are history. "Spas must cater to the executive male," Abrams says. The evidence: "Men's locker rooms are the same size as the women's locker rooms at all the resort hotel spas," he says.

It's the same at sea, where a 7,000-square-foot (650-square-meter) floating spa aboard the cruise ship *World of Residensea* offers guests a 28-session rejuvenation program for $3,150. On shore, the Lizard Island Spa in Australia touts a $400 Aboriginal "pepperberry and peat mud soak," and a spa in South Africa massages guests while they chew antelope jerky and watch leopards dine on warthogs. Turn on a shower head at The Source spa in Bali and yogurt flows out. Buttermilk streams from the spigots at the Ananda Spa in the Himalayan foothills.

In his cloak-and-scissor world, Boellis keeps his celebrated $25 "Spa Shave" and other executive sprucing secrets under wraps. "Big companies want to buy our brand, and people come around at all hours asking compromising questions about the customers and what we do for them. We say nothing," says the barber of Naples, snapping a creamy silk cape at a stray hair atop the only book on the waiting-room table, a leather-bound copy of Robert Louis Stevenson's *The Strange Case of Dr. Jekyll and Mr. Hyde*.

The Boellis motto: "Never Racist, Even to Those Who Have No Hair." He has instructed his nine barbers and two masseurs to remain vigilant and prevent "aesthetic industry analysts" from learning anything about those who strip down for the almost three-hour, $325 cash-only treatment. "In this busines,s it's fatal to give up the client list," the 34-year-old Boellis explains. "We are the friends, confidants, and advisers to our clients."

And if the secrets leak out? "It may well be the end of crony capitalism as we know it," British property tycoon John Perrin jokes through a mushroom cloud of scalding vapor inside La Prairie Spa steam room at the Ritz-Carlton Hotel in Manhattan, shortly after his arrival aboard Concorde's final flight from London to New York.

La Prairie massage therapist Sue Stanley Hass says forty percent of her clients are men, and getting Perrin to plunk down $180 for a one-hour "Executive Stress Break" massage didn't seem to be a problem. In its first year of business the La Prairie attracted more than nine thousand customers, thirty percent of them men willing to spend $260 for a ninety-minute Caviar Firming Facial.

Hass says her appointment book is filled. The pitch is tempting. "Who but the Swiss know how to combine privilege and pleasure for an hour or more of sybaritic delight," reads the brochure in the waiting room. "And why not combine lavish spa services, the finest catering, and elegant private settings to impress your most discerning corporate clients."

Astonishment is certainly the order of the day in the men's locker room, where naked guys with bewildered looks on their faces sniff aromatherapy fumes and examine tubs of de-jowling unguents. "I'm not sure what this stuff does," Perrin says. "But there's nothing better than a massage."

That's good news for McNees. Her statistics show that persuading a man to have a spa massage is always the first step to opening his wallet to purchase concoctions with names like Cellular Cycle Facial Ampoules and Lipo-Sculpting Eye Gel.

"You often must drag them into a spa kicking and screaming," McNees explains of a growth industry fueled by men with an average income of $80,000 and a burning vanity to remain forty years old at any price. Yet, she continues, "I don't know a man who isn't hooked after that first facial and then doesn't say he needs one every month."

"The spa is a very important part of the new executive lifestyle," adds Maria Lorenzo, director general of Spanish marketing at American Express SAU in Madrid. "Spas and wine rank at the top of what American

Express corporate and private clients want to find out about before making a trip. The research into executive male habits is never-ending."

***

Why is this happening now, when since Greco-Roman times men have found it possible to talk business over a steam and a rubdown without being tailed by market researchers? Some analysts suggest that the first man to leverage the secrets of the steam room was the late socialite and Swiss physician Paul Niehans, the illegitimate son of Kaiser Wilhelm and founder of the secretive Clinique la Prairie spa in Clarens-Montreaux.

The year was 1931. Viagra, according to the U.S. Patent and Trademark Office, was a "term with no denotative meaning," and the hypodermic needle Niehans injected into an aging millionaire contained a perky potion of fetal lamb livers surgically removed from pregnant sheep. More than seven decades and at least a hundred thousand inoculations later, Niehans's freeze-dried ovine therapy ultimately did more than promise to combat age, relieve depression, and generate a line of male cosmetics that includes La Prairie Cellular Anti-Puff Eye Gel ($175 for an airline-meal-size jam jar) and Skin Caviar Luxe Cream ($600 for 3.4 ounces). "La Prairie over the years helped bring executives into spas for more than a massage after a game of golf," McNees says.

Indeed, behind the clinical curtains at CLP on the northern shore of Lake Geneva, Dr. Thierry Walli says that each year he injects fetal sheep liver into 1,300 patients who spend more than $7,000 on a six-day mother-of-all-spas treatment that for a few thousand dollars more can include varicose vein removal and a new nose. Trumpeted as "The Fine Art of Aging," Walli says that highly stressed male executives in particular leave his table invigorated, and that most of those injected with unborn lamb liver return every two years for a refill. Walli says he injects the viscous serum into the buttocks and that the needle remains in place for five minutes. "We have many businessmen clients," is all Walli will reveal of the discreet list of high rollers who have visited the clinic over the past seven decades.

Back on the Naples waterfront and sitting in a Sportarredo Trimax sun chair, Boellis says 1980 was the year his family made the decision to offer more than a $40 shave and a haircut. "The men made the money, and getting them to spend it on their outward appearance really wasn't all that difficult," he explains. Today, Boellis says that eighty percent of his customers sign up for the full body treatment, which includes a manicure, pedicure, facial, massage, and Trimax tan. Those in search of steam are ushered to private boats and sent across Santa Lucia Harbor to the natural saunas and thermal baths on the islands of Agnano and St. Germano and the ancient and active Roman spas on Baia Island and the Isle of Ischia.

"We don't have a steam room because, thanks to Mount Vesuvius, Naples has the best volcanic spas in the world," Boellis says. "We would never create something artificial for our clients."

THE DANGEROUS
CURVES OF A
HIGH-HEELED GUMSHOE

THE PORTER AT 116 VIA VENETO had a broken toothpick in his pouchy mouth. "Fifth floor, next to Paradisi the dentist," he scowled. It was a muggy Roman May afternoon, but the ride to the top was fast and filled with the smell of perfume, a high-priced aroma that led directly to the locked office overlooking Federico Fellini Square. I swallowed hard and thumped the buzzer.

Private eye Miriam Ponzi was no Miss Marple. She had raven hair and signature eyes like Bacall in *The Big Sleep*. Pearls weren't a nuisance around her neck, and the small Dutch cigar cuddled between her thumb and trigger finger looked as good as the expensive paintings that lined her steamy office. The daylight was beginning to fade, but I declined the drink and watched the world's most sought-after high-heeled gumshoe slip like silk into a soft leather chair.

"Businessmen aren't afraid to confide in me," purred the president of Tom Ponzi Investigations. "Of course, it's easier for a woman to deal with a corporate executive in trouble." The Italian-kitten voice was chilly and professional. "All right, how did you find out about me?" demanded the daughter of the legendary Italian detective known as Peeping Tom Ponzi, who favored unfiltered cigarettes, used truth serum on the bad guys, and never left home without two 7.65-millimeter Berettas and a pair of Sylvania night-vision goggles.

Tommazo Ponzi was no pulp-fiction creation and, besides, he knew Rita Hayworth. The bullets were real and *Playboy* magazine said he was cool. Upon his death in 1997, his daughter inherited the TPI brand and a business in which she already had clocked twenty-seven years sleuthing for the likes of Vatican priests, wheelmen Gianni Agnelli and Enzo Ferrari, and enough European politicos to fill a circus tent. She'd helped to shake down hundreds of white-collar crime rackets and kidnapping rings, and lent her street smarts to many of the forty thousand conjugal infidelity investigations her father had conducted for the rich and famous. "Cheating wives have to be trapped; unfaithful husbands trap themselves," was his motto back in the 1960s and 1970s.

But sex no longer pays the bills here at what's perhaps the most celebrated private-detective agency since Spade and Archer in *The Maltese Falcon*. These days, divorce cases make up less than fifteen percent of TPI's annual turnover. Investigating insider-trading deals and Chinese box structures—that is, deciphering the intricate global lacing on multinational contracts and bank transactions—is one of the firm's hottest products. "Our growth area is corporate counterespionage," Ponzi says. "All corporations have employees who cheat, and the New Economy has been very good for our business. We have over a hundred contracts with corporations to monitor computer crime." Nevertheless, she says it helps to have good looks and a dozen reformed hackers on the payroll. A suspicious nature is also required when outsiders show up asking questions about big-name clients and large corporations whose lives have turned dark with something more than night. The philosophy of TPI is simple: what's public is propaganda, what's secret is serious. Ponzi threw her head back, exhaling blue smoke toward the tall ceiling. "I'm not telling you anything specific, so don't try," she says. "We don't look for clients. They look for us, and I don't advertise. Our former clients send us more than enough new clients . . . all of them come to see me after they've traveled well beyond a suspicion of something gone wrong."

Although no hatchet-faced men in baggy suits and cheap toupees walk the corridors of TPI, there is a coat rack that's held its share of shoulder holsters, and a secret stash of file cabinets that contain dossiers going back to 1950 on over a hundred thousand individuals and businesses. "A very helpful archive," Ponzi says enticingly. There are also lots of ashtrays on the tables, sophisticated listening devices in the bookcases, and expressionless faces in front of the watercooler. "I start my day with a cup of warm milk and status reports from field agents," she says. It's a business of wildly contrasting logic that orbits around the phrase *l'acqua in bocca,* or "water in the mouth," a Sicilian warning to keep your trap shut. "My work is a film that can never be made," says the windsurfing single mother with a master's degree in criminology from Cambridge University. "Sure, my image is good for the company, but all our contracts contain privacy clauses that prevent me from talking. This firm never has been involved in a double-cross—and believe me, double-crosses happen all the time in this business because someone violates a confidentiality agreement."

✳✳✳

The waiter at the Argentine steak restaurant across the street from the U.S. embassy had a worried face and slightly nicotine-stained fingernails and walked like he had a corn on his left foot. Ponzi stopped talking until he had hobbled back into the kitchen. She unbuttons her creamy calfskin trench coat and says "quick heist" kidnappings are the principal and least-known danger facing the masters of the New Economy. According to British insurance company Hiscox Group, there were 1,644 recorded ransom kidnappings in 1999, mostly in Colombia, Mexico, and the old Soviet Union. The report said the numbers are growing and the victims tended to be wealthy locals, with the ten riskiest countries accounting for ninety-two percent of the abductions. Ponzi isn't surprised no European country made the list. Most kidnappings within the European Union, she suggests, go unreported. "The big, multimillion-dollar-ransom kidnappings aren't a real problem any more in Europe," she explains with a hard look. "It's the small-change kidnappings, the ones that never make the paper or the police."

The quick heist is a predominantly amateur job, a junkyard crime that's grubby in planning, effective in execution, and, Ponzi says, concluded without fanfare, like paying off a nuisance lawsuit before it hits the court. "Wealthy and important people are now frequently snatched and ransomed for $100,000 after usually no more than three days," she explains. "This type of heist is much less dangerous than a big kidnapping. People pay the ransom because it's cheaper than having your life made public."

To combat the trend, Ponzi says, TPI counterintelligence technicians have embedded miniaturized global positioning transmitters under the skin of European executives and their family members. "The procedure is becoming very popular." She puts down her napkin and picks up her mobile phone without looking at it. She says "tomorrow morning" and casually tugs the green gemstone on her ear before hanging up. She says nothing of the call, but reveals a quick, nervous smile, perhaps the result of her recent trip to meet with a "political client" in Moscow, or maybe some unforeseen fallout from successfully nabbing the swindlers who were counterfeiting Italian automotive parts, after hours, on a chocolate-molding machine in a confectionery factory.

"I wear a hundred masks, but I'm not so tough," she says between sips of black coffee. "I talk to doormen. I look in garbage cans. I sleep with a hot-water bottle on my stomach. I should carry a gun more often." Pursuing the hot-water-bottle angle was clearly hazardous material. The gun was safer, particularly since Ponzi and many of her three hundred employees and consultants, who range from eighteen-year-old students to an 87-year-old actor, have been shot at, kidnapped, or run down by speeding cars. Back at the office and fingering like a knife thrower one of the seven antique magnifying glasses on her desk, she recalls her first case, the time her father asked if she was interested in infiltrating a Marseilles drug mob to track down a missing eighteen-year-old girl. Ponzi was twenty years old and almost had her throat slit.

"I had a transmitter in my wristwatch," she says. "My dad brought the cavalry to the rescue just in time. I got the girl out, though." The experience left her with a soft spot for tracking down lost kids. "When a child goes missing, I get angry. Finding children is my personal expertise."

Of course, sometimes it's wiser to walk away from a case. Like the morning when a lawyer representing 122 indicted Mafia dons strolled into the office to solicit TPI's help in proving that half of his clients were innocent. "I believed the lawyer," Ponzi says. "But I said no because it was the Mafia." The Italian attorney returned a few days later with three wise guys to help plead his case. She told them to take a hike. "Dealing with those kind of people is all instinct," she says. "I must be okay, because I'm not dead yet."

To be sure, Ponzi enjoys working the shadows, and the Italian women's fashion magazines love publishing pictures of her. "This is still a mysterious job," she says. "We have over fifty active operations right now in Europe, Australia, New Zealand, Japan, and the Balkans." Ponzi says TPI's security work for European executives traveling into the troubled Balkan region is a big rainmaker for the firm. Tracking the activities of Japanese corporations, she adds, is another boom market. "Japanese firms are big into corporate espionage," she asserts. "Theft is the quickest means of getting ideas in the New Economy. I have to be quicker. War is no longer waged to conquer territory, but to discover the commercial secrets of others."

The tempo of a twenty-first-century private eye might be more high-octane and high-tech than what Dashiell Hammett had in mind when he sent Sam Spade after the Maltese Falcon, but the plots that confront Ponzi more often than not remain the same. Like the time she was hired to investigate a satanic cult in England that had lured into its ranks the son of a wealthy European executive. At first, the young man's father wanted to find out why his heir had joined the group and if he was in danger.

The reason, of course, was a dame. Moreover, Ponzi discovered that a group of nefarious characters had planted the lady in bed with the young man for the sole purpose of harvesting information about his powerful father and intelligence on how he managed the corporation. "What at first appears to be a relatively simple matter for our level of clients has a way of turning into a complex fiscal investigation," she explains. "I'm sure my job is more pragmatic, and certainly more adventurous, than what you see in the movie house."

CONFESSING CORPORATE
SINS TO THE MONKS
OF MOUNT ATHOS

"THIS IS WHERE THEY ALL COME, and I'm the one who lets them in," says Father George, the sentinel monk who patrols the coiling dirt road into Moni Vatopedi, one of the twenty monasteries on the isolated Greek peninsula of Mount Athos.

Today, this spit of cliffs and forests inhabited by 2,400 monks in northeastern Greece is a private pilgrimage site for many elite politicians and businessmen. Long before global paladins embarked on their annual pilgrimage to the World Economic Forum in Davos, Mount Athos was celebrated as the Western world's most fashionable retreat, where leaders came to ponder their souls and the state of the world. The pilgrims they have attracted over recent years have included Italian prime minister Silvio Berlusconi, King Juan Carlos of Spain, and former U.S. president Jimmy Carter.

"The men come from all over the world," Father George explains, sweeping his visitor's log toward the rugged terrain that for more than a thousand years has served as host for the likes of Byzantine emperor Theodosius I, French president Charles de Gaulle, actor Mel Gibson, Prince Charles, U.S. president George H. W. Bush, Cuban president Fidel Castro, the Aga Khan, and Russian president Vladimir Putin. Standing outside his log-built guard cabin, Father George says the visitors come to what he calls "a mountain of saintly men," all seeking to master a balance between the secular and the spiritual.

"Mount Athos was a private moment that I'd rather not talk about," Peter Armitage, president and CEO of Capital International Fund Management, says through his spokesman, Chuck Freadhoff.

"The visits are kept very secret," says Paris Kritikos, proprietor of Kritikos Restaurant in the port village of Ouranoupoli. "The boats to the Holy Mountain leave from here," he explains while grilling lamb over an open fire. "I feed all the big names before they go in and after they come out. I have seen the change on their faces."

Other than those making pilgrimages, which usually last three days and are free, the monks allow about 120 daily visitors to the heavily guarded Mount Athos, where entry is by boat or helicopter and women are strictly forbidden.

Each day at four A.M., a lone monk dressed in a flowing black cassock and habit walks the cloister of Vatopedi and pounds a wooden mallet against a ten-foot-long oblong plank to awaken the 150 brothers and the pilgrims of many faiths to an almost five-hour Orthodox Christian service before sitting down to a silent breakfast of wine, vegetables, and prayer. At the same time, similar rituals are taking place inside the nineteen other Orthodox monasteries sprawled across the 135-square-mile peninsula.

"Deciding on a monastery is a metaphysical management decision," is how Greek hedge-fund manager George Karaplis describes the process of selecting a retreat. "The spirits, God, call it what you want, tell you what monastery to go to. Every CEO needs to visit Mount Athos. I've accompanied senior executives from Lehman Brothers and Morgan Stanley, but the privacy of the experience, the transformation these men experience on Mount Athos prevents me from revealing their names."

The monks, too, say there are no names on the Holy Mountain. The only illumination in Vatopedi's tenth-century basilica comes from candles, their glow reflected off clouds of frankincense, four massive gold chandeliers suspended from the frescoed dome, and an equal number of fifteen-foot-tall gold candlesticks on the rose-and-green marble floor. From the darkened narthex, chanting monks with chest-length beards emerge, trance-like, to venerate what they say is the belt of the Virgin Mary, a piece of the True Cross, and some twenty-seven saintly body parts that have been left in their care along with more than four thousand priceless icons.

Says Father Matthew, a monk from Wisconsin who manages the abbey's computerized building-supply warehouse from inside a converted donkey stable, "Vatopedi is a place of miracles."

It's also a place of wealth and influence.

The monks of Vatopedi say the Holy Mountain was first settled by the Virgin Mary. The businessmen came in A.D. 985; three wealthy medieval merchants spent their fortunes building Vatopedi and founded the abbey's holy order of monks. According to the guest book, the first global business leader to visit Vatopedi was the Italian grain broker Ciriaco d'Ancona, on November 19, 1444. King Alfonso of Spain followed in 1456. The Medicis arrived in 1472. "All the mules in the Holy Mountain would not be enough to carry the gold in the treasury of Vatopedi," one anonymous sixteenth-century pilgrim wrote in the guest book.

Father Irenaios, a French monk, says he has taken the confessions of many Mount Athos pilgrims. "I've spent hours listening to professionals, businessmen, and politicians," Father Irenaios recalls after an evening meal of grain and mountain grasses.

"All of them have great problems in focusing on what is important. They all come to Vatopedi with a need to understand the difficulties they face in work and in their lives." Filling small glasses with a fiery eau de vie called *tsipouro*, Father Germanos, the deputy abbot, nods his head in agreement and says, "All businessmen come to Vatopedi feeling a great emptiness."

What the monks of Vatopedi see is a global economy in which high-charged and stressed-out businessmen are increasingly tormented by moral obstacles that money and power can't overwhelm.

"Explaining how Vatopedi changes men is a hard question to answer," says Graham Speake, the Oxford, England–based manager of the Swiss publishing house Peter Lang AG and author of *Mount Athos, Renewal in Paradise*. "We read, go to confession, and talk to the fathers. We find wisdom."

Greek deputy foreign minister Petros Doukas says his visit to Mount Athos persuaded him to get married and have a family. Athens lawyer and former parliamentarian Stratis Stratigis says his pilgrimage along with a Russian army general allowed him to recognize the "Godly provenance of nature."

"I drove ten companies into bankruptcy by the age of thirty-eight to make money," George Karaplis explains. "I traveled the world, divorced and with a bag of pills. By chance, I went to Mount Athos. I got off the boat and for no reason started running. One of the monks handed me a piece of cake and said, 'George, why did it take you so long to come here?' I'd never seen the man before. That's not a very CEO-like scene, is it?"

Still, Father Matthew suggests that speaking in fractured parables instead of profits is a strategy unlikely to curry much interest in boardrooms. "These are my future roommates," he quips, walking across a lawn piled high with the remains of Vatopedi's deceased monks, chalk-white skulls and bones waiting to be entombed in the church crypt. "My job is to pray."

ALL SPONGES ARE GREEK

THE KNIFE RARELY LEAVES the blistered left hand of Stavros Valsamidis. Twenty feet (6 meters) beneath the Aegean Sea, where the warm tourist waters of Kalymnos Island turn cold and emerald, a sharp diving blade remains the cutting-edge technology for the $100-million-a-year Greek sponge industry—as it has for millennia.

Entering an underwater tunnel twelve hours by boat from the clamor of Athens, Valsamidis points his well-used scalpel toward the rock face. The 55-year-old sponge diver rips a gelatinous, cantaloupe-sized black creature from its mooring, severs its remaining umbilical cords, and deposits the prized *kapadika* sponge from the Dodecanese Islands in a pouch strapped to his weight belt. Behind his face mask, the lifelong sponger's brown eyes arch into a grin.

Kalymnos has been the global headquarters of the sponge industry since Homer first raved about the product's absorbent properties in *The Odyssey*, almost three thousand years ago. However, in the summer of 1986, a sponge plague of unknown origin swept through the Aegean, and marine biologists have yet to find a cure.

"Sadly, the Aegean is not so rich in sponges any more," laments Aristotlis Pavlidis, Greek Minister for the Aegean and Island Policy. For Pavlidis, formulating the government's sponge "immigration" policy is serious business. "Recognizing sponges as Greek is critical for the economy of our islands," he says. "Thousands of jobs are at stake." And a great deal of national pride: "Everyone's life would be a lot better off without artificial sponges."

But the millions of synthetic sponges manufactured each year by 3M Co. ("Sorry, we don't provide numbers on sales or manufacturing quantities," says 3M sponge product manager Katherine Hagmeier) are the least of Pavlidis's diplomatic headaches. He is also in the throes of negotiating a sponge treaty with Libyan leader Colonel Muammar Qaddafi that after eighteen years of talks could finally allow Greek divers access to the largest known luxury sponge reserves in the world, about forty renewable tons annually.

Back on Kalymnos, a pork chop–shaped chunk of rock that's home to sixteen thousand people and sponges as big as living-room sofas, the identity crisis began when a bacteria infected Aegean sponge beds, forcing thousands of Kalymnian divers to seek unsullied sponges in the Caribbean, the Philippines, and the Gulf of Mexico. Local production plunged from thirty tons in 1986 to three and a half tons in the opening years of the twenty-first century. Sponge analysts say divers on the bone-dry island in the future will be lucky to harvest a little more than a ton from the Aegean and seven tons from the rest of the Mediterranean Sea. Yet Athenian merchants continue to tag the immigrant sponges as Greek. This accepted marketing mischief now has the country in a lather about how to explain all this to tourists.

Zinos Bantabanos says he has decided to carry on labeling his shop's five thousand sponges as Greek stalwarts. Since the government says seventy-five percent of the raw sponges taken outside of Greek waters return to Kalymnos to undergo the process necessary for commercial sale, the sponge retailer reasons that his critters are Greek. "I have more sponges than any other store in Athens," Bantabanos says. "But I have no idea where most of them come from." He also doesn't know the name of his shop. "My family never gave the store a name. Call it the Sponge Shop," he suggests, flicking a $220 garbage can lid–sized "elephant's ear" sponge into a wicker basket.

"I'm flexible about what makes a sponge Greek," says Emmanuel Sakaleros, president of Sponge Traders International, an Athens-based company that annually processes and sells thirty tons of sponges and millions of Egyptian-grown loofahs to customers that have included Queen Elizabeth II, American organized-crime boss Meyer Lansky, FBI director J. Edgar Hoover, and opera star Maria Callas. Chewing an unlit Cuban cigar beside a fluffy knoll of sponges inside his factory, the sixty-year-old Kalymnian bathroom-product executive and former Miami restaurant owner reluctantly admits that the homegrown Greek sponge is now mostly a myth. In the same breath, he says that ten percent of the world's hundred thousand sponge-industry workers are Greek, and all of them are divers, processors, or clippers. In the U.S., for instance, Greek spongers working out of Tarpon Springs, Florida, each year pluck and prepare about 360,000 sponges, worth about $1.4 million, from the Gulf of Mexico.

"Only a Greek knows how to dive for a sponge and then turn it into a thing of beauty," explains Sakaleros, pointing his cigar toward a burlap sack of "fina," silk sponges from the Bahamas destined for the shelves of Harrods department store in London.

The sponge magnate lights his stogie and takes a thoughtful puff.

"All sponges are Greek" is his verdict.

"Our divers even traveled to Australia to find the best sponges," seconds the dethroned King Constantine.

Sakaleros says that despite the bacterial infestation, which continues to ravage most of the Mediterranean and causes harvested sponges to disintegrate into glop, the few to have survived the blight are cherished by connoisseurs. Sakaleros says the seven tons of Libyan silks that annually reach the market fetch more than $300 a kilogram. "Ahh, if I could find more Libyans," Sakaleros says. "They are clean and soft as air. Only the sponge pirates dare go in for them."

George Moussas, who has sponged the Aegean currents for twenty of his fifty-seven years, says it is hazardous work, and pretty much follows the script of *Beneath the 12-Mile Reef*, the 1953 Academy Award–nominated high-seas sponge thriller starring Gilbert Roland, Robert Wagner, and a giant octopus. "Sponge diving is the most dangerous business on Earth," Moussas reckons through a cloud of cigarette smoke as dawn breaks over the bow of the sponge boat *Marianna*. In the halcyon years of 1965 to 1970, the men and children of the Moussas family would make four 197-foot (60-meter) dives each day, remaining submerged for thirty minutes and returning at the end of the summer season with a hundred tons of sponges. Experienced recreational divers with scuba tanks are advised to venture no deeper than 131 feet (40 meters). "We made more money than a government minister," Moussas recalls. "Fear was never an issue."

It was also an Olympic sport—sort of. At the 1900 Summer Games in Paris, the first and last time the International Olympic Committee awarded medals to athletes who could hold their breath, Frenchman Charles de Vandeville took the gold in underwater swimming. De

Vandeville dog-paddled 197 feet and the rules allowed him to take a few gulps of air along the way.

Even after the invention of the closed diving helmet and air hose in 1840, Kalymnians continued to drape a stone around their necks, plunge in naked to reduce friction, and regularly reached depths in excess of 230 feet (70 meters) on one breath of air. The cost was heavy. According to Greek government figures, between 1930 and 1977, divers with or without compressed air gear accounted for ten thousand deaths and twenty thousand cases of paralysis from the bends, the decompression sickness that appears when a diver surfaces too fast and nitrogen bubbles form in the body.

Valsamidis is skeptical of the statistics. "During those years, we lost three sponge divers each day, some fifty-one thousand children and men," he says.

In 1979, researchers from the Institute of Human Physiology at Gabriele d'Annunzio University in Italy visited Kalymnos to investigate the fantastic tales of local lung capacity. They discovered that Kalymnian men seemed to have evolved lungs better adapted for life beneath the waves.

"I'm sure we Kalymnians are part seal," Valsamidis says. "I've spent more of my life underwater than I have sleeping in bed." When not submerged, Valsamidis ushers visitors through his sponge museum, greets guests at his seaside tavern, or selects merchandise for his family's supermarket. "Kalymnians don't like artificial sponges," he says firmly. "So I don't sell them."

As for the sponges fated to beautify bathtubs and sinks, they all first arrive ashore covered in a rubbery slime and filled with gray jelly. Valsamidis violently stomps his smelly *kapadika* sponge with bare feet until the juice spews out. The sponge is then washed and immersed in seawater for a few hours, and then whacked with a stick to remove any remaining foreign objects. The stinky process is repeated until only the soft skeleton remains. From there, the sponges often head to the Papachatzis Sponge Export House, one of the island's nine wholesalers that first wash and then use shears to clip and shape the bulk of global production. It's a mom-and-pop operation, where Nicholas Papachatzis and his wife each year bathe some 1,300 pounds of sponges in concrete tubs of seawater, hydrochloric acid, and, for those customers who prefer blond sponges, a further solution of potassium permanganate.

"The uneducated public wants blond sponges, but they don't last as long as a pale sponge," says Aphrodite Papachatzis, wrapping a satchel of "Greek" silks for a German tourist. "For the body, what you want is a natural dark silk sponge that's been well sheared and is soft on the skin."

And that's precisely the sort of rub the Greeks want to give the world. "The tourists will go home with their sponges," Sakaleros proclaims. "And they will be Greek sponges."

15

MOVIE CATCHES SPARTA
UNPREPARED FOR A CRAZE

THERE'S A SHORTAGE OF SWORDS IN SPARTA. Greek merchants from Athens to Thermopylae are also concerned about a scarcity of spears as they prepare for summer visitors obsessed with the hit film *300,* the gory story of the 480 B.C. clash between King Leonidas of Sparta and his archenemy, King Xerxes of Persia.

"My Spartan swordmaker died a few weeks before the movie opened," laments Theodoros Tzamalas, whose shop, Greek Souvenirs, has been the main retail outlet for Spartan battle gear in Athens since 1940.

"Until *300,* there was no rush for Spartan swords," Tzamalas says from behind a counter cluttered with strap-on sandals and miniature-soap Parthenons. "Our Leonidas sword was lightweight steel, cost $22, and was archaeologically correct," he adds. "Now hundreds of people are specifically asking for them and I don't have any."

The Greek deputy foreign minister, Petros Doukas, the highest-ranking Spartan in the government of Prime Minister Costas Caramanlis, says he's aware of the *300* weaponry crisis and its cascade effect on Greece's economy.

"The movie's lesson is: fight for your country, even if it's a losing battle, and have enough swords and hotel rooms on hand for tourists," says Doukas, squeezing lemon on a clearly un-Spartan lunch of broccoli spears in his office.

Diplomacy dictates that Doukas remain a noncombatant in the war of words between *300* fans—who so far have spent more than $435 million on tickets—and Iranian hard-liners who argue that the film is part of a wider Western agitprop campaign that smears their country's Persian heritage.

The Iranian poet Bahram Bahrami, who translated Samuel Beckett's play *Happy Days* into Farsi, has called the film an exercise in "blood libel." The British historian Tom Holland, whose book *Persian Fire: The First World Empire and the Battle for the West* recounts the events that led to Thermopylae, described the battle as "the model of a martyrdom for liberty."

"The Greek government takes no position and offers no official criticisms of the film," Doukas says, picking up a photo of his father, a World War II fighter pilot in North Africa.

"It's not like the old days," he recalls. "Until the late 1950s, Spartans acted exactly like the ancients: laconic, aristocratic, with a class structure that didn't care about money. Pedigree was everything." As was widespread public support for sword ownership.

"That's now gone, too," frets the historian Despoina Stratigis, owner of Synergies, a Sparta-based cultural tour company. "Last season, I put visitors in touch with Spartan cheesemakers," she says between slicing wild asparagus in her home and fielding calls from U.S. and European families seeking to retrace Leonidas's march from Sparta to Thermopylae. "Now everyone wants a swordmaker. We don't even have an original sword in our museum, and there's only one swordmaker left in Sparta."

That would be Costas Menegakis, a 42-year-old Greek-Canadian blacksmith who specializes in horseshoes and hasn't made a sword since 2005.

"It was a Viking sword," Menegakis says, sitting atop an anvil alongside his charcoal-fired forge and brandishing a homemade French rapier.

"I'm ready to make Spartan swords, $118," he adds. "I pound swords and spear tips from steel, but if someone wants an original poured in bronze, I can do that."

No matter the model, Menegakis guarantees that his hilts are the real deal. "Many were made from goat horns," he says. "We have lots of goats in Sparta. The hills are filled with them."

Global interest in Spartan swords has also caught the eye of a local police inspector, Panayiotis Skaras. He has spent the past eight months trying to discover who hacked off the 11-kilogram, or 25-pound, sword measuring 1.5 meters, or 5 feet, from Sparta's towering bronze twentieth-century statue of King Leonidas.

There are no leads, though Menegakis says he suspects a "band of Gypsies." Café gumshoes suggest that the robber was an Athenian envious of Sparta going to Hollywood, or perhaps Persian pranksters out for revenge.

Whoever the culprit was, Sparta's deputy mayor, Metaxia Papapostolou, recently had a replacement sword fitted in Leonidas's hand—before the onslaught of tourist buses reaches the southern Greek city. She says the perpetrator won't be shoved into a pit, unlike in the movie.

"Sparta doesn't plan on launching any invasions over this," Papapostolou promises. Instead, the city is investing $10.9 million to refurbish the crumbled tourist sites.

"Our big attractions are the Sanctuary of Artemis Orthia and the olive-oil museum. We're staging ancient Greek plays in the ruins of the outdoor theater. Trouble is, Spartans weren't theatergoers; the Athenians were the ones who went to plays," Papapostolou bemoans. "We Spartans did things for real, and many other Greek cities are jealous about what the movie's popularity has brought us."

Back on the warpath between Sparta and Thermopylae, Shelagh Meade, an 84-year-old British archaeologist, says the 162-kilometer, or 101-mile, walk she recently completed with a few dozen other Sparta buffs along Route Leonidas obliged her to reflect upon her decades of studying the region.

"I didn't particularly like the Spartans," Meade says. "I'm afraid the movie will make young people more violent. Of course, I didn't like *The Charge of the Light Brigade*, either."

PART TWO:
THE GAMES
BILLIONAIRES PLAY

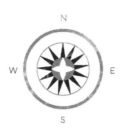

16

THE REVOLUTION
BEGINS WITH A 3-IRON

O N THE EVENING OF JANUARY 13, 1986, Robert Trent Jones Jr. yanked a golf cap over his eyes, strolled off a plane at Manila International Airport, and gambled that Philippine president Ferdinand Marcos was just too busy trying to suppress a revolution to remember that he had marked him for assassination.

"I was expecting all hell to break loose," recalls the chairman of Robert Trent Jones II Golf Course Design LLC, a family-owned architectural firm that since 1931 has built or refurbished 570 of the more than 30,870 golf courses around the world. "I'd built six courses in the Philippines, and Marcos cheated on every one of them to keep a phony seven handicap," Jones says. "He used barefoot caddies, who curled their toes around his bad lies and moved the ball into the fairway."

Why Marcos wanted the marquee architect of the $24-billion-a-year golf industry dead had nothing to do with his refusal to design a course that could accommodate the military dictator's woeful slice. Since 1975, Marcos had known that Jones was serving as the global point man to raise money and political support for the island nation's pro-democracy People Power movement led by Benigno Aquino and dozens of Jones's Filipino partners. A frequent witness before U.S. congressional committees investigating Marcos's human-rights abuses, Jones had privately lobbied for regime change in the Philippines while playing golf with Georgia senator Sam Nunn, U.S. secretary of state George Shultz, and other senior officials in both the Carter and Reagan administrations.

What Marcos didn't know was that Jones had been shuttling messages between Reagan administration officials and People Power leaders while playing golf with both groups in the U.S. and the Philippines.

"Bob is a really good golfer and very competitive in everything," Shultz says. "I wasn't in the Philippines. Bob was, and he was an influential voice. He was a good and trusted back channel, and he kept me well informed."

Adds Jones, "I didn't need a cover story. I really was in the Philippines building golf courses."

Two weeks before Marcos's Aviation Security Command assassinated Benigno Aquino as he stepped off a plane in Manila on August 21, 1983, Jenetta Sagan from Amnesty International phoned Jones in Hawaii with instructions to warn his friend of the plot that awaited him upon return from a three-year exile in the U.S.

"I told Benigno, and his silence was overpowering," Jones recalls. "He knew, and there was nothing I could do to prevent him from going home."

On August 23, two of Marcos's henchmen in San Francisco blocked Jones from entering the Commonwealth Club for lunch. "They told me not to go back to Manila, ever, or I would 'follow my friend's fate'," Jones says. And then Jones went back to the country, with instructions from Shultz to assure widowed People Power leader Corazon Aquino that the U.S. would recognize her new government if the uprising proved successful.

"I'm here to build a golf course and play a few rounds with my partners," Jones told the Aviation Security Command agents before climbing into the car Aquino had sent for him. Jones shut the door. People Power organizer Jose "Peping" Cojuangco Jr. handed him an AK-47 assault rifle.

"Marcos will torture all of us for the information you're carrying," Cojuangco said. "We must not be taken alive."

Reaching for one of the clubs piled on the backseat floor atop golf balls and ammunition clips, Jones selected a 3-iron and tapped Cojuangco on the shoulder. "Bobby looks me in the eye and calmly says, 'Peping, you got a 7-iron back here? I'd be much better with a 7-iron'," Cojuangco recalls over lunch with his sister, former Philippine president Corazon Aquino.

"Bobby put his life at risk for us more than once, even though I never played golf," Aquino says as the laughter turns solemn. "There's no doubt you used the game of golf to influence U.S. politicians to support me instead of Marcos," Aquino tells Jones. "You helped me become president."

Jones sips lemonade and brushes the praise aside. "It was the honorable thing to do," he says. "Golf is an honorable game. You play the ball where it lies."

***

Robert Trent Jones Jr. has no physical or mental fear. Detail fascinates him, particularly when sculpting raw land into environmentally friendly golf courses or indulging in his other passions: politics and poetry. His constitution is extraordinary; he sleeps only a few hours a night, catching "combat naps" as he commutes between each of the no more than ten bespoke golf courses he builds annually.

His client list is global in scope and includes Kim Jun Ky, chairman of the South Korean industrial conglomerate Dongbu Group; Jackson Ling, chairman and chief executive officer of Enhance Holding Co., the world's largest maker of neon signs; and John Tyson, chairman and CEO of Tyson Foods Inc., the world's largest meat-packer.

The cost of a signature RTJII course runs from $950,000 to $1.2 million. The price doesn't include construction.

"Anything more than ten is production architecture by a computer and a committee," Jones says. "I don't do that. When my name is on a course, you can be damn sure it was designed in my head and that I built it with my own hands."

Jones learned the craft from his father, a second-generation Welshman who began his career as a teenage caddy for Eastman Kodak Co. founder George Eastman at the Rochester Country Club in New York. "Dad left the caddy shack and started to play, then he learned how to design," Jones says. "Eastman taught him how to run a business."

Trained from birth by his father to continue the family legacy of building "masterpiece" golf courses ("Dad threw a rattle in my crib and showed me how to grip a club," he says), Jones has spent his entire life turning everything from the scrubby semi-deserts of the Middle East to the swamplands of Thailand into championship golf courses.

He spent twenty years bulldozing through the Soviet bureaucracy, finally convincing President Mikhail Gorbachev that the bunkers he intended to build at the Moscow Country Club in Nakhabino—Russia's first and so far only eighteen-hole golf course—were not Pentagon-inspired tank traps to slow down Russian armor during any armed confrontation with the West.

"I closed that deal by inviting a group of Soviet Central Committee members to the Bohemian Club in San Francisco," Jones says. "They were the first communists ever to visit the club. We sang songs and read poetry in the dining room."

In 1979, the White House called Jones away from a course construction site on the Japanese island of Hokkaido to fly to Seattle for a meeting with President Jimmy Carter and Chinese leader Deng Xiaoping to discuss what ultimately became the 7,025-yard, par-72 Shanghai International Country Club.

"Carter and Deng didn't play golf, but they both understood that golf was a great way to attract investment," Jones says.

"We finally made it to Shanghai in November 1983," says Blakeney Stafford, Jones's attorney. Accompanying the duo was President George H. W. Bush's brother, Prescott Bush Jr., who arranged for a group of Japanese investors to underwrite the course.

"Shanghai was a dust bowl and we were absolutely the only foreigners in the city," Stafford recalls. "We went to the zoo with thousands of Chinese to see the pandas, and we were the most exotic animals in the place."

Three months after the Chinese government's crackdown on protesters in Tiananmen Square in 1989, Jones, Stafford, and Bush returned to Shanghai and built the course.

"There's always a lot of 'deal fatigue' and lost time building a course in a politically sensitive country," Stafford says of the ten-year project in Shanghai. "We charged the Russians $387,000 for Nakhabino and lost a bundle, but Bob views these courses as political labors of love and doesn't care how long they take."

"Bobby is a living brand in China and the man who single-handedly brought golf to Asia," explains Robert Theleen, a former U.S. Central Intelligence Agency officer and now chairman of investment capital firm ChinaVest Inc. in Shanghai.

"The greatest gift an American doing business in China can give to any government official is two golf gloves, and Bobby is responsible for that tradition. The politicians don't want anyone to know they play golf," Theleen explains. "They all use two gloves so neither hand will be tanned by the sun."

Today, Theleen says China boasts two hundred golf courses, with a hundred more being built—so many courses that the government has slapped a three-year moratorium on all new construction.

"I'm going to have Bob build me a course alongside the Great Wall anyway," says Enhance Holding CEO Jackson Ling. "The economy is like water and it can't be stopped. Golf is essential to doing business in China," says Ling, who has invested $85 million in the RTJII course Jones built for him at the Anting Enhance Golf Club in International Automotive City, northwest of Shanghai.

The 7,200-yard, par-72 course is the centerpiece of a 46-square-mile industrial patch that Allen Matis, chairman and CEO of investment bank Oriental Development Ltd., describes as the "boomtown home for the Chinese automotive sector and twenty thousand foreign manufacturing firms."

Indeed, Ling is so enthralled with having Jones as his personal golf-course architect that he has lined the road between Shanghai and International Automotive City with billboards festooned with a picture of Jones and the RTJII logo.

Smoking a Cohiba and piloting his Mercedes S600 like a tank over the unfinished bunkers along the monster 620-yard eighteenth hole, the neon-sign mogul says he doesn't care how much money it costs for an RTJII championship course. "Shanghai is flat, so I need to spend money on lots of bunkers," Ling explains, stepping on the accelerator.

"I threw up my hands, told Bob I wanted the best and that price wasn't an issue," Ling says as the car blasts over the fortification and slaps down on the fairway. "Business over golf is a way of life in China, and a lot of people cheat. I find out who cheats on the golf course."

In Washington, Jones's willingness to play risky shots while partnered with the likes of Gorbachev, Jack Nicklaus, Deng Xiaoping, and Tiger Woods spurred President George W. Bush to give his golf companion the nickname "Renaissance Man."

"I am practicing but don't seem to be making much progress—how about a lesson?" reads the handwritten note Bush sent Jones, which is now taped above the coffee machine at RTJII headquarters in Palo Alto, California.

***

"Reagan didn't like to play golf," says Jones, who built the putting green on the south lawn of the White House. "Ford was a keen golfer. Nixon hacked around. I've hit balls with all of them, and all of them recognized the importance of golf as a diplomatic tool."

Jones, a card-carrying Democrat, says his global view was forged on fairways that weren't necessarily built with American soil.

"My family for nearly seventy-five years has been into globalization and using golf for regime change," Jones says. "Golf is an honorable game that must be played by honorable men and women," is his guiding principle, and friends say Jones can turn furious with any politician or businessman who mocks this deeply entrenched conviction.

"Bobby is one of our most important operatives," quips Rep. Nancy Pelosi of California during a late-afternoon lunch at a restaurant on San Francisco Bay on the eve of the 2004 U.S. presidential election. "He builds golf courses for Republicans."

Jones doesn't smile at Pelosi's description of his status in the Democratic Party.

"Look at it this way," he tells Pelosi, who is now Speaker of the House. "Both Bush and his father like to play a fast round. Clinton likes his mulligans."

As for status, it's hard to beat your own golf course. John Tyson calls the one Jones built for him "an okay goat yard."

Standing on the practice tee of his 7,506-yard, par-72 Blessings golf club near his corporate headquarters in Springdale, Arkansas, Tyson says hitting a golf ball is a "secondary function" in any outing with Jones. "Bob gives you a walking lecture on golf design and global politics, and you learn how his mind works," Tyson explains.

He says Jones has a willingness to take risks and believes any challenge can be overcome by the disciplined application of the rules of golf. And he adds that Jones, like the game of golf, has a knack for humbling people quickly.

"Golf is the definition of diplomacy," Tyson explains. "The parties are together on the same ground, going in different directions to reach a common goal. After eighteen holes, all the parties are exposed and all the baggage disappears."

The American Society of Golf Course Architects counts 166 members on its rolls, and thirty of them have worked for the Jones family.

Although golf legends such as Jack Nicklaus and Gary Player charge from $400,000 to $2.2 million to build eighteen holes, a 2003 analysis by the Golf Research Group in Dallas showed that Jones's courses outperform the competition in generating green fees, membership sales, and the attendant value of real estate connected to the course. "It is noticeable that the value of the memberships at the courses designed by RTJII have endured better than at courses by other designers" such as Nicklaus, Player, Arnold Palmer, and Tom Weiskopf, the report said. "RTJII memberships are roughly double their launch price today, while memberships at other courses are roughly half their launch prices."

In the industry's fastest growth area, Southeast Asia, for instance, the report said Jones's eighty courses there annually generate about $56 million in green fees as well as membership sales and dues. Nicklaus finished third with $37.5 million; Player bottomed the field with $18.4 million.

"Jones is the man," explains Peter Walton, CEO of the International Association of Golf Tour Operators, a 900-member industry group that caters to the desires of the world's fifty million golfers. "His name is magic. When Jones creates a signature course, customers literally come running with their clubs and wallets," Walton says.

Pouring wine in the Dongbu Group corporate dining room in Seoul, chairman Kim Jun Ky says the epiphany came to him in 2002, after he putted out on the eighteenth green of the Four Seasons Resort golf course on the Caribbean island of Nevis.

"I went right to the clubhouse, called my office, and told them to immediately find Robert Trent Jones Jr.," Kim says. "I'd discussed Mr. Jones building a course for me in 1987 and 1990, but decided on a Japanese architect. Then I played his course on Nevis. I finally realized it is easy for someone who has played golf for thirty years to score par on other courses, but not so easy on one built by Mr. Jones."

Kim walks to the giant floor-to-ceiling windows that encircle his penthouse, raises his glass, and offers a toast to his guest. "Mr. Jones, you are an honorable man," Kim says through his interpreter.

Jones thanks his host for the compliment, but warns that the tribute might be fleeting. The architect says the mountain he's about to spend a year sculpting into a 7,200-yard, par-72 golf course, with fifty-five lakes and waterfalls, is severe, and that Kim will have to "think and play well" to survive the championship challenge.

"I must explore the prevailing winds and how the light falls on the land to create tight tee shots and tight fairways," Jones tells his new client. "But I must also apply Korean culture to the course, and to accomplish that I still have much to learn."

Kim grows excited, and interrupts his interpreter.

"As of now," Kim announces to the senior Dongbu executives gathered for the celebratory dinner, "the course will be named The Robert Trent Jones Jr. Golf Course."

The following morning, Jones is juggling a pair of golf shoes and a plate of toast in the back seat of a truck sliding down a hill near the summit of Mount Soori, site of the bespoke 7,400-yard, par-72 course he's now completing for Hyundai Cement Co., and in mortar range of the demilitarized zone that separates North and South Korea. On the other side of the mountain is Jones's Oak Valley Golf Course.

"That's the one where I had to incorporate poles on either side of the fairways so the army can stretch out cables to prevent North Korean troop gliders from landing at night," Jones says. "Whoa, stop the truck," he barks.

Yang Kim, managing director of the Hyundai Sungwoo Resort, nestles the vehicle alongside a boulder. "These are diamonds," Jones says, climbing out of the truck and scooping up a handful. "Silica sand, baby, made by volcanoes, easy to shape and the best soil you can have for a golf course."

Jones fills both palms with dirt. "The only difference between investing in a Picasso and a great golf course is you can't move the golf course," he adds. "Michelangelo preferred Carrera marble; I'm the silica sandman."

Still, Jones says geology confronts him with an often insoluble dilemma not faced by other artists. All golf courses start with the practical consideration that their design is limited by what the earth has to offer and, more important for Jones, who the client acquired the land from.

"It's frequently a life-or-death situation that has nothing to do with green drainage," Jones says. "The golf industry is so big with money, power, and superstars that everyone forgets we play an agricultural peasant game. Before I work on land, I want to know where it came from. You can't just go around filling in somebody's rice paddies."

Indeed, a 1997 *Smithsonian* magazine review of the ecological hazards attached to golf-course construction described Jones's method of design as "a case study of how a golf course can have a surprisingly low impact on even a sensitive environmental area."

Shortly after the 1994 opening of the Moscow Country Club, for instance, Jones discovered that villagers were shagging tee shots and trying to sell the balls back to the players. In response, club officials blocked off much of the course, built on land that for centuries had been the region's richest ground for mushroom picking.

"The villagers didn't know about golf and I didn't know about the mushrooms," says Jones, who helped broker a compromise that left the balls in play and the mushrooms available for the skillet.

"Where fairways come from is a serious political issue," explains Alan Timblick, senior vice president of InvestKorea, a South Korean government agency with a mandate to attract foreign investment to the country. "Much of the world perceives golf as a rich man's sport, and right now the government here is about to stop subsidizing thousands of peasant rice farmers and plans to move that agricultural land into the golf leisure industry."

Timblick, a British banker and the highest-ranking foreigner in the South Korean government, says the shift from paddies to putting greens is essential to stop South Korean golfers from leaving the country with $571 million each year to play on Japan's 2,400 courses or the eighty-two courses in the Philippines. "We don't have enough golf courses," he rues. "You can't have a business hub without golf. Golf is necessary to remain competitive in attracting direct foreign investment."

At the same time, Timblick says South Korea's four million golfers, who currently vie for tee times on 195 local courses, must employ camouflage to describe their sport. "In South Korea, golf must be referred to as 'exercise' or 'field research'," Timblick explains. "It's too ostentatious and politically incorrect to say you're playing golf."

Jones says politically motivated disaffection with the golf industry, once begun, acquires a momentum all its own. "I've spent over twenty years putting the Reds on the greens in Russia and China," Jones says. "The only argument that works is to explain that golf is not slash-and-burn capitalist agriculture and that the entire community must share in the economics of the sport. That's what I told Deng and that's why the Chinese government gave us one dilapidated bulldozer and three thousand stoop-laborers to build the Shanghai Country Club golf course."

Asian operations director Michael Kahler harbors no doubt that Jones's poetry also helps seal politically sensitive deals. "Never seen anything like it," he says. "You're sitting around a conference table, discussing a multimillion dollar contract with clients and government officials, and Bob pulls out his poems and starts reading them. He gets applause."

During his meeting with the chairman of Dongbu Group, for instance, Jones explained the mission of RTJII with two lines from his poem "Greens":

Creating great greenscapes now,
Green lungs against the urban plow.

In Beijing, during a meeting with Hu Jian Guo, vice chairman of the China Golf Association, Jones read verses from "Sixty on the Seventh of September," a poem dedicated to Russian deputy foreign minister Ivan

Sergeev, the director of the Soviet state company that helped him battle the communist hardliners to build Nakhabino:

Celebrate the essence of Nature
Not the victory of temporary games.

***

It's wintry and after midnight on the Old Course at the Royal & Ancient Golf Club of St. Andrews, where locals on May 14, 1775, reckoned all courses should be eighteen holes long because there are eighteen "jiggers" of whiskey in a bottle of Scotch.

It was along this 6,609-yard, par-72 pasture that shepherds six hundred years ago boiled gull feathers and stuffed the downy porridge inside a spherical leather sack to first play golf with jury-rigged farm implements. As Tiger Woods said after charging to victory here at the 2000 Open, "To win at St. Andrews is the ultimate."

Peter Dawson, secretary of the game's rulemaking body, says Jones's courses tap the spiritual energy of the game as it was first played on the Old Course in the Scottish seaside town. "Bob is very high on the list of great golf-course designers," the British engineer says on the balcony of his office at the R&A. "The Old Course is the game's sacred yardstick, but not all golf-course architects look at these eighteen holes as such. Bob does."

Walking the Old Course blindly alongside Jones is not an experience easily forgotten. He is swept up by the occasion and, for him, it is a ritual now in its fortieth year. His body is immune to the cold, his voice firmly solemn with every word. "This is a spiritual place," Jones says as a bitter North Sea wind slaps against the invisible flagsticks. "To build a great golf course or play a great game of golf, you need to feel the land," he adds, running his fingers across the consecrated turf.

Even at more than $100 a round, the Old Course is an elite tabernacle. Only forty-four thousand visiting golfers by lottery each year win starting times on the Old Course, and the links are closed on Sunday.

"Demand outstrips supply by a margin we can't even calculate," Old Course superintendent Gordon Moir says, pointing to a street of multi-million-dollar row houses strategically clustered alongside the eighteenth green. Much of the real estate is foreign-owned, giving titleholders residency status and the right to take advantage of the eight A.M. to ten A.M. starting time reserved for locals.

"A holy place?" Moir asks. "For a golfer, this is God's proving ground."

Jones's golf partner, William Swing, the Episcopalian bishop of San Francisco, reckons there's no blasphemy in viewing the game as the Lord's work. "Ninety percent of the events that happen in the Bible take place outdoors," the prelate reasons. "Golf gets you back in the direction from which we came. The game is complicated and you must be accountable. There's redemption, and a great deal of grace. You can hit a horrible shot and still have a great result. That is life."

Sitting in his owner's suite at the Old Course Hotel in St. Andrews, Herbert Kohler, chairman and president of the global plumbing and engine-supply giant Kohler Co., puts down his drink and scratches his white beard. "Is Jones really a good golf architect?" asks the proprietor of the 2004 PGA Championship course Whistling Straits near Kohler, Wisconsin, and the £35 million Dukes Course in St. Andrews.

Kohler points toward the early-evening snow flurries outside. It's dark and cold, and a foursome is playing the eighteenth hole. "That's the Road Hole, the most famous hole in golf, and it was built by grazing sheep," he explains. "For a course to be called great, every hole must try to be as memorable as that one. The Old Course is a fluke of nature and remains the touchstone for greatness in all modern golf-course architecture."

"Toilets or golf courses, you must make the best," he says. "Jones built one of the great golf courses in the universe, The Prince, in Hawaii. There are fifteen thousand golf courses in the U.S., and The Prince is one of the very few where every hole meets my definition of great. That doesn't make Jones a good architect, it makes him good-God amazing."

***

The day was hot and showery, with a tricky pitch shot to the green on the 212-yard seventeenth hole at St. Elena. Majestic trees surrounded Jones with a canopy of branches ready to wreak havoc on any chance of a par three. A short backswing, a clean follow-through in the rough, and the ball plops down on the Philippine green looking at a bogey.

"I made this hole too darn hard," says Jones, as he putted out on the 7,170-yard-long course he carved through the jungle in 1994. "Right, I know what's coming," he adds, tugging the ever-present golf cap over his brown eyes. "Everyone's going to ask what's my favorite place to play golf. The answer remains the same: the next hole."

PROPULSION **IS A REAL PLUS WITH CLUBS** MADE **IN A MISSILE** FACTORY

THE IDEA TO BECOME A GOLF PRO FLEW OUT OF THE SKY and hit Alexey Nikolov on the head.

"I was visiting a family in Florida," explains Nikolov, chewing a red wooden tee in the pro shop of the Moscow Country Club, twenty-five miles east of the Kremlin in the village of Nakhabino. "One morning, I left the house and strolled into a beautiful park. Within seconds, faraway voices started screaming at me, and I was hit by what seemed to be a petrified egg. I had no idea what was going on. Turned out, I had wandered onto the third fairway at the Pine Oaks Golf Club in Ocala."

Eight years and a lot of golf lessons later, the graduate of the former Soviet Academy of Physical Culture is Russia's first golf pro and the chief spokesman for the Czar. "But this baby is no Romanov," says Nikolov enthusiastically, as he swings the Russian royal family's namesake—the first driver ever made in Russia—at a ball on the country club's 7,005-yard championship course. "Pure titanium head and, at $360, thirty percent cheaper than anything comparable on the market. The pro shop can sell you a full set of Czars for under $2,000."

Promoting Russian drivers, irons, and putters, coaching the national golf team, and juggling the tee-off times of the club's golfers leave Nikolov little time to play the game he is determined to popularize in a country that once denounced golf as capitalist decadence. When he is not in the clubhouse organizing corporate tournaments or on the course shooing sunbathers off the greens, Russia's would-be Arnold Palmer can be found in the caddie shack, painting balls red for winter play. "I don't even know what my handicap is any more," he says, "but I do have a fifty-year plan for Russian golf. By 2042, we will have two hundred thousand players, a hundred courses, and two Russians on the PGA Tour who are winning events."

Nikolov's blueprint is the audacious offspring of a Russian golf strategy sealed with a handshake in Kuala Lumpur in 1974. It was on the junglefront course at the Royal Selangor Golf Club that Vladimir Kuznetzov, the Soviet ambassador to Malaysia, spotted the American golf-course architect Robert Trent Jones Jr. approaching the first tee. "What's your handicap?" Kuznetzov recalls asking Jones. "About a six," Jones replied. "That's pretty good," said the ambassador. "I'm a fourteen myself." "Really?" asked Jones, his curiosity aroused. "Where do you play in Russia?" "That's the problem," said Kuznetzov. "I must go to Czechoslovakia to play on my vacation."

According to both men, that chance encounter was the first step in a strange twenty-year commercial effort that culminated in the official opening of the $3.5 million Moscow Country Club in the spring of 1993, which included Jones's presentation of a Czar driver to President Bill Clinton. "The entire Russian golf project was quite a military comedy during the Cold War," says Jones. "The Pentagon thought I was going to build bunkers that could stop NATO armor from rolling across the fairways, and the Red Army thought I was building secret NATO tank passages into Moscow under the guise of a golf course."

But in the new Russia, the biggest challenge has been to speed up the play of golfers representing twenty countries and two dozen multinational corporations.

According to Nikolov, the Japanese, who make up a quarter of the membership, like to stop for a fairway sushi picnic after nine holes. British players demand at least two club-sponsored tournaments a month. Americans wander the tees in search of nonexistent refreshment stands, and Korean companies organize impromptu tournaments that cause green gridlock. "You think Brezhnev had headaches with detente," Nikolov chuckles.

The Russians, who make up more than twenty-five percent of the membership, present a unique set of hazards for the cheerful club pro and his staff of Nakhabino schoolchildren, who are Nikolov's caddies, greenskeepers, and golf students. "My countrymen are not yet wise to the ways of golf," reflects Nikolov. "They arrive for the first time, think the driving range is the first tee, and head off to play beneath raining range balls. The staff risks their lives to steer them in the right direction."

Meanwhile, over at the nineteenth hole—a modern two-story log cabin with a pro shop and a Western-style restaurant—Englishman Mark Hamilford is trying to persuade Russia's new millionaires to buy memberships. Sipping a beer at a table overlooking Nakhabino's pine-and-birch forest, he opens his pitch by asserting that memberships have appreciated thirty percent since they were first offered.

"We've already sold a few hundred," says Hamilford, who works for the division of the Russian foreign ministry that owns the club. Memberships kicked off at at $23,500 for an individual and $95,000 for a corporate affiliation. Hamilford also manages Nakhabino's twenty-seven dacha residences. Located near the back nine, each Finnish-built home has a sauna and heated floors. Rents range from $80,000 to $140,000 a year, and there is a waiting list. "We're going to build 103 more," he says. "The demand for the dachas is enormous."

So is demand for Nakhabino's mushrooms, said to be the best in Russia. Every weekend, nearby villagers scale the concrete wall encircling the course and root for them. Trying to fade drives around the mushroomers and putt through the frogs that hop across the greens in the summer make the par-72 course quite a challenge.

At Metal-Park Ltd., a joint venture with Russia's state-owned aircraft manufacturer Strela, they make golf clubs the old-fashioned way: by hand, and in the same forges that produce Russian Kh-35 naval cruise missiles, Kh-31 air-to-surface missiles, and the titanium fins of MiG-29 fighters.

"We make the MiGs in one room, the 5-irons in another," says Metal-Park's vice president and marketing manager Vladimir Maksimov, whose company turned out its first club head in 1993. "Our original model looked like a potato," he adds, "so we had to make some design changes." Metal-Park has thirty employees, fifteen types of drivers, two lines of irons, and four devilish putters. After fabrication inside a closed military complex outside Moscow, the heads are shipped to Korea, Taiwan, and the U.S. to be fitted to shafts and grips. The Czar's overseas assemblers have so far fitted Metal-Park's 95-percent titanium heads (and a line of titanium–beryllium composite heads) on forty thousand clubs, including the driver Jones carried aboard Air Force One to give to President Clinton.

And what about the story making the rounds that the Czar is made out of genuine Soviet nuclear missiles, Maksimov? "A wonderful ad strategy, but unfortunately a myth," he admits. "Perhaps I shouldn't dispel the story, because we feel our propulsion technology does make the ball go farther."

THE BALLYBUNION CHALLENGE:

IRON AGE GOLF

ED VAUGHAN IS WHISTLING past the graveyard. But the moss-draped tombstones that have marked death for thousands of golfers here on the 392-yard first hole of the Ballybunion Old Course on the western shore of Ireland are the least of the hazards waiting to disrupt the chief executive of U.S.-based Electronic Transaction Systems Co. Before the sun and his golf game disappear over the cliffs along the Atlantic Ocean, Vaughan will become one of some twenty-five thousand global executives who this year will be savaged by offshore gales that empower a hillside of wind turbines, bunkers the size of medieval battlements, and undulating traps filled with seashells, stones, and the decayed bones of Ballybunion's Iron Age inhabitants. The 445-yard second hole is less kind.

"I couldn't sleep last night," Vaughan says of his dream to experience what the likes of Tiger Woods and Tom Watson suggest is the toughest and most spectacular links course in the world. "I've heard about the Old Course since I was a child," he explains. "My heart is pounding." Vaughan, whose game averages in the mid-80s elsewhere, believes his soaring tee shot past the Killahenny cemetery is an omen of birdies to come. Today the sun is out and the wind is rustling a mere fifteen miles per hour. But Ballybunion is provoking him, a prank that will turn ugly on the fifteenth hole, a staggering 216-yard par 3 pounded by Atlantic whitecaps and encircled by hostile banks of reeds and a series of trenches that could repel a tank battalion.

Ballybunion is a place where it's impossible to exaggerate the passions of those who play here, or the harsh reality of the adventure that awaits them. Sure, fourball on the hallowed flatlands of the Royal and Ancient at St. Andrews is a duff through history, and wooing a member at Augusta National to let your Big Bertha run amok among the azaleas can be a rewarding escapade. But make no mistake. Ballybunion is nemesis: the world's only golf course where players have as good a chance of shooting par with a spherical leather bag stuffed with boiled feathers as they do with the latest in aerodynamic golf balls. As Vaughan lamented after shooting a nine on the fifteenth hole, "Who the hell built this place?"

No one knows for sure, but the links' land—sandy rolling hills and high-grass dunes imprinted along a coastline beaten by wind, waves, and burrowing rabbits—clocked its first player in 1893. The vastness of Ballybunion's seaside setting does not provide the natural markers golfers usually rely on to judge distance.

And though there are some 130 links courses in the world, there's only one Ballybunion: 6,953 yards where talent with jiggers and cleeks (4-irons and shallow-faced irons) must be used with the precision of a surgeon's scalpel.

"You play a links course by Braille, with fourteen clubs, a white cane, and a trustworthy seeing-eye dog," warns golf-course architect Robert Trent Jones Jr. And don't even think Jones's advice might work here on the Old Course. "The distortion at Ballybunion is overwhelming," he says. Indeed, less than five percent of the golfers who play Ballybunion manage to break 100.

It's perhaps no wonder that a nineteenth-century priest was the first person ever to have recorded a hole-in-one on the par-71 Old Course, or that the thrall is so strong that nearly every day, helicopters full of golfing executives brave the pelting elements and touch down alongside the driving range. Says Ballybunion secretary-manager Jim McKenna, "I've seen top corporate executives so awed over finally getting here that they arrive at the first tee in tears."

McKenna, a retired criminal investigator with the Irish police force, is not one for irrational exuberance. "All the tales about Ballybunion are true," says Marty Carr, chief executive of Carr Corporate Golf Travel Ltd. in Dublin. Carr's company specializes in the niche market known as heligolf, this year shuttling a thousand executives and their entourages from Dublin and Shannon airports to Ballybunion. "God neglected to make roads when he made Ballybunion," Carr says. "Our clients think nothing of spending $3,000 an hour for a helicopter ride." A former stockbroker with Paine

Webber in New York, he says his past life "helping people lose money in the stock market" prepared him for handling Ballybunion.

"Green fees at Pebble Beach are more than $400. A round at Ballybunion is 75 Irish pounds," Carr says. "It's a deal and a pilgrimage for wealthy golfers used to manicured courses in the sun. A lot of folks are adventure seekers who don't play golf all that often. That's how exciting Ballybunion is."

Never mind the weather. "The worse it is, the more they want to play," Carr says. "They come with ski jackets and woolly hats and hand-warmers." He adds that what makes Ballybunion so different from the other championship courses he represents is the overwhelming number of corporate customers willing to sacrifice a confirmed round at Royal County Down or Royal Portush on the off-chance of a tee time on the Old Course. "I deal with thirty Irish golf courses, and clients demand Ballybunion as their top choice," Carr explains. "With chopper time, they pay over $3,500 a day to play the Old Course. I have executives prepared to spend a week at Ballybunion, playing thirty-six holes a day with a helicopter on call."

At times during the summer, the lawn across the street from Ballybunion's concrete-block clubhouse resembles a military landing zone, with businesspeople jumping off choppers in golf cleats and scrambling up the hill with their bags to find the old course starter known as Small Patsy. "I've seen them all and tell them all not to hit the blessed turf when they tee off—even Bill Clinton, who shot a respectable 87," Small Patsy says of the three hundred golfers allowed to play each day.

"The big hitters of the political and business world don't come here to enjoy themselves, they come here to play golf," says Aoife Brock, the innkeeper of the Teach de Broc guesthouse, a ten-room bed-and-breakfast that has served as the nineteenth hole for top executives from all over the world. "We don't even count the helicopters any more," says Brock, who's baked scones for the likes of former Irish foreign minister Dick Springs and global financier Wayne Huizenga. "All they want is good coffee at dawn and a powerful shower in their room. They arrive stressed out and tunnel-visioned on the Old Course."

McKenna says the draw of Ballybunion is so strong, so consuming, in fact, that over the past twenty years the cremated remains of at least fifty golfing businessmen from around the world have been scattered from the bunker above the seventeenth tee, the highest point on the course. Friends of deceased Ballybunion linksters also have returned with the clubs of their playing partners, burying them in the Killahenny cemetery.

Then there's the late Martin McDermott, a California corporate attorney who died in 1987 and willed that his body be freighted six thousand miles to rest with the other golfers buried in Killahenny. After that, McKenna says, the town ruled that only locals and their relatives could spend eternity in the "boneyard," ensuring an afterlife of errant tee shots knocking shards off their granite gravestones.

"Ahh, yes, what a marvelous way to go," muses Australian pharmacist Bob Keane, who earlier in the day carried his golf bag off a nearly thirty-hour plane and bus expedition from Sydney to Ballybunion to tee off before lunch.

Clambering down the misbegotten scrub-brush ravine that guards the eighteenth green, Keane's playing partner, a bloodied and bandaged Peter Turnbull, digs into his wallet and proudly displays the note from Dr. Derry Gibson, a local physician who twenty-four hours earlier had sewed five stitches in his forehead after it was whacked by a rogue ball shanked off a 4-iron. "The doctor said I could play Ballybunion today if I didn't drink last night," Turnbull says. "I was concerned Small Patsy wouldn't let me tee off because the injury might slow down our foursome." The rules stipulate that the Old Course must be played in four hours or less, and groundskeepers wander the links to speed up stragglers and collect the many Cuban cigar butts players leave behind on the tees. Robert Lauglin Jr., who works in the trust division of J.P. Morgan in New York, says his cigar helped him get over blasting his first two tee shots into the boneyard on his second visit to the Old Course. "The first time, I played in a windstorm and couldn't see a thing," Lauglin says. "I promised never to come back, but here I am."

Nonetheless, the Cohiba *robustos* in the clubhouse are easier to score than a tee time. The club doesn't start taking spring and summer reservations until November. As for the heligolfers willing to slap down any price for unlimited mileage on the Old Course, McKenna cocks an eyebrow and says raising the green fees would be unfair to those who can't afford the big ticket prices charged by most other duality golf courses in Ireland. "We could raise the green fees to two hundred Irish pounds tomorrow and get it," he says. "That's not what the members want."

McKenna also balks at inflating the membership roll. "Now we have a foursome teeing off every fourteen minutes, and I'd like to get that up to fifteen minutes," he says. "It helps preserve the course." Memberships cannot be resold and since 1997 have been frozen at 2,018, including 650 overseas members who pay a one-time fee of $5,000 for as much golf as they want. McKenna reckons sixty percent of Ballybunion's non-member players are American, the remainder a mixture of Swedes, Italians, and South Americans. Marty Carr adds that ninety percent of his Irish heligolf business comes from U.S. executives and corporate incentive programs. Much of it is repeat traffic destined for Ballybunion.

"All repeat players remember the caddy who first carried them through the course," McKenna says. "It's the caddies who carry this club." Veterinarian Jackie Hourigan says the "wildness of the Old Course" also has contributed to Ballybunion's status as one of the toughest links in the world. Around town, Hourigan is widely revered as the man who saved the Old Course from the sea. In 1977, during his tenure as Ballybunion club captain, some eighteen thousand square feet (1,672 square meters) of the Old Course slipped into the Atlantic. "The Irish government didn't want to come up with the money to fix the environment," Hourigan recalls. "There were no golfers in government, and the tourist board didn't believe anyone would be daft enough to travel to Ireland to play golf." So Hourigan launched a global campaign among golfers to save Ballybunion, including a limited sale of life memberships for one-hundred-fifty Irish pounds.

Money poured in from around the world, enough to reclaim the eroding fairways and perk the interest of U.S. professional golfers tantalized by the rich history of Ballybunion and seeking a rugged and secluded links to prepare themselves for the British Open. In 1981, five-time British Open champion Tom Watson played Ballybunion for the first time, eventually supervising upgrades on the Old Course. Jack Nicklaus arrived a few years later and immediately sliced into the boneyard.

"Real golfers know Ballybunion always has been the greatest piece of golf terrain in the world," Hourigan says.

But does a course *Golf Magazine* rates as only the eleventh best in the world—below Augusta National, Pebble Beach, and the Old Course at St. Andrews—deserve such tributes? Those who have played Ballybunion insist the blarney is justified, particularly since one of the few things all golfers can agree on is that every course must first earn its reputation by successfully hosting major professional tournaments. The first and only pro gathering at Ballybunion was the 2000 Murphy's Irish Open, a pit stop along the European PGA Tour that fails to attract the stars from the more lucrative U.S. PGA Tour.

"What Ballybunion has achieved is unheard of in golf," Ed Vaughan says after shooting a 28-over-par 100. "I'd play this course every day of my life. Oh, yeah, I'm coming back," he vows. "Ballybunion beat me up bad. I want revenge."

HEY, TIGER,

BET YOU CAN'T BEAT ME

ON AN OIL SLICK

"**Y**OU'LL GET USED TO THE SMELL," Laxman Singade promises, selecting a 3-iron and setting off in his E-Z-Go golf cart to whack the wild hounds nearing the fifth "brown" of the Dubai Country Club. "No greens here," says the man who has spent more than thirty years refining the game as the club's chief brownskeeper. Singade is an authority on golf as it's played here in the Persian Gulf. The local version of the sport is the only officially sanctioned game played amid dogs and lizards chasing balls across a glutinous mix of sand and thirteen thousand gallons of upper Zakum Crude oil.

"The perfect brown is built from choice Emirate *subka* sand and light-weight crude generously watered with used engine oil," Singade says of the pastime concocted shortly before World War II by expatriate British oil executives in Iran. "Some courses in Saudi Arabia also oil the fairways, but that gets messy."

A noxious frolic? Think again.

The Royal & Ancient Golf Club of St. Andrews, the sport's global governing body, says playing golf on an oil spill is perfectly up to par. The Royal & Ancient rulemakers gave their approval to the use of oil handicaps on grass courses. The guardians of golf also have validated the dimensions and texture of the portable AstroTurf mat that many of the Middle East's estimated fifty thousand tar golfers, a mix of expatriates and locals, deploy for fairway shots.

"The game should be a must for all keen grass golfers," says Royal & Ancient rules secretary David Rickman. "There are no luxuries."

James McClean has seen firsthand the hazards of the game the Royal & Ancient recognizes as sand golf. The thermometer is nudging up to 118 degrees, and a two-foot-long spiny *dhub* lizard appears to have stolen McClean's ball on the fifteenth hole of the Abu Dhabi Airport Golf Club & Sand Golf Academy, one of about twenty fuel-and-dune links scattered throughout the Middle East, Australia, Nigeria, South Africa, and even in Kangerlussuaq, Greenland.

"I thought the lizards stopped doing that," the club's British managing director says, scraping a syrup of sand, sweat, and crankcase lubricant off his face with a 7-iron. "The lizards first thought the balls were eggs, but gradually learned to push them out of their burrows."

Despite the gallery of canines and reptiles and an unruly mob of camel spiders, which travel at eighteen miles an hour and possess jaws strong enough to bite through golf socks, Jeff Sheldon, director of the fire-security division at Tyco International Ltd., reckons the 6,450-yard, par-71 airport course is a pussycat compared to the eighteen-hole oiler on nearby Futasi Island.

"Ospreys nest in the trees and have a horrid habit of relieving themselves on you in the middle of a backswing," says Sheldon, a veteran of the sand game. "The stuff shoots out like cannon fire. And the heat is so bad that golf balls either split open or get distorted out of shape."

Over at the Abu Dhabi Golf & Equestrian Club, Bob Lapointe says that there are no more than a hundred thousand sand golfers globally, and that they all need to ruin a set of clubs during one round before they can claim expert status. "Whoever said the desert is made of sand was lying," says Lapointe, a technical instructor for the Abu Dhabi National Oil Company and chairman of the Emirates Gentleman's Golf (and Girlies) Society. "Irons are completely destroyed hitting balls off rocks, and the fairways are covered with a filthy dew of oil. It's a great game."

Mohamed Mounib, managing director of Abu Dhabi Airport Catering and Duty Free, says that all sand golfers are "nuts" and that he accepts full responsibility for the plight of the 250 members at the airport club. "My company owns the land," Mounib says in the refrigerated clubhouse. "A few crazy guys came to me in 1997 and said they wanted to build a sand course and I said yes. I didn't know the first thing about golf. Now I have a twenty-one handicap and go home coated with oil."

Aficionados insist that the oil game has a friendly side. Economically, they point out, sand makes sense. "It costs around $8 million just to build eighteen grass holes in the Arabian desert and a million gallons of water a day to maintain it," says McClean, the club's managing director. "A sand course costs $20,000 and needs ten thousand gallons of water each week to smooth the fairways."

***

Even though more lavish and popular grass courses are opening through-out the Middle East, the Royal & Ancient's Rickman says that "sand golf is an admirable endeavor with great enthusiasm in a climate that works against players." Which is just what the founding foursome of sand golfers from British Petroleum had in mind when they invented the sport. Old-timers say the Bobby Jones of the Persian oil game was a British Army officer in Iran named Dixon.

"Dixon went to Kuwait after the World War II and helped build the course at Magwa," says Roy Connor, a senior engineer at the Abu Dhabi Oil Co. "Magwa is our St. Andrews, the home of sand golf." The game's oral history suggests that it was at Magwa, which was blown apart during the 1991 Desert Storm campaign and later rebuilt, that petroleum engineers fleshed out the original formula for making browns. "The brown was a science for those men," Connor marvels.

The earliest known recipe called for Kuwaiti crude oil mixed with smooth sand harvested deep in the desert and trucked to the course. After using rakes and pitchforks to mold the sludge into browns, the putting surfaces were further greased with a precise three-to-one ratio of spent lubricating oil and fresh paraffin and then left to bake for six to fourteen days before play. In the inferno of the desert, sprinkled with engine drainings and swept with brooms after everyone putts out, browns keep nicely for a year.

The so-called Magwa Method changed as the game rolled into Saudi Arabia and the UAE, where brownskeepers tweaked the process to accommodate regional differences in oil and sand. Mark Hutton, general manager of the Dubai Country Club, the oldest sand course in the UAE, says the Dubai Method was developed in the late 1960s by the revered Portuguese brownskeeper Ignacio Roderick near a scorched trailer that sits on the club oil dump off the 205-yard fourth hole.

Connor prefers the browns of Magwa. "We cared for them like English gardens," he says.

"Oh, phooey. Dixon's course is overrated and I never liked it much," retorts 92-year-old Irishman Mike Daly, a retired executive with the Bahrain Petroleum Co. "The Abu Dhabi Airport and the Dubai Country Club have the best formula and are the toughest sand courses in the world," is Daly's view. And who's to doubt him? "No one who's still alive, I can tell you that," says Daly, who plays eighteen holes of oil each week and doesn't like golf carts because they get stuck in sand drifts.

For Daly, the only controversy likely to erupt between the sandmen and Royal & Ancient regulators centers on the portable fairway, a twelve-inch-diameter slab of AstroTurf that looks like a pizza with short, curly green hair. "Before the invention of AstroTurf, we hit fairway shots off the sand, though you could improve your lie," Daly says. "There are four sand clubs in the Emirates and they all use a different sort of mat."

Rickman says that "it's rather hot in the desert" and that the Royal & Ancient is happy to endorse the UAE Golf Association's position on the issue of plastic-fairway density.

"I'm relieved to hear that," Dubai Country Club manager Hutton says. "Our research shows that businessmen who play sand golf have a more colorful vocabulary and drink a hell of a lot more beer than grass golfers.'"

ISRAEL'S SACRED GOLF COURSE CONVERTS BOMB CRATERS INTO BUNKERS

IT'S A SOFT 3-IRON SHOT BETWEEN MIRACLES along the Sea of Galilee, where Jesus of Nazareth walked on water and New York-based Americas Partners LLP General Partner Joseph Bernstein is spending $46 million to build the first 36-hole championship golf course in Israel.

"This is God's proving ground and the most exciting deal I've done in my life," Bernstein says of the Galilee Golf Club seaside course atop Mount Arbel, where the fairways are sculpted from the "green pastures" that inspired the Jewish King David to compose the Twenty-third Psalm and where the multitudes gathered beneath myrtle trees to hear the Christian savior deliver his Sermon on the Mount.

"It took them years to get the Israeli government to approve the deal," says Bernstein, whose past property developments for American Partners include the Crown Building and Americas Tower in Manhattan. "The project is unique. It's like building a golf course on Mount Rushmore, and that doesn't get close to the historical significance of Mount Arbel."

For Israel, the significance of a championship course with the cachet to lure marquee players such as Tiger Woods, stage professional tour events, and host affluent corporate golf outings flows even deeper. "Mount Arbel is the symbol for the booming Israeli economy," Bernstein says. "The Galilee Golf Club is a leitmotif for a country that has rid itself of isolation to become part of the global economy."

Although Hebrew University Professor Robert Aumann, winner of the 2005 Nobel Prize in Economics, politely suggests that the God of Abraham might prefer a less secular tour guide for the Jewish state, Bernstein is right. International investors in 2006 pumped a record $23 billion into Israel, fueling economic growth by 5.1 percent and pushing unemployment down to a ten-year low in the fourth quarter. Israel's central bank says foreigners purchased $1.4 billion of property in 2006 and $262 million in the first two months of 2007, and that consumer spending rose nearly five percent in 2006.

"Our economy certainly works best when everybody is looking out for themselves, but there are two big dangers," Aumann says while playing with his grandson in Jerusalem. "Israel simply being physically wiped out is the first. The second is the lost character of the Jewish state. Idealism created the state, it's what we strive for, what makes us unique in the Western world. Yet the survival of Israel is paramount."

***

On July 4, 1187, near the site of the Galilee Golf Club pro shop, Saladin, the Sultan of Egypt, Arabia, Syria, and Mesopotamia, crushed the Crusader army dispatched to recapture the Holy Land. Today, Saladin's decisive victory at the Battle of Hattin arouses al-Qaeda, Fatah al-Islam, and other jihad groups such as the al-Aqsa Martyrs' Brigades to adulate his name and venerate Mount Arbel's soil. Bathed in the angst and delirium of fanatics, the ancient battleground is a main terrorist target for Iranian president Mahmoud Ahmadinejad and his satraps in the West Bank, Gaza, and Lebanon. During Israel's 33-day war against Lebanon in 2006, Iranian-funded Hezbollah terrorists to the north pocked what the Galilee Golf Club prospectus describes as "a cozy citadel in the Promised Land" with twenty Katyusha rockets.

"We'll convert their craters into bunkers," says Moshe Shapira, Bernstein's partner in the venture and general manager of Israel by the Sea Resort & Club, a sprawling estate of luxury golf villas and spa residences coordinated by Ritz-Carlton hotel chain co-founder Horst Schulze and scheduled to open in early 2009 alongside the first eighteen holes.

The club will accommodate 1,500 full-time and one hundred founding members, including former New York state attorney general Robert Abrams. Membership costs range from $37,500 to $150,000, and Shapira says he isn't having trouble finding takers. "I'm more concerned about what the government intends to do about a peace agreement with the

Palestinians and continue Israel's economic growth into the future," Shapira says after whistling past the graveyard that doglegs left off a wheat field earmarked to become the eighteenth fairway. "Israel must be a country that welcomes everybody's business—Jews, Muslims, Christians—and I want all of them to come to Mount Arbel for golf before visiting the holy sites in Jerusalem."

As Aumann tells it, the word of the Lord doesn't always mix with the principles that govern gross domestic product. Israel's GDP was to a degree underwritten by "Jews throwing away their religion, throwing away their cultural heritage," he explains. "Jews now don't any longer know why they are here in Israel," Aumann frets. "What people want is a golf course. They pursue this and don't want to join the Army and be bothered with all the conflicts. This is not a good thing." Says Bernstein: "Nowadays, all young Israelis want to be Bill Gates. They have a mad sense of needing to achieve. It's not about money and the old stereotypes."

Still, the clash between the profits and prophets, in a nation that counts thirty-six political parties in no small part governed by people waiting for the Messiah, has lumbered the Israeli economy with a unique set of truly unseen market forces crying out in the wilderness. Chief among them, Aumann says, is the voice of Moses, Israel's chief spiritual officer. In Exodus, Moses heeded God's word and punished the Israelites for worshiping the golden calf. A few chapters later, during his farewell speech in Deuteronomy, Moses warned the nation about the downside of venture capital. "And when thy herds and thy flocks multiply, and thy silver and thy gold is multiplied, and all that thou hast is multiplied; Then thine heart be lifted up, and thou forget the Lord thy God, which brought thee forth out of the land of Egypt, from the house of bondage," the Torah quotes Moses as saying.

"Moses made a very good point," Aumann reasons. "We're beginning to pursue the gold calf, forgetting our ideals, forgetting why we're here."

Outside the headquarters of Jerusalem Venture Partners, in the hip capital-city quarter of Malha, young men sipping coffee-flavored soda pop and listening to iPods make their way to work alongside young women with babies and BlackBerries. Malha is the festive epicenter of Israel's thriving high-tech sector, where managing partner Erel Margalit handles a $680 million portfolio of investments in some forty Israeli and foreign technology companies. Raised on a kibbutz that manufactured irrigation systems and armed with a doctorate in philosophy from Columbia University in

New York, Margalit started JVP in 1993 and now compares Israel to a corporation that must reinvent itself to survive.

"We're reinterpreting what Israel is all about," says Margalit, whose forty employees work in New York, Jerusalem, London, and Shanghai. "Idealism was the engine of Israel's growth, but idealism today is not measured by the same process we used before. We no longer reflect back to Biblical times. Judaism is a culture, not a religion, and I think we've demonstrated how to make a profit and still be idealistic."

Margalit's long-term challenges are elaborate, complex, and perhaps eternal. "This company has survived two Intifadas, two Gulf wars, and too many suicide bombings," he says. "A peace settlement between Israel and its neighbors must happen. Why? Because our neighbors are a market waiting to happen. Israel is the new economic gateway to the Middle East."

Israel Borovich, chairman of El Al Israel Airlines Ltd., remains skeptical of the high-tech Moloch. "The path to the Middle East is through Dubai," he says. "They have developed an infrastructure that makes it very difficult for us to attract new visitors."

Avishay Braverman, a former World Bank senior economist, also harbors doubts about Israel's economic path. "My fear is Israel becomes a capitalist oligarchy," says Braverman, who represents the Labor Party in Israel's parliament. "Listen and listen hard: economic growth is problematic. Only seven percent of the Israeli labor force is in the high-tech sector, and it accounts for a mere ten percent of our economy. There is no trickle-down." Pausing to quench his thirst at a Tel Aviv café, Braverman, who spent sixteen years as president of Ben Gurion University, puts down a tumbler of water and continues a well-practiced history lecture. "Simple materialism destroyed Israel two thousand years ago. If we neglect the collective, Israel is finished. Privatization was a process we had to allow, but the government is incapable of managing privatization. Oligarchs run the country, and we have some of the worst corruption in the world."

Indeed, at the bar of the American Colony Hotel in Jerusalem, the joke goes that Israel has more corrupt politicians than Jews. A recent poll conducted by Israel's Dahaf Institute found that eighty-five percent of Israelis considered their political leaders to be corrupt.

Police investigations into Prime Minister Ehud Olmert's private real-estate deals and his involvement in the state sale of Bank Leumi Le-Israel Ltd. are under way. There are also official probes into the conduct of Finance Minister Avraham Hirschson; Israeli president Moshe Katsav, who was forced to take leave after being accused of rape; and Justice Minister Haim Ramon, who stepped down for kissing a female soldier against her will. Ramon's predecessor, Tzachi Hanegbi, has been indicted for illicit appointments when he was environment minister. Olmert's long-time aide, Shula Zaken, was put on leave during an investigation by the Income Tax Authority. Israel's ambassador to El Salvador, Tzuriel Raphael, was recalled in 2007 after police there found him outside his home drunk, naked, bound, and gagged with sex toys.

At the same time, thirty-five percent of all Israeli children, and twenty-four percent of the entire population of about seven million, live below the poverty line, according to the government's National Insurance Institute. Among Israeli Arabs, child poverty is more than fifty percent.

"We represent a Third World country," Braverman says. "How we conduct ourselves internally will define our future. The corruption is the greatest crisis in our history, and we are battling now for the survival of Israel," he says. "I don't like a country that takes the money and runs. Eventually, everyone will want to leave."

Until then, Eran Ophir's job is to keep the Israeli workforce alive. "It's not easy; maybe it's my destiny," says Ophir, the brigadier general in charge of building the $2 billion, 800-kilometer (497-mile) security barrier between Israel and the West Bank. "The fence involves legal considerations, engineering, and psychology. It's the biggest project ever to have been built in Israel." Huddled around the fence command desk with his aide inside a bespoke trailer at the Tel Hashomer Military Area, Ophir stirs a cup of robust black coffee laced with cardamom and says his mission is to give Israelis a normal life. "The economy is growing, and the fence has played a crucial psychological role in that growth," he says. "Helping the economy wasn't one of the original goals when we began construction in 2002. It's an added benefit. When the civilian population has confidence, they can do their jobs."

Retired Israeli Air Force general Ran Ronen, chairman of Aquaria Ltd., a $300-million golf and entertainment complex being constructed with Americas Partners in the Red Sea town of Eilat, describes his investment in the future as a "cold and calculated risk," given the continued failure of Israel and its neighbors to implement a peace accord. Ronen is a seventy-year-old veteran of four Arab wars and dozens of dogfights in the cockpit of everything from secondhand Spitfires to F-15 jet fighters. "We must attract non-Jews to the Israeli economy," is his verdict on Israel's economic survival. "The only way to do that is by peace through strength with the Palestinians. That's the solution, but it might be too late if we wait for the peace before we invest."

Back on Mount Arbel, Chaim Cohen says he is ready to switch on his television to watch Tiger Woods play at the Masters. Standing knee-deep in a field of purple and yellow wildflowers, the manager of Moshav Kfar Hittim (Wheat Village) says he didn't know much about the sport until Bernstein and Shapira explained the game and offered the 150 families who manage the highland farm and ranch cooperative a 26-percent stake in the golf-resort project. "I never thought we'd be involved in a golf course," Cohen laughs through his thick white moustache. He says there was a different kind of shooting when his father and the others arrived on Mount Arbel from Bulgaria in 1936 to obtain the land and start the farm. "Back then," Cohen recalls, "you didn't go into fields with a gun, you went with *five* guns."

The guns of Moshav Kfar Hittim are now silent. The only sound is the breeze, rushing up the cliffs from the Sea of Galilee. Beneath a waning copper sunset, the farm's 2007 wheat crop is in final flutter, the land soon reseeded with what master golf architect Robert Trent Jones says will be a "crowning achievement." Shapira says the result will be eight hundred new jobs and thousands of golf balls rolling around the holy mountain, along with the four million eggs the farm's chickens lay annually. "They are very good eggs, and we'll serve them to our guests," Cohen promises. "Golf is an opportunity for our families to build a new chance in the new Israel. Now I must learn how to play."

Slapping Cohen on the shoulder, Shapira says he's eager to include his new partner in a foursome. "What Chaim and I are doing represents what we as a nation want to achieve and is very much a part of our legacy," Shapira explains.

"Israel is trying to be a normal country," Cohen says, as evening storm clouds scud from the north and cluster above Mount Arbel. "We must do this."

CORPORATE PIRATES PILLAGE
THE ISLE OF WIGHT

THE ROYAL YACHT SQUADRON IS NOT AMUSED by the fire-breathing horse that hangs beneath its waterfront artillery here on the Isle of Wight—historic cannons which have, since 1826, blazed the start of Cowes Week, Britain's premier sailing regatta.

For the Squadron, perhaps the most exclusive and secretive yacht club in the world, the logo of Skandia Life Assurance. might as well be a skull and crossbones. Corporate sponsorship has breached the squadron's castle keep and, according to one glum-faced defender, the broadside is a salvo in a uniquely British conflict that hearkens back to Queen Victoria. "The Squadron refused to give her a membership," he reveals, "so she built a house next door to annoy us. Now the island needs Skandia to keep Cowes Week alive, and the Squadron doesn't like that either."

As with the cryptic currents beneath the Solent, the spit of water on which yachting informally began here in 1800, gauging the changing fortunes of the English sailing scene is a treacherous task, particularly when Squadroneers can be blackballed for talking about their club or the regatta, which started as a sprint between pirate frigates laden with contraband and the revenue cutters out to sink them.

But dashing captains and spurned queens are all part of Britain's seafaring legacy, a tradition that's now fighting to stay afloat along the English Channel. Indeed, the Cowes Week regatta, firmly established almost two centuries ago by the Royal Yacht Squadron, has made the most radical transformation in its history in order to enter the stormy seas of the twenty-first century.

A lack of money forced island officials to set sail for a corporate treasure chest, and when they found it, the regatta of the rich and royal hoisted a new ensign: "Skandia Life Cowes Week," complete with $1.2 million of sponsorship loot and, according to the Skandia marketing department, a directive to demystify yacht racing. "The old yachties just don't like us," says Skandia's corporate relations director, Peter Roberts. "Corporate sponsorship is a steep learning curve for them."

Roberts's curve already has churned up some distinctively British swells. Like when King Harald of Norway sailed right past the Royal Yacht *Britannia* to enjoy a few beers with the T-shirt crowd in the Skandia beer tent. Even H.R.H. Prince Philip, who races here every year, joined in the Yacht Wars by voicing his distaste for the Skandia pennants flapping from the masts of the 872 boats that sailed in thirty classes of racing events.

According to one annoyed gentleman in a Squadron tie, the club perceives Sweden's Skandia Life Assurance to be a "plague of Viking invaders." Royal Yacht Squadron secretary Major Robin Rising, R.M., refuses to comment on the conclusion, but, according to Isle of Wight officials, an invasion was long overdue.

Cowes Week began floundering as Britain's Woodstock-on-water in 1990, when petty quarrels erupted between the Cowes Combined Clubs, a loose organization of the eight rival English yacht clubs who then arranged the week's various races, including the biannual Champagne Mumm Admiral's Cup. "Many islanders wondered if an albatross was hovering over us," recalls Chris Brammall, marketing director for the Isle of Wight Council, the local government authority.

A hex certainly seemed to be in the air by the end of racing in 1993. Cowes Week had opened with a fine breeze and was looking to persuade Land Rover to extend its low-key three-year sponsorship deal, then in its final year. But then Land Rover brought its off-roader down to the beach for a spin in front of cheering islanders and news cameras.

"A Mercedes-Benz jeep barrelled past the Land Rover," recalls one witness to the event. "It went into the Solent and drove toward Southampton. Everyone thought it was going to sink. Then the tailgate opened up and another engine took over."

How Mercedes's ersatz yacht secured the authorization required to get on the tightly controlled beach remains a mystery, but many islanders suspect that the promotional prank had to do with the palace intrigues and competing business interests within the Cowes Combined Clubs, which include the Royal Yacht Squadron and its foe, the Royal Ocean Racing Club in London.

While the Land Rover chugged back to the mainland aboard a ferry, the Isle of Wight set a course to change the regatta's organizational framework in hopes of luring a new patron able to navigate the dangerous currents of England's yachting establishment. The council created Cowes Sponsorship Ltd., a corporation structured to include the local government and the Cowes Combined Clubs. To involve the town, the politicians hailed aboard the Cowes Business Association, as well as Cowes Yachting Ltd. and Cowes Yacht Haven, two local institutions.

"We're absolutely delighted to have Skandia," explains a relieved Chris Brammall. "Cowes didn't have a sponsor in 1994, and the island had to spend £150,000 to stage the event. The expenditure really hurt, but we had to do it because Cowes week draws over a hundred thousand visitors who spend some million pounds. What we have now is the old elite temperament of the squadron versus the exciting marketing tactics of Skandia on an island with the worst unemployment in southeast England."

"Skandia is an eager sponsor of this event," says Peter Roberts. "Cowes became available at a time when we needed to publicize our brand, but we couldn't have a booth hawking pension plans and autographed posters of famous brokers. We had to figure out a way to do something more."

According to Roberts, Skandia's first order of business was to transform the regatta into an event more interesting than a bunch of insurance executives watching coastal erosion. "And the best way to stir things up was to use the sponsorship money to lower the entry fees," explains Joe Morant, the Skandia executive in charge of overseeing the firm's interests here. "Without us, the yachts would have been looking at entry fees of nearly £200 per race. We've lowered the fees to £20."

Other innovations include a first-ever video camera to cover the start and finish lines, and the funding of a research project to develop a transponder system that can more accurately signal when a boat finishes. "Skandia has really opened up Cowes Week and made it affordable," says Bob Kemp, the managing director of Kemps Quay, a Southampton boatyard. "Everyone is here, from the big racers down to kids looking for a trophy aboard a squib." Adds Roberts, "Our corporate message is simple: if you have a boat, Skandia will ensure you can race it during Cowes Week."

More than five thousand sailors responded in the first year of the sponsorship, a record that Roberts admits is ironic for an insurance company that doesn't insure boats and is prohibited by law from selling its financial products directly to consumers. But to get its message across, Skandia has raised its logo atop nearly every building and yardarm in Cowes. They've also chartered racing yachts for visiting brokers to sail, with Skandia awarding special trophies to the first corporate-sponsored boat to finish in each of the thirty classes.

"There are twenty thousand independent financial advisers working in seven thousand organizations throughout the U.K. who can sell Skandia products," reels off captain Tim Sewell, a Skandia executive in command of one of the firm's yachts; "we have sixty of them racing and another 450 watching aboard five cabin cruisers."

For David Pickens, the helmsman of the Skandia yacht *Charlie* and the director of St. Peter's Square Investments Ltd., the corporate sponsorship is an extraordinary opportunity. "My clients are high-net-worth individuals who like to sail," he says. "This is a perfect match."

Unless perhaps you're the radioman at the Royal Yacht squadron castle in charge of choreographing the movements of 872 boats.

"No one on the water understood a damned word he said, so all the captains signaled the castle and told the Squadron to find someone who could speak English," explains Pickens. "The squadron is so aggravated that before this sponsorship runs out, we expect them to open up on us with their cannons."

22

THE **SAIL** SALESMAN
OF MONACO

DURING THE HALCYON DAYS of the Industrial Revolution, the man who broke the bank in Monte Carlo likely parked his canvas-rigged sailboat near the jetty where luxury-yacht builder Luca Bassani today lands his helicopter.

"It was *de rigueur* for wealthy businessmen at the turn of the century to have a large sailboat to travel the world," Bassani says, easing the green Eurocopter over the belle époque Casino de Monte Carlo and into the Monaco heliport. "And the same thing is happening down there today."

While visitors to this principality on the Mediterranean peek into the legendary gaming rooms hoping to glimpse the high rollers at play, they would be better off gathering outside the rose-marbled offices of Wally Yachts. A mile's walk from the nearest roulette table is the headquarters of the shipbuilding firm that Bassani named after the American cartoon alligator Wally Gator. This is where the new rich now come to seek their off-hour pleasures in the form of sailboats that exceed a hundred feet (30.5 meters) in length and can cost in excess of $50 million.

"Wally owners aren't concerned with economic factors," Bassani says. "Building sailboats isn't risky, it's just expensive."

Fingering his stubbly gray beard from behind the two solid-silver sharks on his desk, the yacht-maker from Milan cracks a smile and describes his lucrative business as the ultimate in niche marketing. It's a trade where size matters. Bassani says the jumbo sailboats, which include one-mast sloops and two-mast ketches, went out of fashion between 1930 and 1990 but have soared back into vogue since, adding that technology has made them simpler than ever to operate. His ambition is to bring the new rich down to the sea in these very big ships, even if the only knot a prospective client knows how to tie is in his or her shoelaces.

"The Wally concept is to make sailing a yacht as easy and comfortable as a powerboat," Bassani explains in his office. In the background, Shirley Bassey is wailing the title track from *Goldfinger* over the Wally Yachts promotional video. It's a fitting tune, particularly for Wally clients who have the Midas touch but prefer wearing loafers. "Some customers love our sailboat design, but just don't like tying knots," Bassani concedes. In 2002, he launched a 115-foot (35-meter) speedboat for a customer based on the specifications of a Wally sailboat. Powered by two diesel engines torquing over ten thousand horsepower and with a cruising speed of sixty knots, the boat carries twenty-five thousand tons of fuel and a price tag of $10 million.

"Until recently, there were very few sailboats over a hundred feet because the old technology required crews of twenty people to sail the vessel for one hour," Bassani explains. "Computers and hydraulics have changed all that. Today you can sail a 160-foot (49-meter) yacht with three people, and two of them are needed just to tie the ship up to the dock."

Jeff Flood, the president of Balearic International Yacht Brokers in Palma, Majorca, says Wally Yachts has cruised into a boom market created by landlubbers fascinated with the notion of taking their Great Gatsby lifestyles to sea. "The trend of people buying boats over a hundred feet long is absolute," Flood says. "If you have to ask how much a Wally costs, you can't afford it."

For a "rebel boat-building company" that, Bassani asserts, "breaks every yacht-club rule," Wally Yachts so far has managed to remain the darling of the sailboat set and is facing little real competition. The U.S. consumer magazine *The Robb Report* consistently hails the company as the best sailing-yacht builder in the world.

But rebellion doesn't come cheap at Wally Yachts, where the base price for a hundred-foot-long boat starts at around $10 million and 55-foot- (16.7-meter-) long sailboats are referred to as "tenders" and "dinghies." Bassani describes a "medium-size boat" as an "eighty-footer," and says yachts upward of 107 feet (32.5 meters) long will soon replace them in that category. Indeed, Flood adds, Wally has targeted and is now globally leveraging a wealthy Mediterranean market that currently boasts over 1,500 sail- and powerboats over a hundred feet in length. Wally owners, however, spend an average of only thirty days a year aboard their super yachts, Bassani says. Time is money, of course, especially if you have to maintain a super-rich lifestyle and pay the insurance on one of these boats.

An energetic promoter with grand plans to create a line of clothing and home furnishings based on his jazzy yachts, Bassani since 1993 has constructed sailboats that mimic mansions, complete with servant quarters. The smallest Wally ever built, the 67-foot (20.4-meter) Slingshot, was sold for $2.2 million in 1998 and is about to be purchased on the second-hand market for $2 million. Yet the big boys in the Wally fleet are over a hundred feet long, and all of them are massive computer-operated vessels whose hydraulic-powered, carbon-fiber sails propel hot tubs, laundry rooms, speedboats, and wardrobes tooled from waterproof Florentine leather by Roman saddle-makers.

Perhaps more critical for those who have to spend their time at the wheel, a big Wally is exceptionally swift. Consider: America's Cup racing yachts, which are built to hustle, normally reach speeds of no more than fifteen knots. Wally's can easily exceed twenty knots. "The Wally is a very clever cruising yacht that's neither classic nor modern in design," Jeff Flood says. "It's a pleasure boat built like a regatta racer for extremely wealthy people who want to sail very quickly, very fast, and very comfortably."

And hopefully unnoticed. Invisibility—though difficult to achieve aboard a teak-decked Goliath that speedballs over twenty-three knots—is desirable. "My customers prefer their privacy," Bassani explains. Nevertheless, it's hard to remain inconspicuous aboard a boat that from stem to stern can be taller than a lot of buildings in Paris. So far, Wally skippers have included Gucci chairman and CEO Dominico De Sole, cosmetic kingpin Lindsey Owen-Jones of L'Oréal, Pirelli tire boss Marco Tronchetti, and Norwegian shipping magnate Martin Bergensen.

Sipping a drink with Bassani on the dock in Savona, Italy, the owner of the 107-foot (32.6-meter) *Kenora* surveys his nearly $10 million Wally yacht. "The only problem with this boat is that it shrinks once you put it in the water," the Mexican oil tycoon chides his shipbuilder with a wink. "Maybe I'll have to order a bigger one."

And why not go for a sailboat that could take on Moby Dick? That's precisely what a growing number of Bassani's deep-pocketed customers seem to have in mind. And should there be concern that Wally's $25 million, 160-foot (48.7-meter) sloop might shrivel as it rounds the Cape of Good

Hope, on his drawing board are plans to build for a European client the world's biggest two-mast sailboat: a $50 million, 275-foot (84-meter) ketch. "It comes with a helipad," Bassani adds.

Wally engineers say the 500-ton ketch with a 195-foot (59.4-meter) mainmast will run at thirty knots under optimum conditions. No wind? No worry. "There's space on board for four jet skis and two twenty-foot tenders," Bassani says. The boat also boasts eight large cabins and, he promises, "Only three people are needed to physically sail it." But caveat emptor: "It will take twelve people to moor the ship dockside," he cautions.

"Ahhh, if I could only get Bill Gates interested in sailing," Bassani muses. "Imagine what I could build for him."

Wally general manager Giorgio Magrini visibly turns pale when Bassani starts talking like that. Magrini is the man responsible for the seven engineers, eight naval architects, sixty-five carpenters, and some three hundred other people who lend their skills to building each Wally yacht in six shipyards from Italy to New Zealand. The former America's Cup raceboat designer is Wally's numbers cruncher, massaging into mathematical reality the big ideas Bassani and Wally customers excitedly bring into his office on a regular basis. "Custom boats of this size and scope don't first come with a production model," Magrini cautions. "Our first product is our final product. We can't afford any mistakes."

Though he estimates the 275-foot ketch will take three years to build, most Wally yachts, all of which come with independent desalination systems that convert seawater to fresh water, require five months of planning before construction begins, and then around eighteen months until the vessel is launched for sea trials. The company currently has facilities to build seven super yachts at once and has plans to increase that capacity to ten boats. "Owners take a lot of time to decide if they want a Wally, but once they make the decision, they want the boat yesterday," Magrini says.

But no matter the price tag, all blueprints must first past muster with veteran English naval architect Paul Berry and structural engineer Nino Ascone, whom Bassani shanghaied from Ferrari after the Italian designer helped develop the new Ferrari 360 Modena. Berry and Ascone are the self-described "algebra men." "All dreams must pass this desk," Berry says. Adds Ascone, "There are limitations."

A much bigger headache, Bassani says, is negotiating the 196.5-foot (59.9-meter) gap beneath the Bridge of the Americas that spans the Panama Canal. "I like building large boats. I like building tall carbon-fiber masts," he enthuses, spiraling his hands in the air. "But the mainmast on the 275-foot (84-meter) ketch can't extend higher than 195 feet (59.5 meters), otherwise the boat won't clear that damn bridge when crossing the canal. What's the customer to do if he doesn't want to sail around Cape Horn?" Perhaps strap the boat to the on-board helicopter and fly it over the bridge? At these prices, why not?

Despite the computer modeling and high-tech hull evaluations in sophisticated water tanks operated by the Swedish Navy, the bone and root of Luca Bassani's yacht business is contained in naval architect Paul Berry's dog-eared copy of *Roark's Formulas for Stress and Strains*, the bible of structural engineering. After *Roark's* blessing, all designs undergo seven thousand hours of engineering. "But this is what always happens," Giorgio Magrini explains. "Luca defends the customers who want lighter, faster yachts with quieter engines. I want bigger engine rooms and defend the guys who have to do the real work on the boat."

SLOSHING **THE SEAS**

WITH A CREW OF CHAMPAGNE-

SIPPING **SPORTSMEN**

S TANDING ON THE VERANDA of the Costa Smeralda Yacht Club in Porto Cervo, Sardinia, Commodore Gianfranco Alberini brushes rogue shards of Mediterranean lobster shell from his blazer and surveys the impressive array of ships that fills the harbor below. "This is spectacular sport with a glamorous lifestyle ashore," he says.

But in this purpose-built seaside village of opulent shops and boisterous boats on the northeastern tip of Sardinia, is "sport" merely a trade term? In any case, the $100 million worth of sailing ships that fill the harbor here each year for the annual Maxi Yacht Rolex Cup testify to their owners' very serious—and very costly—interest in yachting. "The owners of these twenty-five yachts are a club that moves around the Mediterranean," explains Rolex official Stewart Alexander. "It's a swish."

What's certain is that no sport is swisher than racing 85-foot (30-meter) sloops and 185-foot (56.3-meter) schooners around the rocky islets of Sardinia while cabin girls serve ostrich-meatball sandwiches on linen napkins. For the most part, athletic ability aboard these super yachts is more dependent upon business muscle than it is a result of hours toiling in the gym. And mere millionaires need not come down to this sea in their ships: unfurling jibs in the Mistral-driven winds off Porto Cervo and in Europe's other maxi-yacht competitions is a luxury pastime reserved for billionaires.

"The Rolex Cup is the highest concentration of super yachts in the world, and everybody wants to come," asserts Luca Bassani, president of Wally Yachts. Indeed, those few affluent "sportsmen" who aim to compete in this year's competition are no doubt already planning their strategies and, most importantly, seeking to assemble the strongest crew. For Bassani, who has a small fleet of Wally yachts racing here every September and at equally posh maxi-class regattas in Portofino and St. Tropez, gatherings of the world's wealthiest boat people provide an ideal showroom for his vessels.

The global economy may be in need of a life raft, but this fleet seems to be steaming ahead. And at between $4 million and $20 million a vessel, the industry doesn't need to build a lot to remain afloat. Italy's maxi-yacht shipwrights were set to manufacture a total of 428 boats. "But," chimes in Rolex chief executive Patrick Heiniger, "business? Selling watches? No, we're all here to have fun."

At the same time, maxi-yacht–class ships are vessels of the Old Economy: Italian designer Salvatore Ferragamo's *Swan Solleone*, Pirelli tire and cable boss Marco Tronchetti Provera's *Kauriusti*, and German banker Thomas Boscher's *Tiketitan*. But the big lady of the Porto Cervo waterfront is the *Adela*, a 185-foot, two-masted schooner owned by George Lindemann, the bearded chairman and chief executive of U.S. natural-gas company Southern Union Co. Lindemann is an avid sailor who made his fortune selling contact lens designs for $60 million before branching out into pharmaceuticals, cable television, and cellular phones.

"Sailing the *Adela* is fun," he says of his labyrinthine, $20-million schooner built of Cuban mahogany and stuffed with sterling silver fixtures. A few years ago, he spent $3 million to saw the 98-year-old ship in half in order to add the twelve feet (3.7 meters) needed to install a walk-in refrigerator and a walk-in freezer. "This is my summer home, and it floats," he explains as the crew hoists the mainsail and checks the satellite telephones. "A motorboat is a floating Marriott hotel room. *Adela* is a great excuse not to attend meetings."

More accustomed to spearheading whaling expeditions in the North Atlantic than trying to capture calm Mediterranean winds with nine tons of fuel, the *Adela* is a seafaring mansion, too overweight to race in the breeze. Nonetheless, Lindemann grouses as the lighter and much faster maxis zip past his gothic dreadnought: "This is an old-fashioned boat and we sail the way they used to sail." Aboard the *Adela*, that means never failing to curse smaller vessels equipped with hydraulic winches and pushbutton sailing technology. Though the maxis are separated into four divisions and handicapped for racing purposes, Lindemann insists the scramble for top honors is "serious fun."

Back on shore and wearing a scarlet T-shirt emblazoned with *Adela* and a color-coordinated baseball cap, he wanders the marina, posting handwritten signs seeking crew members to help him out. "We serve a very good lunch," he says. "Smoked reindeer." As for conducting business aboard the *Adela*, "I take forty-five minutes of calls from the States each night," he explains. "The *Adela* is truly an amazing boat," says Charles Dana, commodore of the New York Yacht Club and a deckhand aboard the *Adela*. "The size of George's yacht gives him real independence to go anywhere."

The *Adela* might look big, but it's a toy boat in comparison to the 243.9-foot (74.3-meter) *Phocea*, the largest sailing yacht currently afloat, and the 358-foot (109-meter) *Sea Cloud*, a four-masted barque that's the largest yacht ever built. Yet no matter the size, the high maintenance costs and rapid deterioration of these dramatically restored early-twentieth-century vessels have convinced most wealthy sailors to climb aboard the high-technology luxury vessels. It's perhaps the nichest of niche markets and one dominated by only five shipwrights: Jongert, Perini Navi, Swan/Navtor, Baltic, and Wally Yachts.

"They're the real go-fast luxury boats," explains Jeremy Morse, the helmsman aboard the 69-foot (21-meter) *Onawa*, a restored and speedy wooden vessel that's too small for the maxi races.

Gianluca Vacchi's 80-foot (24.3-meter) Wally sloop is big enough, and he's christened his speedster *Genie of the Lamp*. The chief executive of IMA SpA, a maker of packing equipment for the pharmaceutical industry, is at the wheel of his gizmo-filled super yacht with the wind at his back. The fifteen-knot wind suddenly changes direction, and Vacchi gives the order to shift the position of the spinnaker, a large sail festooned with the cartoon genie from the Disney movie *Aladdin*. But the flapping $20,000 sail becomes ensnared in a cable and rips in half. The boat lurches, Vacchi groans, and the eight-person crew furiously hauls the torn spinnaker in from the water. "It's real good business to be on the water," Vacchi says, cracking a sardonic smile and watching Lindsey Owen-Jones's *Magic Carpet* overtake his *Genie of the Lamp*. "Lindsey always manages to beat us, and our boats are exactly the same," Vacchi says. Still, he adds, "This sport introduces you to a group of like-minded people and it helps me in business."

It's also good business for the sail-haulers and winch-grinders, the hired crews who aspire to serve aboard one of the yachts competing in the America's Cup. Many of the deep-pocketed maxi owners plying these waters help keep afloat the syndicates that underwrite America's Cup yachts. "Sailing is a very competitive sport on the crew level," says Mauro Pelaschi, the helmsman of the Italian America's Cup challenges and a former world-champion skipper. "The crews want to look their best. They know people are watching."

Also eyeing the festivities through binoculars from the machine-gun deck of the patrol boat *D'Agostino* are sailors from the Guardia de Finanza, Italy's tax police. They scribble notes and chirp over walkie-talkies as the fleet sails back into the harbor after each race, their crews scrambling ashore to the handsome white canvas hospitality tents filled with polished dining tables, wood chiffoniers, and a hastily built Bentley automobile showroom. Over beer, much of the talk centers on the difficulty many of these owners now have in chartering their vessels.

With costs of between $45,000 and $60,000 a week, plus twenty-five percent for food and fuel, it's perhaps easy to understand why vacationing businesspeople aren't keen to hoist the sails of a maxi yacht. Still, says Patricia Aste, director of the Omega Watch Co.'s marketing office in Italy, "Sailing is a rare world and a rich world." So atypical and affluent, in fact, that Omega annually sponsors the maxi yacht *Rrose Selavy*, named after a Marcel Duchamp pun, in the race underwritten by one of the company's chief competitors. "We know Rolex doesn't like it so much," Aste says, "but these days there aren't many sports for high-end luxury products to sponsor."

24

GREG NOLL STILL

WALKS ON WATER

G REG NOLL HAS AN ENDLESS SUMMER COLD. "But that doesn't prove he's human," insists Robert Rabagny, the president of the annual Biarritz Surf Festival and Longboard Classic, Europe's biggest surfing tournament. "Even the gods must rest," he says.

And who's to argue, particularly when there are seven million surfers in the world ready to kick sand in the face of any landlubber who might disagree with Rabagny's incorporeal evaluation of Noll, a former California lifeguard who rode the big waves to become the most celebrated surfer and surfboard designer on the seven seas.

"There are two things never to forget about surfers, no matter their age or income," sniffles Noll, boss of Da Bull Inc. and the French government's guest of honor at the annual surf fete: "they sleep anywhere, and they never miss a meal."

And let's not forget that each one spends on average $1,000 a year on boards, wet suits, and other surfing hardware, spawning a near $7 billion global industry in which a pronouncement by Noll packs the authority of a hurled stone tablet. "Not bad for an ol' surfer," he chuckles. "Of course, you had to be a bit crazy to do what I did."

What he did to earn his reputation as one of the world's greatest athletes took place off the Hawaiian shore in 1964, decades before the razzle-dazzle of televised surfing tournaments and suntan-oil sponsorship transformed the sport into a wet Formula One racing circuit. Standing alongside his homemade board in a pair of trademark black-and-white-striped trunks,

Noll spent an hour studying the treacherous tubular waves along Pipeline, arguably the Pacific Ocean's most notorious piece of breakwater. After isolating the risks, he paddled furiously through the churning soup and beyond the reef. He glided back aboard a majestic twenty-five-foot (7.6-meter) wave—a feat yet to be equaled at Pipeline.

The legend of "Da Bull" was born. Five years later, Noll became an immortal. A December storm blasting south from the Aleutians was pounding gargantuan typhoon waves onto Makaha Point in Oahu, the ancient birthplace of surfing. Setting off with his board into the worst hurricane to ever hit the Hawaiian islands, he returned to shore in command of a monstrous forty-foot (12-meter) swell—the largest wave ever to be recorded as ridden by man.

"I've been able to eat out on that wave for years," laughs the jovial Noll, over the safety of a tall iced tea at the Paris Hard Rock Café, where a valuable painting of the historic Makaha Ride is on exhibit and a few dozen of Europe's five hundred surf-shop owners are scrambling for his autograph. "Tens of thousands surfed during the sixties," he adds, pointing to a gaggle of wide-eyed forty- to fifty-year-old men who have come here to meet Da Bull. "Now all the guys are returning to the sport. All it ever really took was one wave; after that ride you were hooked."

According to Rabagny and other surf watchers, the global rebirth of the sport among older men and women is thanks largely to Noll, who single-handedly brought back the easier-to-ride longboard he first began to build in 1951, when he had just entered his teens. "The eight- to nine-foot longboard died in the late 1970s," says Rabagny. "Teenagers wanted the new and smaller four-foot boards, but they're useless to most people over thirty."

During the late 1980s, Noll started receiving calls from what he describes as "lost surfers" looking to see if Greg Noll Surfboards Inc. was still making boards. The company, which in the 1960s had had sixty employees and made 150 boards a week, had been out of business since 1973.

"I started making boards in my garage when I was eighteen years old," recalls Noll, who says there were perhaps ninety surfers at the time in California. "I went formal in 1959 and hated it. Surfers don't like dealing with guys called 'Inc.,' and they're right. The new formality has really hurt the sport. The guys you surf with are your friends, not your competitors."

Although Noll continues to decry the regimented structure of the beachwear and watersport businesses in tones perhaps more appropriate to describe a wipeout on a coral shoal, surfing experts credit Greg Noll

Surfboards with pioneering the design changes that first gave the sport its mass popularity.

Before 1958, surfboards were expensive and heavy wooden behemoths. So Noll and a few other young California dreamers went casting for a new mold that could cut a board's weight from over sixty-four pounds to under twenty-five pounds. One member of Noll's surfing safari was Bob Simmons, a California Institute of Technology engineer who realized that the foam, fiberglass, and balsa wood being used by aircraft-wing designers could also be fashioned into lightweight and inexpensive surfboards.

"Foam technology made surfing take off as a business," explains Noll. "It also created the Beach Boys, a zillion bad beach-party movies, and surfing mothers naming their children 'Tube Steak.'"

For Da Bull, the world-wide resurgence of the sport means watching over a "laid-back" $2-million-a-year retail surf-clothing company, a hectic international travel schedule, and an exclusive line of new garage-built longboards engineered "for us guys with some beer under our bellies."

"I have hundreds of middle-aged executives begging me for boards," says Noll, amazed that his hand-tooled wave-riders fetch between $3,500 and $5,000. "Even my old $125 boards are being auctioned off for thousands. Some stinker in Los Angeles was busted for making forgeries and selling them as the real thing. The cops who nabbed him were all surfers."

If you can find one, a vintage Greg Noll "Da Cat" model can sell for upward of $5,000. (Named after his surfing pal Miki Dora, its 1965 price was $175.) Compare that with the $600 cost of a new top-line, off-the-rack surfboard, and it's perhaps even harder for non-surfers to understand why people have demolished houses to find an intact Noll original with its classic oval decal of Da Bull riding down a curl.

Although Noll has no idea how many of his original boards are still out there, he does know one lost surfer who wanders the world looking for them beneath beach houses. "He found one," recalls Noll, "but the homeowner had built an addition onto the house, and the board had become part of the support structure. Had to call in a full crew of contractors to get Da Cat out."

Noll guesses that he made over fifty thousand boards between 1951 and 1973, and that most of them are now either forgotten pearls or crushed fiberglass at the bottom of some faraway reef. Yet wherever he goes, he's swamped with appeals to aid lost surfers in their quest to find or authenticate one of the originals.

But that's not likely to happen again: Noll's new surfboard company is a one-man operation, and Da Bull has a two-year waiting list for delivery. The sixty boards he's made since 1990 have already spawned a brisk resale market. Many of them hang in American museums. Over a dozen of his new signature boards have been sold to European and Asian surfers, with rare vintage Nolls having been spotted in the Netherlands, Spain, France, Belgium, and Switzerland.

"Jeez," says Noll, flashing a boyish grin. "Surfing in Switzerland. We ought to look into this."

THE SURFING ELITE
GOES TO BIARRITZ
FOR BOARDS

THE STORY OF HOW THE FRENCH came to dominate the luxury European surfboard industry begins on an autumn morning in 1956, when the actress Deborah Kerr played out what surfers in Biarritz insist is still the second most famous moment in beach history. At the time, Kerr's adulterous romp in the sand with Burt Lancaster in the 1953 film *From Here to Eternity* was number one.

"Kerr was sitting alone on the beach, watching her husband Peter Viertel ride the waves on a surfboard he had brought from America," recounts Philippe Barland, president of the French surfboard-maker Barland SA. "It was the only surfboard in France, and my father walked by and asked Kerr what he was doing with it in the water."

Within a year, metal-shop owner Michel Barland was in the surfboard business and the locals had crowned Kerr Queen of The Waikiki, the country's first surf club. At that time, nobody—outside a few tube steaks washed up on the beaches of Biarritz—thought the French Atlantic coast was good for anything except oysters.

Nearly five decades later, France boasts at least thirty luxury-surfboard makers, and the concierge at the swank Hotel du Palais knows a "tube steak" is a surfer who wipes out in a curling wave pipe. Olivier Pasquet has been riding waves for more than twenty years and says the time he spent surfing is now a big help in dealing with unusual queries from visitors to Biarritz, a vacation town that has a reputation for catering to wealthy executives and European royal families.

"Quite a few of our Russian guests now ride waves," Pasquet says. "Part of my job is explaining shore breaks and directing them to surf ateliers. French surfboards are chic."

French fashion designers are renowned, of course, for their ability to embroider reputations into everything from hand-fed escargots to a ramshackle farmhouse in Provence. Yet even here in the land of Saint Laurent, there is something unusual about bestowing luxury status on a foam-and-fiberglass plank.

So what makes a French surfboard so special?

"It has attitude," says Olivier Turrauba, owner and master shaper at the French board house Choka, which annually exports around three hundred surfboards costing between $600 and $1,000. "You know us French, everything we make must have an attitude."

Philippe Barland's boards have more than attitude: they have naked women painted on them. "Artisans fashion our boards, and those who desire them must come to France," Barland says, running a finger across his fluffy black moustache. "The Far East makes too many cheap, mass-production surfboards for me to profitably export to the U.S. and Australia."

Barland shapers go full-tilt boogie, turning out more than a thousand custom-built, $800-to-$1,200 longboards and another ten thousand off-the-rack, low-price models in all shapes and sizes. Barland spends a minimum of forty hours hand-molding each luxury longboard before the Parisian art deco painter Serge Fargues puts his brush to the fiberglass shell. "About sixty percent of our market is over thirty-five years old," Barland says. For these surfers, who come from around the world, high-quality artwork is very important, he adds.

"Surfers aren't just kids, you know," says Hugue Pinol, a middle-aged physician who owns a dozen surfboards and has been riding Bay of Biscay swells since he was ten. "I surf with lawyers and businessmen from all over the world."

Still, shooting the curls off this old whaling port with "Da Doctor" (a native Hawaiian surfing honorific) is a cinch compared to charting France's role in the global surfboard economy. "Surfboards are now a category of art work," says Greg "Da Bull" Noll, a champion U.S. surfer and shaper who since 1951 has built over fifty thousand boards, including some that fetch $15,000. "French riders and shapers have a lot of local pride in their boards."

For Phil Jarratt, senior marketing executive for the U.S. surfware company Quiksilver Inc., identifying even one French shaper or any of Europe's active surfers is a vital part of his job. The global surfing apparel and lifestyle industry annually sells some $4 billion worth of merchandise. Along with some twenty-six other surf-apparel makers, Quiksilver more than a decade ago established its European headquarters in one of the villages tucked into the rocky cliffs of southwest France.

"This is where the world's surfers come and a new generation of boards is being built," Jarratt says. "There's no surf-apparel industry unless we have local boards and surfers for customers to identify with."

Finding a good wave is the easy part. *The Stormrider*, the *New Testament* of the surfing set, has identified 150 beaches along France's three coastlines, and 850 more throughout the rest of Europe and North Africa, as surfing hot spots. Noll says the first professional American surfer to ride the French wave was the famed Miki "Da Cat" Dora, who in the 1970s ditched the warmth of Hawaii's outside Pipeline for the cold curls off the Basque surfing village of Guethary, where he stayed until his death in 2002.

Surfers are mostly independent-minded and travel frequently, making it difficult to track their habits, industry analysts say. They are reluctant to talk about how many boards they buy and what brands they prefer, Jarrat says. "The French board business got hot in 1989, when all the American surfers followed Miki to see if the big waves were for real," he says. "Many guys arrived without surfboards and went French. The word on France started to spread."

Americans annually spend around $200 million on surfboards, says Angelo Ponzi, a senior analyst at the California-based research company Board-Trac. His research was the first time anyone tried to track industry-wide surfboard sales. "The numbers were hard to come by because most shapers work in garages and aren't big on talking," Ponzi says.

Board-Trac reckons about thirty-three percent of the 407,280 sold in 2001 were luxury longboards, the eight- to ten-foot models favored by older surfers. The U.S. is the leader in producing and selling surfboards, mainly the mass-produced variety, Board-Trac estimates, followed by Australia, excluding Asian knockoffs, and France. Board-Trac officials were unable to cite precise figures. "How many French boards are out there is anybody's guess, but there are a lot of them," Ponzi says. "American surfers for years have been traveling around the world buying boards to ride and then bringing them back to the States."

Surfboard analyst Alan Tiegen, the European general manager of the Surf Industry Manufacturers Association, says that the French produce about five thousand luxury boards each year and that he has his own way of following the market: he sips chilled glasses of rosé wine on the terrace of Guethary's Hotel Madrid and counts the people buying lumps of Mr. Zogs Sex Wax for Surfboards at the village surf academy, one of over seventy wave-riding schools along the 25-mile coastal stretch between Biarritz and the Spanish border.

Pointing toward a clutch of Guethary storm riders streaming to shore, the U.S.-born Tiegen says France is a new mile zero for those seeking the endless summer. "Hanging out at the Hotel Madrid and counting the boarders walking to the beach is a critical part of our research," the surfboard researcher explains. "The waves out there reach twenty feet in winter. That's Hawaiian big."

26

THE MAN WHO LEFT
WALL STREET FOR LE MANS:
"HAD TO DO IT, BABE"

LEO HINDERY JR. IS WEARING a chalky white suit with blue stripes
that guarantees his survival in a 1,300-degree Fahrenheit fire for
twelve seconds.

"After that, I'm toast, babe," says the founder of the U.S. cable television
giant Yankees Entertainment & Sports Network, his 205-pound body
crunched behind the wheel of the Porsche 911 GT3 RSR grumbling to leave
Le Mans pit 14.

On a noisy Saturday in June, along the rolling hills of western France,
Hindery for the third consecutive year will attempt to become the first U.S.
corporate chieftain to win the grueling 24 Hours of Le Mans endurance
race. Some 250,000 people will be at the track and millions more around
the globe will witness on TV Hindery's attempt to finish what he calls the
"biggest deal" of his life: capturing the checkered flag at Le Mans.

It's the largest annual gathering of sports-car fans in the world, and
Hindery and his two fellow drivers are crowd favorites to win the GT class,
a stampede of eleven high-velocity Porsches, two TVR Tuscans, a deuce of
Ferraris, and one Morgan, going bumper-to-bumper with thirty-two other
race cars for twenty-four hours over three thousand miles and through
whatever fate hurls against them.

In 2003, Hindery led his team across the finish line in second place, a
feat that Steve McQueen could pull off only in the movies, in his role as a
race-car driver in the 1971 cult film *Le Mans*.

"Hindery has the skill to actually win Le Mans," says Janos Wimpffen, director of Motorsport Research Group LLC, a Washington-based firm that analyzes racing results and tracks the provenances of drivers and race cars. "That Hindery took the second-place GT finish in 2003 is simply astonishing."

Bathed in sweat and the aroma of Elf Racing Fuel, sporting fire-retardant jockey shorts and a helmet that can muffle an impact load of 40 G's, Hindery tightens the Velcro straps on a fresh pair of gloves. He says Le Mans is a place where his more than two hundred broadcast-industry deals with an aggregate value in excess of $100 billion are meaningless indicators of authority and influence.

"To qualify for a really big Wall Street deal, you're talking about a transaction worth at least $5 billion," Hindery hollers as the pit crew harnesses his six-foot frame to the Porsche's black carbon-fiber seat. "Le Mans is bigger than any deal, and it doesn't care about shareholder value."

For the 56-year-old Hindery, a Le Mans hot lap in his silver-and-blue Porsche with the New York Yankee logos above its exhaust pipes takes four minutes and ten seconds. His speeds range from sixty miles per hour at the clogged Amage Curve to kissing 200 mph down the four and a half miles of the Mulsanne Straight, avoiding collision with Le Mans prototype-class cars that can whip past at 258 mph. Mostly, Hindery will average 140 mph, three to five percent slower than his two fellow drivers, Marc Lieb and Mike Rockenfeller, who are less than half his age.

Hindery adjusts the plastic pipe snapped to his body webbing, a series of microscopic hoses that distribute water to cool his torso during the race. He taps at the prescription sunglasses wedged into his helmet. His cheeks are crimson from the pressure of the headgear. His knees and lower back are in pain, lingering reminders of near-fatal racing crashes in 1996 and 2000.

"Le Mans is a place where nobody cares about anything except how you drive," Hindery says, flipping an electronic-fuel-meter reset switch to "race" position. He revs the engine, adjusts the two-way radio built into his helmet, and speaks over the same microphone the U.S. Army uses in Apache Longbow attack helicopters. "You can distract yourself in business and at worst lose a deal. If you distract yourself in here, you are dead. I find that exhilarating."

During his staggered eight hours in the cockpit, Hindery's heart rate will reach ninety-five percent of its capacity, or 150 to 200 beats per minute. His eyes will vibrate and cause blurred vision; his feet will cramp from delivering more than a thousand pounds of pressure on the brake pedal. The flat-6 Boxer engine will heat the Porsche's interior to 150 degrees Fahrenheit, and Hindery will sustain a body temperature of 103 degrees. He is also likely to dislocate his thumbs and fracture a few ribs while downshifting from 130 mph to 60 mph in a blink, in order to reach the 180 mph straightaways without lethal incident.

This isn't a hobby, and Hindery says he has learned to coexist with the thundering nausea that results from driving the 8.48-mile (13.65-kilometer) Le Mans circuit in four minutes and fifteen seconds.

"Chief executives live in an artificially rarefied air of numbers and accomplishments, but you can't bluff with impunity in a race car," Hindery shouts above the overture of a 450-horsepower engine in a vehicle with a muzzle velocity in excess of 190 mph and a warning label on the door that reads: "This car is not road legal."

The drive from Hindery's Manhattan home to the Circuit de la Sarthe in Le Mans is no ordinary rush-hour commute. He has successfully passed four hundred other three-man professional racing teams who each year compete for some fifty Le Mans starting slots in four separate classes of race cars: the LMP1 and LMP2 prototypes, as well as the GTS and GT categories. The entry fee is $50,000; the GT class winner goes home with a trophy and a check for $15,000.

"You beg to drive here," Hindery says of his investment.

* * *

The place is Tacoma, Washington, a small food market on the corner of Twenty-sixth and Proctor. It's 1962 and Leo Hindery, the son of a shoe salesman, is fifteen years old, bagging groceries to make ends meet and watching his pals ogle *Playboy* on the newsstand. He recalls the moment in his office on the thirty-sixth floor of the Chrysler Building in midtown Manhattan: "I'd just finished stocking the shelves. I picked up a copy of *Road & Track* and opened the page to a picture of a green Lotus. I couldn't catch my breath. I fell in love." Suddenly there's a roar from the store manager to get back to work, and reality slaps the teenager in the face.

"I knew sports-car racing was a rich man's hobby," Hindery says of the day he started to chase his dream of racing at Le Mans. "It was a sport handed to wealthy, East Coast, Ivy League kids, not a poor boy from the Northwest. I decided to become a businessman, a privateer, and chase my ride like a Gypsy."

Hindery's pursuit lasted almost thirty-two years. It ended at a March 1994 board meeting of Intermedia Partners Inc., at the time the fastest-growing cable company in the U.S.

"I was the managing general partner and chief executive," Hindery says while walking the Le Mans track, kicking errant gravel off the rubber-scarred tarmac. "The previous fall, I'd bought an Acura NSX and took it out on the Sears Point Raceway in Napa Valley. I nearly got myself killed, so I went to North Carolina and signed up for the Richard Petty Driving Experience Challenge at the Charlotte Motor Speedway."

In the middle of the Intermedia board meeting, Hindery says the dream that he had deferred in Tacoma came out of nowhere and kicked into top gear. "Now I was really hooked," he says of the epiphany.

Hindery headed for the track the next morning.

For the next six months of 1994, he would spend every free moment learning how to drive, and survive, a racing car. Hindery was forty-six, kicking out of curves on heated "gumball" tires at 135 mph and hacking power slides on asphalt ovals built for the raw nerves of a twenty-year-old. Off-road, he lived in ramshackle trackside motels and hung out under the grandstands with mechanics who don't like chrome trim on their racers or Coca-Cola without a splash of bourbon.

In May 1995, Hindery qualified for his first NASCAR race at the Charlotte Motor Speedway. He finished thirteenth in a field of forty-three.

Jack Welch, Rupert Murdoch, and Liberty Media Corporation Chairman John Malone were Hindery's big-buzz industry running buddies back at his personal table at the Four Seasons restaurant in New York, but that sort of wheeling and dealing didn't register for the growing number of global race-car fans who were now asking: "Who is this guy Leo Hindery?"

"We never cared that Leo was a multimillionaire," says John Warner, sales manager of the British pest-control company Igrox Ltd. and president of the Two Wheel All Terrain Society, the BAM! Racing team fan club. "Leo has always made the effort to get close to the fans. He's a throwback to sports before the sponsors took over. The rest of these professional racing teams are run by corporate snobs who want us to buy their cars and give us the cold shoulder. Leo is one of us. He drives for us."

***

Over the past eighty-one years, Le Mans has been the scene of numerous tragedies: fires, explosions, and the worst accident in motor-racing history. In 1955, a prototype magnesium Mercedes-Benz 300 SLR driven by Pierre

Levegh slammed into the rear of an Austin-Healey, burst into flames, and catapulted into the crowd at 140 mph, killing eighty-two spectators and injuring hundreds of others.

"Le Mans is no place for a wealthy executive with a $500,000 sports car in his suburban garage," says BAM! business director Peter Baron, who with Hindery and German driver Marc Lieb drove the BAM! Porsche to a 2003 podium finish. "They will be killed, instantly."

The winding track through the Sarthe River basin is also no two-lane blacktop for enriched executives seeking high-speed entertainment inside a fashion statement. The course spools out along cordoned-off public roads that snarl around apple-tree forests, shredded-pork-paté sandwich stands, and industrial parks wrapped inside hurricane fences. Private homes are encircled by protective battlements of discarded tires. Traumatology specialists patrol the perimeter aboard ambulances and medical evacuation helicopters.

***

Hindery has driven in seventy-five professional races, and his body feels the pain.

A 1996 crash into a concrete wall at the Concord Motor Speedway in North Carolina compressed two of his vertebrae and bent his spine like a sapling. Arriving at the hospital with a broken neck and his jaw fractured in eight places, Hindery was in shock. His liver shut down and the doctors feared he would die.

Four years later, while driving his red Ferrari 360 Modena at the Road America Track in Wisconsin, Hindery smacked into another wall, causing doctors to replace his right knee and leaving a perpetual throb in his leg. "The Road America crash was bad," he says. "I had to fly directly from the track to a meeting in Singapore. Didn't know my knee was gone and that I was bleeding internally until I got there all swollen up. I went from the meeting to the hospital."

On a muggy April test afternoon at Le Mans, Hindery's right hand embraces the metal stick that controls the Porsche's "dog type" six-speed gearbox. He is moments away from triggering an engine release of 8,500 RPM, a thunderous 405 newton meters of torque, or about five times the power of a family sport-utility vehicle.

"Corporate America has never been comfortable with its CEOs being involved in professional sports car racing," Hindery says. "Welcome to my secret life, babe."

And perhaps the most cunning cover-up on Wall Street.

"I didn't really know about Leo's other job," says Robert Davis, executive vice president of communications at YES Network. "Leo tells me nothing. And when he took second place last year at Le Mans, we didn't issue a press release."

Davis says he left Hindery's Manhattan office that July afternoon in complete disbelief, and in no small part because Hindery was heading to the Fun City Tattoo Parlor on St. Marks Place to have the son of big-band leader Artie Shaw tattoo the Le Mans track and the inscription "24 Heures du Mans Podium 2003" on his left shoulder.

"The tattoo is a traditional rite for Le Mans winners," Hindery says. "I'm saving the right shoulder for first place."

YES human resources director Grace de Latour vividly remembers her reaction to the news that Hindery was having a racetrack permanently etched on his body. "My God," de Latour says, "no one in the broadcast industry ever knew of Leo's stature in the racing world."

Indeed, Hindery's YES Network, which cablecasts New York Yankee baseball, New Jersey Nets basketball, and a cavalcade of other big-ticket sports events including Manchester United soccer games, didn't even televise any of the boss's races.

"I still don't believe Leo is a race-car driver," says Hindery's longtime friend Matthew Blank, chairman and chief executive officer of Viacom's Showtime Networks division. "Wall Street doesn't tolerate its CEOs racing cars," says Blank, sipping white wine alongside Fox News Chairman Roger Ailes at the Four Seasons, the official restaurant sponsor of the BAM! Racing team. "It's too dangerous. But Leo never paid attention."

Almost never.

"Back in 1997, when Leo was president at TCI, the board of directors thought he just liked to drive sports cars," says Mark Coleman, Hindery's personal attorney for nearly twenty years. "Come on, who on Wall Street would ever believe that Leo Hindery is a professional race-car driver?"

John Malone certainly didn't.

At the time, Malone was chairman of the TCI board and ringing Hindery's cell phone at the most awkward hours to talk about pulling the company out of a $15 billion debt crisis. "Once I'm testing a new car at Indy and John calls to discuss a major congressional regulatory push related to promoting high-definition TV," Hindery says. "He couldn't hear me over all the engine noise and asked where I was. I told him I was at an airport."

The "loud-plane" excuse was a stock fib, and Malone and the rest of Wall Street kept buying the story Hindery spun at tracks from Road Atlanta in Braselton, Georgia, to Canada's Mosport International Raceway in Ontario.

"My cover didn't last too long, though," Hindery says. By late 1998, Malone and the TCI board finally realized that their multimillion-dollar president was moonlighting as a professional race-car driver.

"They went completely nuts," Coleman laughs. "Leo was told to stop immediately because he could get killed and dangerous recreational activities were expressly forbidden in his TCI contract."

Hindery told the board that he would walk if TCI didn't renegotiate his contract. "They expected me to take up golf," Hindery says.

"It was an interesting renegotiation," Coleman says of the new deal, which allowed Hindery to continue his breakneck pursuit of an invitation to Le Mans in return for instituting a "key man" life insurance policy and a promise to be careful and behave in the best interests of the company.

Hindery punched out of NASCAR in 1998 for the Ferrari Challenge Series, a sequence of eight races that leads to a 24-hour endurance race at Daytona. If he was very fast and very lucky, an invitation might follow from the Automobile Club de L'Ouest to attempt to qualify for Le Mans.

The French told Hindery to show up for the test runs in April 2002.

"It was my first visit to Le Mans, and it happened again: I couldn't catch my breath," Hindery says of the moment the flowing steel-and-concrete grandstands came into view and his head filled with the sound of the greatest sports-car drivers in the world whizzing beneath the track's trademark Dunlop Bridge. "I walked along the track and into our pit," Hindery continues. "The team was preparing the Porsche, and I was in a church. Speechless reverence, babe."

Hindery finished seventh in the GT class of eighteen cars. French children swarmed around him, asking for autographed photos. Old men ran through the crowd to kiss him on the cheeks. Women threw bouquets at his feet. Jubilant Le Mans officials asked him to come back in 2003 and try again. Wall Street was never so far away.

***

"It's time to throw up," Hindery says, looking up from a bowl of Cheerios and a side order of baked beans ninety minutes before the flag drops on this year's twelve-hour endurance race at Florida's Sebring International Raceway: 3.7 miles, seventeen turns, and the last stop before Le Mans.

"No problem, babe. I've reserved us a stall for sixteen visits," Hindery says. "Everyone who's anyone is there and we shall throw up together."

In an age when Wall Street recognition is often measured in degrees of disgrace—L. Dennis Kozlowski of Tyco International Ltd., Jeffrey Skilling of Enron Corp., and Bernard Ebbers of WorldCom Inc. come to mind—Hindery suggests that it might be refreshing to watch him, a former merchant mariner and graduate of Stanford Business School, barf in the toilets made famous by high-rolling race-car drivers such as A. J. Foyt, actors Gene Hackman and Paul Newman, and lunar astronaut Pete Conrad.

Originally built in 1941 as a training field for U.S. Army Air Corps bombers, Sebring's Quonset huts and ten-foot-thick concrete runways in 1950 were jackhammered into what Hindery calls the most stubborn sports-car track on earth. Unlike the silky tarmac laid out fresh each year at Le Mans, there's nothing smooth about Sebring. The track is coarse, bumpy, and ugly, with potholes haphazardly filled with lumps of asphalt.

"Turn 17, the Sunset Bend," Hindery says, wiping his mouth with a moist paper towel. "I've told the medical team to pay close attention to the buzzards flying overhead. I hold the world record for never taking a line around 17 the same way twice and that's not good. If the buzzards show up, I'm in serious trouble."

Avoiding disaster is the keystone of the professional racing game. Though each team scripts its track strategy before the starter's flag drops, Hindery says the cars and the drivers more often than not forget their lines.

Hindery's ten-member pit team, dressed in fireproof New York Yankee livery and charged with keeping him alive at Le Mans, includes technical director Tim Munday, a retired car-and-motorcycle racer from north London, and BAM! truck driver Rick MacQueen, the "fire-bottle man" and logistics coordinator. Bob Skene handles the transmission. Robin Hayes is the tire specialist. Matt Bishop, Jim Balkanloo, Jim Thompson, and Rob Joy speed-change forty-four sets of tires during the 24-hour race. Steve Johnston pumps the fuel, and Jim "Chachi" Malicki runs the laptop computers and software that record everything that takes place inside the BAM! Porsche. Everyone is a master mechanic.

Then there's Toto, the radioman from Costa Rica, named after Dorothy's dog in *The Wizard of Oz.* "And we're not in Kansas any more," Toto says as Hindery blasts out of the pit and accelerates back onto the Sebring track at 153 mph. The laps pass, but the buzzards don't over Sunset Bend. The BAM! drivers—Hindery, Mike Rockenfeller, and Peter

Baron—are averaging 110 mph with a shattered windshield. The race is five hours old and BAM! is in second place, moving up in the nineteen-car GT field.

Hindery suspects a miracle is going down.

***

On the first day of practice, Baron on his third lap rockets down the Flying Fortress Straight at 150 mph. He downshifts from sixth gear to fourth and flutters the brake to take the Gendebien Bend at 108 mph. Too fast. Baron is now airborne, landing on a concrete barrier with an impact of 40 G's.

Hindery runs to the crash site, praying that Baron isn't dead.

"I can't believe that just happened," Baron mumbles as he climbs out of the wreck.

"Fly the space shuttle and you experience a sustained force of about 8 G's," explains Dr. Vincenzo Tota, a trauma specialist and racetrack physician. "Baron's crash was not a sustained 40-G impact, but it's still a huge hit, long enough to cause problems."

Munday's crew takes four days to bring the Porsche back from the dead, just in time for Baron to recover and Rockenfeller to capture pole position, whipping around the track in two minutes forty-one seconds, one-third of a second off the fastest GT qualifying time recorded at Sebring.

The race is now seven hours old. Hindery is coming out of Turn 5 pushing 100 mph, a refrigerator-white Porsche on his tail, when the orange Lola in front of him spins out. Hindery swerves to avoid the whirling British race car, but "she whacked my ass," he calmly reports over the radio.

"Need a new wing," Hindery transmits, the Porsche's carbon-fiber rear end flopping through Gurney Bend and into the Fanglo Chicane.

"Pit now, Leo. Pit now," Munday replies.

"We got a leak in the cool suit," Hindcry says, climbing out of the cockpit, the crew scrambling to replace the shattered rear end and get the damaged Porsche back into the race. The rear tires are hot and shredded, with the rubber oozing like licorice poured from a furnace.

"No one in the world sweats more than me," Hindery hollers over a Ferrari growling out of pit row, spilling himself into a blue canvas chair. "Gremlins, lots of gremlins out there."

BAM! finishes in fifth place. Still wobbly from the crash, Baron sees the wisdom of offering his seat at Le Mans to Marc Lieb and heads back to BAM! headquarters in Stuart, Florida, to race-ready a fresh 1,100-pound "virgin Porsche" for France.

Hindery, his lower beck in severe pain, limps aboard a private jet for New York and a meeting with Janina Bradauskiene. "My job is to prepare Leo's body for Le Mans," she says. Hindery is lying naked, belly-down, on her table, snoring, with dozens of Japanese acupuncture needles wiggling in his back.

"It's quite simple," Hindery reckons at the gala 2003 Porsche Motorsports Banquet in Weissach, Germany. "Nobody understands the economics of sports-car racing," he explains, gently pointing a champagne glass toward Wolfgang Duerheimer, executive vice president of research and development at Porsche AG.

"You have no ceiling, Wolfgang," Hindery continues. "I spend $1.5 million a year and we both know guys who will drop $50,000 just to take one pound of weight off the car you give us, and another hundred grand to make it go faster."

Porsche's top executive mechanic nods in agreement. There's a huge temporary stage behind him in the Porsche workers' cafeteria, and a Teutonic pop band is playing Beatles standards for the thousand people here to celebrate the company's cars and drivers. Photos of Hindery and the other "Porsche pilots" flash on giant screens erected around the room.

"Your private customer team is vital to our sales," Duerheimer says over the music and with a sly smile on his lips. "Remember the old Ford motto: race on Sunday, sell on Monday."

The cordial relationship between Hindery and his racemaker is often bittersweet, and it has nothing to do with money. It's about bragging rights.

"There's always been tension between the privateers who drive Porsches, and the Porsche factory driver teams the company runs against us," Hindery explains. "Porsche is at Le Mans to sell cars and presumes that first and second place will go to their factory effort. That didn't happen last year."

Bob Carlson, a manager of Porsche Cars North America Inc., discounts the contretemps as friendly bickering among hot-rodders. "Of course all the private Porsche teams would love to have factory drivers and the full weight of Porsche behind them," Carlson says. "But Leo's victories justify the reason why fifty thousand retail customers in 2003 bought Porsches. Leo helps create Porsche aspirants. He attracts customers with an average age of forty-five to fifty and an average income of $200,000 a year."

"Yeah, right," Hindery says back in his New York office, pointing to the gold Le Mans trophy he took home for capturing second place in 2003.

"We beat the damn socks off the Porsche factory team and the boys back in Weissach didn't like that one bit."

Thomas Dattilo, chairman and president of Cooper Tire & Rubber Co., reckons puckish spats are part of life in the fast lane. "Race-car drivers create a buzz around you, whatever your product is," says Dattilo, whose tire division sponsors the Cooper Championship Series racing circuit. "It's unwise to overanalyze how the investment plays out on the market."

Reaching Le Mans as a privateer isn't cheap. Porsche provides fitness training, insurance, spare parts, and a corporate track for its eight factory drivers, who are paid to do nothing but win. Track time alone for a privateer can cost $6,000 an hour. "You win Le Mans by paying attention to the details, and Porsche has all the details covered," Baron explains.

"Insurance runs from $1,500 a race to $1 million for the season," says race-car driver John Gorsline, president of the Gorsline Company, an insurance firm that specializes in "retirement and estate planning strategies and insurance for high-risk professionals and athletes."

And then there's sticker shock. Hindery's Porsche costs $200,000, but only if Porsche agrees to sell him one of about twenty-five of the 911 GT3 RSR models the company builds each year specifically for the professional racing circuit.

"This is a business where money buys acceleration and control," Hindery says. "What's interesting is how quick you can get to 187 miles per hour, and the GT3 gets you there real quick."

Hindery's ride at Le Mans will go through 176 tires, all underwritten by Michelin. The New York Yankees, Porsche, YES Network, and the Four Seasons restaurant foot the remainder of a 2004 sponsorship tab in excess of $1 million.

"Le Mans is why I spend my money," explains Seth Neiman, a managing partner of the California venture capital group Crosspoint Venture Partners and journeyman driver for the Flying Lizard Motorsport Racing team at Sebring. "I got into racing for entertainment, but now I'm climbing the mountain. I want that invite to Le Mans."

A man in a crisp white Brooks Brothers oxford-style shirt is standing in the semidarkness of Le Mans pit 14, observing the scene like a director at the final dress rehearsal before the opening night of a Broadway play. The BAM! crew members see him and acknowledge his presence with nods and smiles. "Brock is here," one of the mechanics whispers as the energy in the garage seems to pick up pace.

Peter Brock made General Motors cool.

In 1956, at age nineteen, he was the youngest automotive designer ever hired by the U.S. carmaker.

In 1958, he designed the prototype fiberglass Corvette Stingray. Superlative.

In 1965, he designed Carroll Shelby's Cobra Daytona Coupe. Legendary.

Today, he's the president of Brock Racing Enterprises and one of Hindery's closest friends.

The custom-car builder and retired race-car driver says it takes more than money for a shot at Le Mans. Brock cites an incident he witnessed at Le Mans in 1970, the year a Hollywood film company, Solar Productions, entered a Porsche 908 roadster mounted with three movie cameras and co-piloted by Herbert Linge and Jonathan Williams. The two cameramen, both proven racers, entered the field to film Steve McQueen and Jackie Stewart drive a 700-horsepower prototype Porsche 917 in the race for the movie *Le Mans*.

Brock says the race was treacherous. It rained the entire twenty-four hours, and it was so wet that the Mulsanne Straight turned into a wading pool. Ferraris turned into fireballs along the Dunlop Curve, Alfa Romeo gearboxes littered the White House Straight, and the Amage Corner looked like a junkyard in a thunderstorm.

At three A.M., six-time Le Mans winner Jacky Ickx accidentally plowed his V-12 Ferrari 512S into a trackside official and killed him. Only sixteen of the fifty-one cars that officially started the race were able to finish.

"The favorites were crashing out or breaking down," Brock recalls. "About four hours before the end, the cameramen realize they have a damn good chance of actually winning Le Mans."

Linge pulled into the pit for a fresh roll of film, told director Lee Katzin that *Le Mans* was no longer a Hollywood fantasy and asked him to cancel further film stops in return for an almost certain victory.

"Katzin ordered them to keep coming back for film," Brock says. "It was tragic. Linge and Williams lost their chance at every boy's dream come true."

***

Belgian classical scholar, religious historian, and Le Mans fan Raoul Vaneigem explains the other reason why Hindery keeps coming back to Le Mans: "There are more truths in twenty-four hours of a man's life than in all philosophies."

Hindery says the 24 Hours of Le Mans is an allegory.

"Le Mans is the only experience where in such a short amount of time a man can compress together all the emotions that make up his entire life," Hindery says, leaning against a tower of tires in his Le Mans office and watching BAM! pit man Steve Johnston pour fuel into his dream. "There's nothing the business world can offer to rival this," he adds, waiting for the green flag to drop on the biggest deal of his career. "Nothing."

Twenty-four hours later, Hindery squeezes himself out of the Porsche and utters three words: "We lost bad."

He returned to Le Mans the following year and captured his dream.

"Had to do it, babe."

27

GASOLINE **SMOKE AND**

ANTIQUE SPEED

THE YEAR WAS 1989, and Malcolm Barber was looking out his window at the rain rattling the Christmas lights strung up outside Sotheby's Auction House. Barber was rubbing an ivory gavel, thinking about the wet drive home, when his secretary put through an unexpected transatlantic phone call.

On the line was Robert M. Rubin, vice president of commodity operations at Drexel Burnham Lambert Trading Corp., the precious-metals–trading arm of the soon-to-collapse company that made junk bonds famous.

"Rubin asked me to sell the Holy Grail," Barber says.

The chalice placed in the auctioneer's hands: a Ferrari 250 GTO, one of only thirty-six built by the Italian automaker between 1962 and 1964. The wholesale factory price then of Enzo Ferrari's first Gran Turismo Berlinetta Competition GTO was $9,700. Chip Connor, president of the Hong Kong investment company William E. Connor & Associates Ltd., paid $9 million for the Rubin GTO, driving off in a street-legal race car that comes with a bare aluminum floor and plastic sliding windows.

The details of the auction, recounted by Rubin, who is retired, and Barber, now a group managing director at the London auction house Bonhams, illustrate the intrigue and passion behind an investment that first drove off the showroom floor with a sticker price of $13,600. Forty years later, the Ferrari 250 GTO is an asset so secretly held that Peter Everingham, secretary of the Ferrari Owners Club of Great Britain, says his club's bylaws forbid him under threat of legal action to reveal the name of any owner or how much they paid for the vehicle.

Rubin and Barber were set to shatter the unwritten rule of the elite and secretive GTO market, launching a global marketing campaign to sell one. A few weeks before Rubin had instructed Barber to put his car on a jumbo jet and take it on a global marketing tour, another red GTO was privately sold to a Japanese investor for $13,837,500.

This is a hot car. "The GTO without doubt is the most significant race car ever built," says Tim Watson, the public affairs director at Aston Martin Lagonda Ltd., Ferrari's chief competitor on the luxury race-car circuit. Today, all traffic in the three-liter V-12 race car is conducted in silence among a coterie of the global moneyed. The auction of the Rubin GTO, as it would turn out, was the last time proof of a sale price would be recorded in public.

"The private GTO market is a shadowy business full of malicious rumors, and I needed to change that playing field," Rubin says. "Creditors at the time were after Drexel, and I was in the midst of a divorce. I wanted to cut off the negative chit-chat that Drexel's creditors would be coming after potential buyers of my GTO." Nonetheless, Rubin says his decision to offer the car in a public spotlight sparked a backfire among other GTO owners and brokers. "I still receive lots of goofy calls from people who didn't want me to sell the car at auction," Rubin says. "There was no way my GTO would sell for more than $13 million. Everyone in the market knew it, and they were nervous because the sale would lower the value of their cars and create a bear market. The GTO is like a security. There is a lot of volatility and turnover and a lunatic fringe."

On May 21, 1990, fleets of private helicopters arrived in Monte Carlo, their passengers scrambling across the waterfront landing pad and into a circus tent owned by Prince Rainier, who was present. Barber opened the bidding at $2.5 million. Hundreds of hands shot skyward, including those of the eleven phone operators charged with signaling the bids of billionaires who preferred to remain invisible.

"I was no longer an auctioneer," Barber recalls. "I was a referee."

Four minutes into the fray, Swedish real-estate magnate Hans Thulin nodded his head.

"The car is selling for $10.5 million," Barber informed his audience. He thumped the gavel. "A murmur of disappointment immediately filled the tent," Rubin says. "GTO owners had come to the auction believing their cars were worth at least $15 million and didn't think $10.5 million was a lot of money."

Barber then sealed the deal. "The car is sold for $10.5 million," he said, confirming the current benchmark price for a car that comes with wire door handles. There is no speedometer.

A handful of GTO owners and brokers who were familiar with these private transactions and the identities of the approximately three hundred individuals who have over the past four decades owned any of the thirty-six cars agreed to speak about their trades, although many only on the condition that they not be identified.

***

Like all treasure hunts, looking for a GTO involves a secret map, this one drawn by a Frenchman who lives on the shore of the Andaman Sea. Shortly before Jess Pourret in 1987 sold his GTO and moved to Thailand, he assembled the histories of all the cars and published their provenances in *Ferrari 250 GTO*, a rare book that Barber says can itself command as much as $1,000 at auction.

The interviews and published records offer a glimpse into the garages of hot-rodders such as fashion designer Ralph Lauren, who paid $650,000 in 1985 for a red GTO branded with the chassis serial number 3987GT. "All GTOs trade very privately," explains Microsoft Corp. board member Don Shirley, who bought a red one and says he didn't pay $10 million for it.

"That's a ridiculous price," the former Microsoft president says with a laugh. "Many owners and brokers like to inflate the price." No wonder. "The GTO is the most desirable Ferrari ever made, and there are only thirty-three of us who own them," Shirley adds. "It's more of a fun investment than watching boring stocks."

Also able to sit behind a GTO wooden steering wheel and the factory-installed bug deflector are Wal-Mart Stores Inc. chairman S. Robson Walton ($3.5 million, 1994) and West Tech Energy, president Ed Davies ($3.8 million, 1995). Other owners include Japanese property baron Yoshikuni Okamato; Washington lawyer Bernie Carl; former Microsoft programmer Greg Whitten; fashion designer Tommy Hilfiger; and Cincinnati Microwave president Jim Jaeger. In Kobe, Japan, property baron Yoshio Matsuta, chairman of Vintagecars, has three GTOs, in green, blue, and red.

"GTOs are sold quietly by billionaires who don't like their affairs to be known," Ferrari Club secretary Everingham says. "Perhaps the only thing faster than its acceleration is its fluctuation rate."

In 1964, for instance, Texas oilman Tom O'Connor donated his dark blue $15,000 GTO to a high school for students to take apart as an instructive exercise. Eight years later, the school auctioned the car for approximately $6,000, the car's record shows. A bearish Rubin reckons that Pink Floyd drummer Nick Mason, who in 1978 paid $86,000 for his GTO, might today get $5 million for the car. A bullish Barber suspects Mason's red GTO could sell for between $8 million and $9 million.

"I don't think we're going to be able to help," Mason's assistant Julia Grinter said when asked if the rock musician would talk about his investment, which is best run with earplugs and comes without a sound system.

"I only wear plugs when I race," Shirley says. "But when my wife and I go out for a drive, we have to communicate with hand signals."

Despite the collective hush among GTO owners, their asset is anything but static. "To own one and not drive it in a rally defeats the point of purchasing the car," explains GTO hunter Simon Kidston, president of Bonhams Europe SA in Geneva. "You do not mollycoddle a GTO."

Gerald Roush, a former university professor of ancient art and civilization, says buying a GTO right now for $8 million would be a bargain. He should know. For more than thirty years, Roush has published the *Ferrari Market Letter*, a forty-page biweekly magazine of classified ads devoted to the sale of used Ferraris. The magazine has 3,800 subscribers, and thirty-three of them are GTO owners.

"Nobody ever has placed an ad in the report looking to buy or sell a GTO," says Roush, who maintains an index of every Ferrari ever made. "It's just not done."

Michael Sheehan, the president of European Auto Sales Inc. in Newport Beach, California, says financing is the easy part. "All you need is a pulse for a bank to give you a loan on a GTO. I could have bought one in the early 1970s for a few grand, but I was in love with a ballerina just as beautiful and used the money to take her to Europe."

Designed by Giotto Bizzarrini at the Ferrari atelier in Maranello, most of the 300-horsepower GTOs left the stable with a bold white racing stripe painted down their centers, all thirty-six of them tuned to drive the twenty-four-hour race at Le Mans and other international competitions. Enzo Ferrari personally vetted each of the original owners.

"From the very beginning, Ferrari cloaked the GTO in the sorts of myths and mysteries that keep the car an astonishingly valuable object, as desired as any painting by Picasso or van Gogh," Barber says.

And like the art world, Rubin says the GTO owners live in a hierarchical society, with power concentrated in the hands of those whose cars have had the fewest owners and won the most races during the GTO's halcyon years on the professional racing circuit.

Ralph Lauren's GTO, for example, likely wouldn't sell for more than $3 million, because Pourret's book records that the car never raced at Le Mans and can't boast its original engine or body. The leader of the pack is Chip Connor, whose red $9 million GTO (serial number 4293CT) remains factory-fresh, averaged 181 kilometers per hour at Le Mans, and sped to victory at races in France, Italy, and Germany.

Still, Rubin says the GTO's ability to mesmerize executives isn't the result of its rarity. "Thirty-six competition cars is quite a lot," he explains. "That there are so many GTOs is what makes them valuable. If an owner has financial trouble, he has the reassurance of seeing the cars privately change hands among other members of the club."

Blowouts do happen. Copies of bank records from the Midland Bank in London indicate that Sheehan, according to sales records, privately brokered the 1989 sale of a GTO (serial number 3909GT) to Japanese car collector Takeo Kato for a record price of $13,837,500.

On August 25, 1994, John Collins, chairman of Talacrest Ltd., the biggest Ferrari dealership in Europe, privately bought Kato's GTO over the phone for $2.7 million. "You could say the GTO market crashed that morning, but Kato didn't care that he lost money," Collins says.

FERRARI'S SECRET SOCIETY

MICHAEL FUX PAID $1.8 MILLION PLUS TAX to join the world's most select and secretive high-speed society. There is no membership card. Instead, Fux, founder of U.S. mattress maker Sleep Innovations Inc., walks into the garage of his Miami home and awakens one of the only twenty-nine carbon-fiber Ferrari FXX sports cars the Italian automaker delivered to a coterie of überwealthy owners from Tennessee to Tokyo, known as the Ferrari Client Test Driver Club.

"There's absolutely nothing street-legal about the FXX," Fux hollers, his voice a whisper against the discharge of a 6,262 cubic centimeter V-12 engine that kicks out more than 800 horsepower at 8,500 RPM—practically the same performance numbers that empower the Formula 1 racers that Ferrari SpA in Maranello, Italy, constructs for Michael Schumacher. The FXX is about as subtle as an erupting volcano, so potent that Fux says the U.S. Environmental Protection Agency's Office of Air and Radiation monitors all FXX imports, slapping club members with a $27,500 fine should the car enter the country without a proper license. "Once the FXX is legally in the U.S., it's up to state and local law enforcement to ensure that the vehicle is driven only on a racetrack," says Dave Ryan, spokesman for the EPA's enforcement division. As for who's doing the driving, "We don't reveal names," says M. Toscan Bennett, public relations director of Ferrari North America Inc.

For Fux, the track is the only prudent place to exercise the FXX alongside fellow clubbers, who include U.S. automotive mega-dealer Phil Bachman of Greeneville, Tennessee; Florida flea-market baron Preston Henn; United Auto Group Inc. chief executive officer Roger Penske; and

Lawrence Stroll, co-chairman of A&G Group Ltd. and former co-chairman of Tommy Hilfiger Corp.

And with speeds in excess of 240 miles per hour and a gearbox that executes shifts in less than a tenth of a second, the language of the ancient Mongol Empire perhaps contains the only verb to express the action a novice experiences behind the FXX wheel: *temul*, the look in the eye of a horse that's racing where it wants to go, no matter what the rider wants.

"Even good guys look like they're sawing wood with their hands in the FXX," says Le Mans winner Leo Hindery Jr., managing partner in the New York-based buyout firm InterMedia Partners LLC. "It's a display car for guys who want to spend two hundred grand a year to drive around a track in demonstration events."

Bruce Clarke, a track official at the Homestead Miami Speedway, knows about the perils of demonstration. Thirty minutes before Fux and seven other FXX owners make their inaugural run, Clarke tells the group they can go as fast as they want and pass whomever they want. "I sure hope they keep their heads on straight," he cautions. "These cars are dangerous."

The FXX isn't a prancing horse for Wall Street bonus babies to saddle up. Ferrari currently manufactures five retail models, and the FXX isn't among them. "You don't go into a Ferrari dealer and order an FXX," explains Fux, who owns a dozen Ferraris. "Maranello contacted us after conducting a long and private vetting of customers."

Client test-driver Henn reckons his membership car required divine intervention. "Ferrari's North American operation called to see if I was interested in an FXX," says Henn, who has raced at Le Mans and owns twenty Ferraris. "My nomination was reviewed by Maranello, and I was given to understand final approval came from the pope."

Ferrari engineer and production director Giuseppe Petrotta says that more than sixty customers have cold-called the company for membership in the Client Test Driver Club since 2004, when his team began planning the project for vehicle delivery. "The FXX gives us the opportunity to test-drive new Ferraris with our customers," he says while preparing Fux's red FXX for the track. "We must limit the number of owners to twenty-nine because including more would detract from the amount of service, assistance, and hospitality we can provide." Client confidentiality is paramount. Petrotta continues, "FXX owners are made aware of many Ferrari technical secrets that our competition would like to be aware of. Telemetry data from the FXX is priceless, and giving customers access to the information is part of the program because it allows them inside the development process for our future cars."

The FXX comes with a squad of five Ferrari factory mechanics and personalized driving tips and training from Michael Schumacher. Standard equipment includes three gigantic metal trunks filled with specialized helmets, fireproof racing suits, red racing sneakers, a smorgasbord of purpose-built tools, and a 300-plus-page instruction manuscript housed in an FXX carbon-fiber binder. Henn says collectors of Ferrari ephemera are willing to pay $10,000 for the codex. As for the car, "I've already heard about offers of $4 million."

Fux says the greatest joy of the FXX is handing its keys over to Jamie Camara and Ian Beltri, young race-car drivers less than half his age looking for a break on the professional circuit. "If I can find somebody to drive it better than me and showcase their talent for Ferrari, then that's the ultimate thrill. My first car was a beat-up 1950 Ford."

Now Fux's stable of fifty cars includes an Aston Martin Volante, a Formula 1 Ferrari, a Saleen S7, a Ford GT, and two Lamborghini Murcielagos. There's also a $1.4 million Bugatti Veyron. "I swapped the Ford for a 1949 Plymouth with rotted floors. The FXX is a much better investment."

Bonhams auction house in London says the jury is still out on the FXX. "Squillionaires want the FXX to pump their adrenalin, and it will take a generation to see if the car does the same for their investment portfolios," vintage vehicle specialist Malcolm Barber explains.

"The FXX is about macho and nothing else," says Hollywood film producer Mara Beth Sommers, who spends her weekends at the track racing an F430 Spider against men in the Ferrari Challenge Series.

Ferrari's Petrotta thinks any discussion of the FXX's free-market worth is premature. "An owner has the right to sell his car, but unless we approve the sale, the new owner is not a member of the club," he says as the FXX fleet rumbles to life in the paddock. "That means no assistance, no mechanics."

The partnership between Ferrari and FXX owners runs through 2007. The two-year agreement stipulates that Ferrari will sanction seven FXX events a year: two each in North America, Europe, and Japan, with an annual grand finale in Italy. What happens next remains a mystery.

"It's one hell of a public relations program for Ferrari, and we're paying for it," Henn says. "Ferrari's people crank it up, warm it up, and wipe it down after we race. The FXX is a car for someone who lives their life every day as if it's their last."

FXX client manager and Ferrari mechanic Andrea Galleti expects each car will clock about 3,500 kilometers over the term of the contract. If owners want to drive the FXX on their own, "we will do everything we can to have a factory team of engineers and mechanics on hand."

Slipping into the driver's seat of his yellow FXX, Phil Bachman says he intends to permanently garage the Ferrari in Maranello in order to sustain its Italian provenance. "Driving this at Homestead is great, but I want to maintain its European pedigree and keep it on European tracks," the car dealer says over the bawl of eight FXXs revving their engines. "I sell Pontiacs to pay for Ferraris," he shouts, "and this one is over the top with power."

In pole position, Fux gives a thumbs-up and blasts off around the 2.21-mile track. Nausea sets in after the fourth lap and he returns to the pit, his white beard matted with sweat, a top speed of 210 mph on the telemetry system, and a mischievous smile on his face.

"I'm a little boy," he says, the words streaming from his cracked lips. "Wild, just wild. A hundred and sixty miles per hour is slow in this car. There's someone out there doing 240," he continues between gulps of pink lemonade. "The FXX is it, the best of all my cars. The only thing wrong with it that I can't drive it is on the street."

29

ZIMBABWE **HUNT AUCTION**

EXECUTES HYENA **FUTURES**

AND **PUTSI OPTIONS**

THERE ARE SOME REAL killings to be made on the Zambezi Valley Hunt Exchange. Baboon options are opening at $9 per baboon, traders in Harare expect a stampede on bull elephant derivatives, and phone orders from New York and London are overwhelming Zimbabwe's wireless circuits.

It's open season again for bids to participate in the high-risk business of big-game hunting in Africa.

As wildebeest grow fat for the annual Zimbabwe hunting season, over three hundred great white hunters in jungle fatigues and crocodile-hide boots trek in from the bush every April and deploy beneath the onion-domed ceiling in the grand ballroom of the Meikles Hotel, puffing meerschaum pipes and drinking beer served on sterling silver trays. The hunters unload their big-bore rifles and power up the calculators for the business of buying and selling 104 government contracts to hunt some four thousand big-game animals in the Zambezi Valley wilderness.

"These are very strange investments, because there's no hedge against a cape buffalo," warns Anthony Williams, owner of *African Hunter*, a glossy magazine and tip sheet on how to survive the Zambezi exchange without being gored. "The buffalo is born mean and nasty," he explains a few moments before the opening bell. "You get one kill-shot. If you miss, your investment will stomp you bad. You don't die quickly, you don't die easily."

It's not a market for the faint of heart. Williams says investors here best be familiar with how to leverage a .404-caliber H&H single-shot at less than sixty feet (18 meters) against a rampaging three-and-a-half-ton hippopotamus. As hybrid markets go, there's clearly none more volatile than the Zambezi Exchange, where a fourteen-day option to kill a hippo in 2002 sold for $3,700 and traders say U.S. investors pushed warthog futures to $690 from the 2001 high of $327.

But while a pork-belly contract on the Chicago Mercantile Exchange is a bet on which way hog prices will move in ninety days, a pork option here is a gamble on killing the pig over a ten- or fourteen-day period, all the while tracking the investment through the Zambezi Valley, most often with a 6.5 mm Mauser. If the contract holder either wounds or fails to bag the trophy boar, market regulations stipulate that the option cannot be extended and the warthog gets to go home with his bacon.

Investment counselors here advise shareholders to practice with at least five hundred rounds of ammunition a week before executing a contract in the rugged 300-mile-long spine that runs from the Chizaria Hills in the east to the Mavuradonna Mountains in the west. "Zambezi Valley hunting futures are the most dangerous derivatives on earth," reckons exchange manager Ian Ferreira. "To play this market, you must either be very brave or bloody stupid."

Who's to doubt him? Questioning Ferreira's credentials in these parts can cause more of a stink than calling Ernest Hemingway a sissy. Dressed for floor action in a safari vest, Ferreira is an expert on business along the Tropic of Capricorn and can trace his family's mercantile roots in Zimbabwe to 1496, when a relative sailed up the Zambezi River looking for gold with Portuguese adventurer Vasco da Gama.

An auctioneer by trade and a big-game hunter by inclination, Ferreira has run the one-day exchange for twenty-seven of his sixty-one years. The market, he explains, is the descendant of the shadowy Zimbabwe tusker exchange, where foreign businessmen once gathered to haggle over ivory prices with local white hunters and native tribal leaders. In the mid-1960s, the government banned the trade and created a regulated market to curtail the commercial slaughter of elephants and other endangered species.

While traders encircle Ferreira with bids on tuskless elephants, towers of cash tumble out of bags and into the four banknote-counting machines whirring on clerk Penny Carritt's desk. The exchange treasurer bundles the bills in toilet paper and drops the take in an iron box for delivery to the bank. "This is Mickey Mouse money for foreign investors," Carritt says, wrapping cream-colored single-ply bog roll around a stack of a hundred thousand Zimbabwe dollars.

Trading is momentarily suspended by what Ferreira suggests is the most hazardous of market threats: the putsi call, which is actually more of a shriek. It comes shortly after a trader notices that a tiny native insect known as the putsi has laid its eggs under his skin. As the bug's trademark blue welt erupts on the man's leg, Ferreira locks down the exchange and hollers for blacksmith and bush doctor Corn Smit to come in from the lobby with his bowie knife.

"Too deep to cut out," Smit says, sheathing his blade and grabbing an empty beer bottle off the floor. "Putsis are toxic and I don't want the poison seeping into your blood."

"I don't care," the trader moans. "It hurts. Just dig the damn thing out."

Instead, Smit flips open a lighter, heats the mouth of the beer bottle, and presses it hard into the wound. He then pours a pitcher of ice water on the warm glass to create a vacuum. The putsi pops out and Ferreira reopens the market with a $7,000 option for a fourteen-day lioness hunt.

Standing beneath the head of a stuffed blue gnu in the foyer of his home, Ferreira says the exchange is immune to risks that include droughts and bush fires, floods and malaria, armed poachers, tsetse fly infestations, venomous black mamba snakes, annoyed environmentalists, food shortages, and four separate currency exchange rates. Not to mention the government of strongman president Robert Mugabe.

Mugabe's continued refusal to accept a new national constitution and hold free and fair elections after nearly three decades in power has plunged the country into violence and scared thousands of photo-safari tourists into taking their cameras and foreign currency to Kenya.

The U.S. and Great Britain declared the Mugabe regime a fraudulent government and imposed travel sanctions against him and his cronies. Human rights groups here say hundreds of thousands of people have fled their homes in fear of revenge attacks against those who fail to support the government.

But Ferreira says big-game hunters don't care about the perils of politics. "Hunters on this level are naturally tough people," he explains. "They come here for the Big Four: leopards, lions, elephants, and buffalo. Those are the blue-chip trophy animals."

Still, big-game hunter Bill Bedford says he walks into the exchange each year certain that the political climate will cause the market to crash. "It never turns out that way," the owner of Ingwe Safaris explains. "The Zambezi Valley is a globally recognized brand name and the last place left to buy old-fashioned hunts." Kenya banned hunting in 1977, and South Africa offers mostly stocked antelope hunts, leaving Tanzania, Zambia, and Zimbabwe the only countries where sport hunters can go after the Big Four.

Ferreira reckons that the thrill of tracking the Big Four across the legendary Zambezi Valley makes the exchange impervious to forces that would tumble markets elsewhere. In 2002, 240 investors spent a total of $3 million for the right to hunt trophy game from antelopes to zebras, a 131-percent increase over the 2001 close of $1.3 million at official exchange rates. Ferreira says the numbers aren't an inflated indicator of market strength.

"The official 55-to-1 exchange rate between Zimbabwean and U.S. dollars is the same now as it was in 2001," Ferreira explains. "You can buy options with black-market Zimbabwean dollars bought at 400-to-1, but the government will not let you take the trophy out of the country without proof of having exchanged the money at the official rate."

Ray Townsend, the managing director of Chapungu Safaris, who in 2002 spent a record-setting $36,363 on a fourteen-day option to shoot a male lion, suggests there are ways around the currency regulations. He plops his feet atop a scruffy canvas duffel bag packed with millions of the Zimbabwean dollars and declines to spill the beans.

"I'm not telling anyone how we make money," he says to the laughter of other traders. Patting his ample stomach, which he fondly describes as "Mount Kilimanjaro," the big-game hunter grins and pours himself another beer.

"My client who bought the lion is an Austrian timber magnate and money isn't a problem for him," Townsend says. "I've taken out sixty businessman-hunters every year for the past fourteen years, and very few are interested in African politics. They're prepared to mortgage the wife and sell the house for the opportunity to hunt in Zimbabwe. This is a mystique-driven market where the U.S. dollar is king."

That's a continuing problem for Leon Oelsehig, a South African hunter who represents clients with only rand in their pockets. "American dollars now control the Zambezi Valley," he gripes. "I've been priced out by rich

American duck hunters. They want to taste the fear of walking into a herd of angry elephants."

But why?

"Putting your life in danger from time to time breeds a saneness in dealing with day-to-day trivialities," muses local hunter Don Heath. "It gives you the enthusiasm to tackle normal days, when the most dangerous thing encountered is a taxi weaving through traffic on the way to work."

Investors these days are mostly wealthy executives who view a big-game safari alongside renowned African hunters like Charls Grobbelaar in the same light as playing eighteen holes on the Old Course at St. Andrews with Tiger Woods.

Lining up a shot in the Zambezi Valley isn't cheap. "People looking for any of the Big Four are hard pressed to spend anything less than $7,000 for a maximum four-day hunt," says Grobbelaar, owner of CG Safari Services and chairman of the Zimbabwe Professional Hunters and Guides Association. "Big-game hunting in Africa is a sport for American dollars."

Depending on the price of the initial contracts, which can run from $7,500 for a basic ten-day hunt (one buffalo, ten antelopes, and four baboons) to over $100,000 for a fourteen-day safari with options to target the Big Four, local hunters separately charge upward of $700 a day to equip and escort clients into the bush. For the novice, Grobbelaar offers a three-day special $3,250 sable antelope hunt. "We don't let our clients go after the animals on their own," he says. "The rule pisses off a lot of American businessmen used to getting their own way, but if we didn't enforce it, we'd have a lot of dead executives out there." As for who those businessmen might be, Grobbelaar isn't talking.

One businessman-hunter, Bjorn Edlund, communications director at ABB Ltd., Europe's biggest electrical engineering company, says the silence is no surprise. "Big-game hunting in Africa is a taboo subject outside the boardroom," says Edlund, who hunts wild boar in France and bull moose in Sweden, and who has no plans to purchase a $9,000 Zambezi Valley leopard option. "It just doesn't look good for a corporate executive to publicly admit he hunts elephants," Edlund explains. "They're supposed to shoot golf with clients."

That didn't stop a vibrant secondary market for a $45,454 bull elephant from taking place this year beneath the kudu antelope horns downstairs in the hotel's Explorers Club Bar, and market-tipster Williams says it's not unusual for a buyer to resell an option for a thirty-percent profit. But a balanced portfolio in pachyderms and crocodiles by no means guarantees a return on investment.

"A client two years ago bought a $15,000 lion option and we never bagged it," Townsend recalls as a cell phone rings and interrupts his story. Moscow is on the line. "They wanted to confirm another July option for a tusker," he says after booking the contract.

"Some dealers buy on spec, but not me," Townsend continues. "I buy what clients tell me to buy. Americans want the biggest and the best, the Europeans prefer going after older animals," he says, smacking Grobbelaar on the knee. "Though a few years ago there was that Spanish businessman who had the whole elephant stuffed for display in his home, right?" Grobbelaar swears the story is true and says he sees nothing odd about stuffing a six-and-a-half-ton elephant for the living room. "Some of these guys just take home elephant feet and make table legs out of them," he says.

Back on the trading floor, hyena shares suddenly plunge from their 2001 high of $290.90 to $18.18 a share. The hyena market is collapsing, and Ferreira says the ninety-four percent drop is no laughing matter. Though American hunters never have been keen on the carnivorous scavenger, Ferreira is perplexed because local investors have historically favored long positions in hyenas as a hedge against burglars.

"Many criminals believe tribal witch doctors can transfer their spirits into hyenas, so people often hang a hyena head in their home to scare away thieves," Ferreira explains. "The drop either reflects that homes are saturated with hyenas or that criminals are no longer afraid of witch doctors."

30

RUSSIAN SHARPSHOOTERS

TAKE AIM AT **A NEW CAREER**

COLONEL ANATOLY SHEROV is a coach who doesn't like playing games. Pacing his practice field—a claustrophobic, subterranean pistol range some five hundred feet (150 meters) from the Kremlin—the Russian Interior Ministry's chief of athletic development and combat training soberly sizes up the 150 entrants in the government's Annual Criminal-Police Shootout.

The first five shooters step up to the firing line and blast away at individual targets, eighty feet (24 meters) downrange, that resemble the human thorax. Through binoculars, Col. Sherov reflects on the results. "These are world-class athletes who can kill," he notes approvingly.

Col. Sherov's uncommon take on sports might sound merciless, but he says the spread of violent crime in Russia since the collapse of communism in 1991 has made such an appraisal necessary. According to ministry officials, homicide, assassination, kidnapping, and armed street crime are soaring in Russia. At the same time, Col. Sherov's sharpshooters are shedding their ministry uniforms to take better-paying private security positions, and the depleted Russian treasury isn't helping to attract enough high-caliber athletic talent to fill the gap.

Major General Vyacheslav Voronsov, the ministry's chief personnel officer, says the departures have ruptured the morale of many of those left behind. To be sure, the proliferation of violent crime against businesspeople in Moscow has spawned more than three thousand registered private security firms, all of which are vying against one another and the ministry for a dwindling pool of athletes willing to endure the often-ruthless challenge of law enforcement in Russia.

"The best shooters are made from highly trained athletes, and they're getting harder to find," Maj. Gen. Voronsov shouts over the rush of automatic-weapon fire. "None of these men could be on our Olympic shooting teams; the psychology is completely different."

Sharpshooting tournaments are an institutional feature of police forces globally, but there's clearly a unique urgency and perhaps singular history behind this nearly century-old gunslinging competition. Ministry officials hint that past participants have included members of KGB covert-operation units. Legend has it that KGB founder Felix Dzerzhinsky himself once contended for the title of Russia's best shot.

Although Dzerzhinsky's score is believed long forgotten, Col. Sherov says the match over the years has remained a contest to discover the coolest finger on the trigger of a 9 mm Makarov automatic, the standard police-issue, eight-round Russian-made sidearm mythologized in countless James Bond movies.

But no shaken martinis or sultry spies await the hero here. Instead, the big winner usually receives a paltry cash prize of about $150; others take home trophies and chocolate-colored baseball caps embroidered with the logo of U.S. gun maker Browning Inc. Yet with half the 150 contenders—nearly all men—representing fourteen of Moscow's top bodyguard companies, the shootout over the past few years has turned into a vanity gunfight for bragging rights among government and private-sector security outfits.

"This is the most important shooting competition in Russia," says Dimitri Gorovoy, deputy chief of armaments at the closely held Rodon, a private security firm that takes its name from the acronym used to denote the ministry's feared but now defunct Dzerzhinsky division. "The realities of winning and losing when your opponent has a weapon are different," Gorovoy adds. "There are no silver and bronze medals in this game."

There is, however, corporate sponsorship: German sports-apparel giant Adidas-Salomon AG in 1998 provided winners with official World Cup game balls, clothing, and encouragement.

Standing beneath an enormous Adidas banner framed with diagrams of AK-47 assault rifles and rocket-propelled grenade launchers, antidrug commander Lt. Gen. Oleg Sergeev reluctantly admits that Adidas must now help underwrite the event because "the ministry's financial situation is far from good."

Neither is its survival rate. In 1997, rues Maj. Gen. Voronsov, "Three hundred of my troops were lost in shootouts. It's a horrid figure. We need to spend more money on training."

An Adidas official says the company is eager to leverage its brand to promote the ministry and to use its trendy logo to help Maj. Gen. Voronsov attract new recruits. "Adidas is on very friendly terms with the Interior Ministry to solve the criminal problems that hurt law and order and business in Russia," explains Anatoly Osetrov, the senior Adidas executive in the shooting gallery and the company's security chief in Moscow during the 1990s.

On the firing line, the rules of the game are deadly simple. Each entrant gets a hundred rounds of ammunition. Whoever hits the center of the heart cavity the most times is the winner. There is no handicapping.

"This sport is a practical application of gunfire," explains Oleg Khodov, a member of Rodon's team. "We're not here to get a score," he adds, "we're here to show that we can kill a guy before he kills us first."

"Don't believe what you see in movies. There aren't many people who can shoot to kill first at another human being," Maj. Gen. Voronsov cautions. "The difference between Olympic marksmen and these men is steel in the soul . . . an understanding that there's no protection from the first shot. So you shoot first and make it count."

Rodon's Gorovoy, an avid football player, says the most efficient shooters have an athletic background and must remain in superb physical shape if they want to survive Moscow's mean streets. Strength and lightning reflexes, Maj. Gen. Voronsov agrees, are essential because "the criminals are more aggressive, better paid, and better armed" than ministry forces.

"The ministry invites the private security shooters because no longer can we rely on our own troops to fight crime," Maj. Gen. Voronsov explains. And to further develop a working relationship with the private sector, he says, his office helped enact legislation to allow his force to more closely work the streets alongside firms such as Rodon, as well as for laws permitting private sentinels to carry weapons more powerful than the Makarov.

"This work is combat athletics," Maj. Gen. Voronsov says.

"I'm always looking for real athletes," adds Anatoly Mogaesky, president of the privately owned, 400-man Hawk Security Company. "I no longer need to find good men within the ministry forces; once I find a natural athlete, I send him on special training courses with Russian Special Forces or the FBI Academy in the U.S."

Hawk's five-man shooting team is a jumble of athletes originally recruited from football clubs, track-and-field events, and weight-lifting gyms. But finding eagle-eyed men and women immune to the lure of Russia's thriving underworld, Mogaesky says, is the biggest challenge in his job, particularly since most of his clients are no-nonsense foreign corporations such as the Pepsi-Cola Co.

"Too many of the security firms are corrupt," Mogaesky charges. "The only way to isolate an honest one is to make sure the company is authorized by the Interior Ministry and has a yearly turnover of at least $1 million." Mogaesky, a former captain in the ministry's economic-crime squad, says that the best security firms have at least a hundred employees with a government license to carry weapons. "In Moscow," he adds, "clients need guards who know how to shoot accurately."

But not too accurately. "It's an honor for a security firm just to be invited to this event," Mogaesky says. "It would be bad form for any of us to offend the criminal police by actually beating them."

Mogaesky's etiquette might well be on target. The winner of this year's Shootout was Lt. Col. Igor Volosov, with 97 of 100 shots fired precisely into the heart. "Politics," Mogaesky says with a wink, in defense of Hawk's 91-to-100 kill ratio.

31

DEATH **AND LIFE**

AT 5,000 FEET

ABOVE AUSTRIA

UNITED AIRLINES PILOT Rick Massagee loops his plane into a 250-mile-per-hour (400 km-per-hour) maneuver. Pulling back the stick at just above 325 feet (99 meters), the 41-year-old aviator corkscrews skyward at sixty feet (18 meters) per second, the engine's awesome thrust at five thousand feet (1,524 meters) allowing him to now vertically hover the scarlet aircraft like a hummingbird.

"If this was dangerous, I wouldn't do it," says Massagee, the 1994 U.S. Aerobatics Team champion, on the ground at Austria's Wiener Neustadt Airfield to compete in the penultimate third leg of the Breitling World Cup of Aerobatics. "You know if we hit the ground, we die."

The airline industry calls them daredevils, professional pilots call them athletes, and both groups say your average commercial airline passenger feels safer knowing nothing about the downside to Newton's Laws of Motion.

But for the dozen aviators here seeking first prize along the global aerobatics circuit sponsored by the Swiss watch manufacturer Breitling SA, pushing an aircraft's performance envelope to the max is a blend of athletic strategy, engineering prowess, and personal courage that pays huge and often unseen dividends in the commercial cockpit.

"Rick Massagee is one of the twenty best pilots in the world," says Northwest Airlines captain Michael Heuer, a World Cup judge and member of the International Airlines Federation board of directors and president of the group's Aerobatics Commission.

"But Rick and the rest have been invisible," the former U.S. Air Force pilot adds. "The airlines are run by bean counters who are nervous about advertising what these pilots do. The fact is that aerobatics is a safe-driving course." According to Heuer and other aeronautical engineers, competitive flying is much more than a sport and has no room for cowboy antics. Instead, they say aerobatics is a golden opportunity for commercial pilots to hone skills the major airlines claim are of marginal importance when flying today's high-tech equipment.

"Safety is the only factor in a commercial aircraft," Massagee explains. "And the airlines rely on sophisticated technology for the extra edge. What's often lost is how to fly an airplane when the technology breaks down."

And for an aviator, there's no greater challenge than taking to the sky to polish the nanosecond adroitness required to become a sanctioned aerobatics pilot. Yet in the commercial cockpit, pilots rely on computers and hundreds of hours in flight simulators.

"It's great," Massagee says of the technology. "But it's not up there." And many pilots here believe the training should be in the sky but isn't because apprehensive airline executives confuse aerobatics with stunt flying. Although there haven't been any fatalities in thirty-five years of IAF-sanctioned aerobatics competition, there are some twenty pilots killed each year performing stunts at air shows. "The difference is huge," explains Malev Hungarian Airlines pilot Zoltan Veres. "Aerobatic pilots are Olympic gymnasts. Air-show pilots are clowns in a circus."

And after a few days of experiencing World Cup aviators throttling through high-speed spins, hammering stalls, and a near mach-force loop-climb called the "reverse half Cuban," there's no doubt that the sport offers pilots a unique opportunity to measure themselves to the limit.

"The Breitling wing," Heuer says, "allows pilots to test necessary skills that most airline executives and passengers really don't believe are important."

The performance of Breitling's iron butterflies unfolds like a game spread across the sky, and the spectacle seems to defy gravity. Flying in hand-built art-deco monoplanes with top speeds of over 250 miles an hour, the aviators zoom through routines that pull more gravity acceleration (G-force) than any supersonic jet fighter.

"What's going on up there is no frolic," says Iberian Airlines 747 pilot Ramon Alonso. He points to a Breitling plane dropping out of the sky upside down and spinning at 155 miles an hour. "That's critical training."

"It's widely believed that a number of airline crashes are the result of an aircraft flipping over," Heuer explains. "That's a situation pilots rarely experience, and the instinctive reaction is to pull back on the stick for lift. Aerobatics teaches a pilot to instantly push the stick forward. The plane doesn't matter: if it can fly right side up, it can fly upside down."

The Breitling planes are designed to perform around all three of an aircraft's axes, executing a four-minute series of maneuvers to music, which are judged technically by a panel of professional pilots. The group also has nonflying artistic judges, which have included ballet masters, concert musicians, and a kabuki theater specialist.

"I'm leaving here hoping the pilot on my next commercial flight can do this but never has to," says Professor Raoul Herget, the director of Austria's celebrated Hauer Music Conservatory and a first-time World Cup judge. "Such syncopated flying to beautiful music is an extraordinary display of man and machine that rivals anything in modern or classical dance."

And the aviator's preferred partner is the Russian Sukhoi 31, 420 horsepower of propeller-driven flying beast with a climb rate of eighty feet (24 meters) per second. Sukhoi pilots experience G-force rates that stretch from beyond +12 to below –12. In positive-G flight, centrifugal force pushes down from the brain, accelerating a pilot's heart rate to 180 beats per minute.

Negative-G flight, which occurs when a pilot flies upside down, launches blood into the brain and plunges the heart rate to fifty beats per minute. It is also said to lower the "red veil"—a circumstance in which the whites of the eyes fill with blood.

"The pilot and the plane must fit together," says Russian aviatrix Elena Klimovich, regarded by her peers as one of the finest pilots in the world. "We operate above a one-square-kilometer performance box. No margin for error."

"It's tight sport flying," adds Gordon Bowman-Jones, a retired aerobatics pilot who announces the play-by-play. "And it will never be as safe as stamp collecting."

Or perhaps as cheap. Aerobatic planes run over $200,000 each, and—with fuel, lodging, maintenance, and the cost of transporting crews and aircraft around the world aboard cargo planes—the cost can soar as high as $1 million a year. For the Breitling aviators, all of whom are either test or commercial airline pilots, it's the privately owned Swiss watchmaker who pays the fare in an undisclosed multimillion-dollar agreement that's perhaps unique to professional sports.

Unlike other watch companies, who simply wrap their wares around aviation adventure themes, Breitling has historically canvassed pilots to discover what gear they most need inside a conventional cockpit—and what kind of unconventional skills are required should the aircraft break down. In response to an aviator's query in 1913, for example, the firm engineered the world's first wrist chronograph that could tell a pilot how long he had been in the air.

"We are honored to have been associated with the best aviators since the beginning of manned flight," says Breitling president Ernst Schneider, himself a pilot. "It's our responsibility to help tomorrow's aviators increase their level of skill and the quality of equipment. It's disingenuous to label what we do a sponsorship to sell watches."

The president prefers to call his patronage an "aviation test bench" on which new products are developed out of the informal airfield chats he has with pilots along the World Cup circuit. One such discussion led to the creation of the Breitling Academy, an IAF-approved advanced flying school for pilots directed by World Aerobatics Champion Xavier de Lapparent.

According to one commercial pilot who wishes to remain anonymous, Schneider in 1990 heard the aviators talking about how commercial airliners over-rely on the factory-installed emergency location transmitters employed when a plane goes down. "Emergency beacons are often damaged in a crash," the pilot says. "And we told Schneider that a fail-safe was needed." The result is a $5,000 titanium chronograph with a 121.5-megahertz transmitter devised in cooperation with the French aircraft firm Dassault SA. The watch houses an extendable seventeen-inch antenna attached to a beacon that boasts a range of 250 miles, even when buried beneath six feet of snow.

"This is not a toy," cautions Jean-Bernard Maeder, Breitling's marketing manager, who warns that buyers must sign an agreement that legally binds them not to misuse the watch. "The locator signal connects directly to a satellite and stays on the air for forty-eight hours. It's like an airbag: you can't turn it off, and it works only once."

Across the muddy airfield at the Breitling hospitality tent, Schneider is entertaining five hundred guests perhaps more interested in brunch and his firm's line of $6,000 to $20,000 high-fashion watches. "He won't last long in there," laughs Maeder. Almost on cue, Schneider—dressed in a tattered flight jacket, crumpled baseball cap, and wading boots—comes splashing across the old cow pasture, cracking a salute skyward as Massagee whirls into the sun.

In the summer of 1996, the right wing of Rick Massagee's new Sukhoi race plane collapsed during a practice flight in the U.S. He did not survive the crash.

SOMETHING OF A MYSTERY:
STOCKPORT'S ADOPTION
OF LACROSSE

E VERY DECEMBER, A HEAVENLY MIRACLE is quietly recalled along the Mersey River south of Manchester. The godsend is known as *Bag'ata'weh*, and it was in 1876 when the spirit first touched the two hundred thousand people who now inhabit Stockport, a gloomy industrial town of crumbled cotton mills and mysteriously hallowed lacrosse fields.

"*Bag'ata'weh* was supposedly delivered by God, and there are many who believe Stockport is its Bethlehem," says David Shuttleworth, CEO of the 120-year-old English Lacrosse Union. "But step one foot over the ten-square-mile border, and not a soul will know anything about it. Only Stockport treats *Bag'ata'weh* as a blessing. Nobody really knows why. It just always was."

Over three thousand miles to the west, in the medicine lodge of the Turtle Clan of the Onondaga, faithkeeper Oren Lyons isn't at all mystified. "What happened in Stockport was truly a spiritual event," says Lyons, an Iroquois Nation elder in New York whose people say the Life Giver *Sum'guya'dis'sa'eh* first sent *Bag'ata'weh* to walk among them.

Bag'ata'weh, the Iroquois name for the webbed-stick-and-ball game lacrosse, has been played longer in Stockport than anywhere else in the world outside the region once inhabited by the Six Nations of the Iroquois Confederacy, the tribal political union that between 1641 and 1701 ruled what is now the northeastern portion of the U.S. and Canada. Also known as *tawarathan,* the rugged—and often brutal—Native American sport became Canada's national game in the 1860s. It moved into America during the late nineteenth century to thrive under the name "lacrosse" (a French word originally coined to describe any North American colonial-era stick game) at Ivy League schools, giant East Coast universities, and private college-preparatory schools.

"The essence of *Bag'ata'weh* remains godly," explains religious leader Lyons. "But the spiritual realm is an area in which you either have faith or you don't," he says, pausing. "*Bag'ata'weh* bestows great power on the people of Stockport."

But no one in Stockport knows why lacrosse—a game percolating with Native American allegory passed down orally from father to son—drifted from the New World to anchor itself in the rusted heart of Britain's Industrial Revolution.

As in North America, where some collegiate teams even include a Native American medicine man on the bench for spiritual guidance, Stockport players revere the game as much for its sacramental value as for its competitive nature. Many residents say the town's veneration of lacrosse over soccer is eerie, particularly since Stockport borders Manchester United, the most popular and successful football club in the world.

So, is it prudent to suspect the hundreds of players and coaches who characterize Stockport lacrosse as the consequence of divine intervention to be a novel reflection of what local nineteenth-century literary hero Charles Mackay called an "extraordinary popular delusion"?

Well . . . consider:

At least four Native American spiritual leaders are known to have visited the Stockport area since 1876 to conduct religious ceremonies on many of the two hundred fields where sixty lacrosse clubs and hundreds of elementary school children now play. The last medicine man visited the town in 1996.

Since 1877, Stockport has produced over fifteen thousand lacrosse men and a thousand women whom experts regard as some of the greatest to have ever played the game.

At the 1948 Summer Olympics in London, the last time lacrosse was an Olympic event, the entire British team was from Stockport. They tied the U.S. 5–5 in the final, a sports phenomenon that would today rival a British basketball squad going into overtime against the U.S. Olympic "Dream Team" for the gold medal.

At least a dozen Stockport players over the past decade have achieved All-American status, the highest award that can be given to a U.S. collegiate athlete and a feat one British lacrosse coach describes as about as likely as finding four soccer players in Detroit good enough to play for Manchester United.

Some seventeen hundred of England's current two thousand club lacrosse players are from Stockport. Seventeen of the twenty-six players on the 2000 All-England team were Stockport residents, and the rest were from surrounding cities in Cheshire and Lancashire. The proportion pretty much has remained constant for over a century.

T.S. Hattersley & Son Ltd., the world's largest maker of wooden lacrosse sticks—which Native Americans believe are endowed with spiritual properties bestowed by *Sum'guya'dis'sa'eh*—was founded in Stockport in 1870 and has been based there ever since.

"There sure is something mighty strange going on in Stockport when lacrosse can exist on the same spiritual and athletic level as it does in North America," marvels Jeremy Murphy, a former All-American at the University of Massachusetts. "Lacrosse in Stockport makes absolutely no sense," says Murphy, echoing the conviction of two other American coaches who have visited Stockport. "Unless you believe the miracle."

If *Sum'guya'dis'sa'eh* did manifest *Bag'ata'weh* in Stockport, the spirit was likely delivered by a bird of prey on December 22, 1876. Local records indicate that the town's first glimpse of lacrosse happened that day by chance when a team from the Caughnawaga tribe held an exhibition game in Manchester as part of a marketing gimmick to encourage British immigration to Canada to buffer the domination of French settlers.

Sometime during the Caughnawaga game at the Longsight Cricket Ground, a signalman for the London and Northwestern Railroad halted beside the field a train carrying the Stockport Football Club home from a soccer match against the Manchester Grasshoppers. Aboard the train was Harry Barlow, a Stockport footballer seriously injured during the game when an opposing player savagely attacked him and ruptured his intestine. The 21-year-old bricklayer apparently died shortly after looking out the carriage window at the Caughnawaga "running and waving strange sticks around their heads," according to one written historical account.

The Stockport Football Club immediately disbanded, and is said to have resurrected itself the following day as the Stockport Lacrosse Club, its players dedicating themselves to a sport they had allegedly never heard of prior to the death of Barlow. Native American mythology suggests a possible explanation: one legend has *Sum'guya'dis'sa'eh* giving lacrosse to the people to avenge the death of a warrior killed by an evil underground spirit.

But whatever the reason, Lyons says *"Bag'ata'weh* is a powerful medicine game" and, along with other Native American faithkeepers, he has visited the region to burn sacred bundles of Iroquois talismans to protect local lacrosse players.

David Reid at the Stockport Local Heritage Library offers another curiosity: England had five lacrosse clubs prior to the Caughnawaga exhibition game, but all of those clubs either disbanded or relocated to Stockport within a decade of first playing against a local team.

"I want to believe Stockport was so good that the others just tired of being beaten and quit," adds Stockport lacrosse fan Mike Atkinson, an official at the downtown Hat Museum. "That must be it, right?"

Of course, visitors to the Hat Museum won't find any of the Native American headfeathers worn by the area's nineteenth-century lacrosse players. Those are over at the Stockport Lacrosse Club, bronzed into plaques. Lyons explains that tribal tradition dictates a hawk feather be tied to the hair of a lacrosse player because the hawk is *Sum'guya'dis'sa'eh's* messenger.

"Hawks have flown over our lacrosse field for as long as I can remember," says Bill Roughly, the chairman of the Stockport Lacrosse Club's lawn-bowling committee. "They certainly seem to circle whenever there's a game."

Adds John Weatherlit, another longtime member of the bowling team: "Before the Great War, quite a few lacrosse players were cremated and had their ashes scattered over the field. It was so moving that many bowlers requested the same be done with their remains on the bowling lawn."

But for old-timers like Stockport lacrosse star Les Grainger, there is perhaps no better evidence of a miracle than what transpired after disaster befell those lacrosse players who joined the 1/6 Battalion of the Manchester Regiment during World War One. "More than a thousand players—every last stickman in Stockport—signed up with the One-Six and were slaughtered at Gallipoli. But the lacrosse survived, stronger than ever, in fact."

HIGH-SPEED COMPETITION

ON THE WORLD'S

STRANGEST MONUMENT

IT'S SPRINGTIME, AND NATIONAL pastimes are in full swing all over the world. The Americans rally around baseball diamonds. The French turn their thoughts to packs of cyclists spinning down country roads. And the Albanians are in the thick of the Hoxha sliding season.

Hoxha sliding is no Olympic event, but don't let that fool you. As sports go, this game has it all: a funky venue, contestants who go up to twenty miles an hour on plastic bottles, a battle brewing between two potential corporate sponsors, and a cow named "Bardhoshe."

The action starts a hundred feet (30.5 meters) up a mammoth triangular monument that has been alternately compared to a crashed flying saucer, a lopsided loaf of bread, and a fist of knuckles. A crazed medley of marble and concrete, it was planted in a Tirana park in 1988 to celebrate the eightieth anniversary of the birth of Albanian strongman Enver Hoxha, who had died in 1985, though local legend suggests Hoxha was born in 1902 and isn't really dead.

The dates might not add up, but never mind. The point is that the Enver Hoxha Memorial has a roof that reaches all the way to the ground and resembles a series of toboggan chutes: they're steeply raked, perfectly smooth, and utterly irresistible to anyone with a thirst for speed.

And speed is very much the point. The rules of Hoxha sliding are simple: find an empty plastic bottle, preferably a three-liter Pepsi-Cola container, scramble to the top of the slippery slope, sit down on your non-returnable sled, and slide. Forget about grace or artistic merit; they don't count in this game. Clambering up the roof, Klodian Murati gives some pointers. "No technique," counsels the mop-haired eleven-year-old, who is widely regarded as the All-Tirana Hoxha sliding champion. "Go for speed."

In the field below, a crowd gathers. Lutfi Tota, a 72-year-old farmer, looks up wistfully. "I wish I were young enough to slide," he says, recalling the days when he went sledding in the mountains near his home village. "If I were ten years old, I'd be up there with them."

Tota's cow, Bardhoshe, lies across the finish line, lowing peacefully. She is an essential safety feature in the game, serving as a bovine backstop to keep sliders from landing in a concrete drainage trench at the bottom of the piste. "The cow wasn't there last year when I broke my leg in the ditch," the young Murati explains.

The game's roots trace back to the reign of Hoxha himself, a dictator with a taste for the weird. According to the sport's oral history, Hoxha ordered the entire population of Tirana to stand in the rain without umbrellas one nasty spring day in 1983 so that he and his wife could drive around the city and observe the spectacle of a few hundred thousand people getting wet. Inspired by this performance, the legend goes, Hoxha told his wife to build a pyramid after his death to house everything he had ever touched in life. And so it was that the memorial was stocked with the collected artifacts of Hoxha, including some of his toiletries, until the crumbling of communism in 1991, when they were removed to furnish office space for the Soros Foundation and other institutions.

All of this matters little to the children of Tirana, a dirt-poor city with little going for kids except the meteoric sliding surfaces of a six-sided memorial that they call "the pyramid." Here they come day after day, their ranks swelled by Kosovar refugee children. "It's really, really, really fun," says Ramiz Frashei, a ten-year-old from the Kosovar city Pec.

The sport does have a few drawbacks. Crash helmets aren't available, but since when has that ever stopped kids? More worrisome is the presence of Genc Arra, a government functionary who is paid to patrol the monument and chase the children away. "It's very difficult to keep them off," says Arra. "All of the kids are very strong-headed. The ones from Kosovo don't understand the danger."

All in all, though, things are looking up. For one thing, it was more dangerous to be a Hoxha slider during the construction phase when Hoxha ruled the country. "Back then, there were soldiers here and they would shoot anyone who tried to slide," Arra says, brandishing a small club. "All I have is this stick."

What's more, a breakthrough in sliding technology is revolutionizing the sport. The transformation began when jumbo-sized, three-liter plastic bottles of Pepsi started to pop up in local street kiosks, says young Murati, the sliding champ. Until then, the chariots of choice were the smaller 1.5-liter containers of Fanta and Coca-Cola or, in a pinch, a discarded green bottle of San Pellegrino water. Trouble was, the 1.5-liter sleds got chewed up pretty fast.

"You get about fifty slides with the Coke bottle and about seventy-five with the Pepsi," the champ explains. "The bigger bottle will take you down faster," as well as giving older guys more room to sit. The only edge that the smaller Coke bottle offers, he and other sliders say, is better maneuverability.

Coca-Cola Co. spokesperson Jennifer McCollum defends the tactical aerodynamics of the Coke bottle, saying they "leave nothing to the seat of the pants." But Jeff Brown, a PepsiCo Inc. communications executive, says his company's jumbos have "opened up" the sport. He likens Hoxha sliding to gymnastics: "In both sports, size and body weight have historically limited competition to younger children," he explains. "The three-liter Pepsi chariot allows you to take Hoxha sliding into your teens and well into adulthood."

Back atop the monument, the young Murati is giving a last-minute, $2 lesson to a newcomer. The feet-first slide works best, he advises, even though it offers "no direction control." The novice squats down on his three-liter sled, grips the neck, and asks what to do next.

"Lift your feet in the air," Murati says.

With a swoosh and a shout, the rookie is off. But just fifteen meters into his slide, he executes an ominous 180-degree turn that launches the sled skyward and ends his shot at the title.

But, hey, there's always next season, the cow willing.

34

BOVINE ATHLETES
ARE GROOMED FOR A SHOT
AT STARDOM IN SPAIN

THE SPANISH INQUISITION IS COMING TO TOWN, and Marc Jalabert is nervous. And when it arrives, says Jalabert, his destiny will be written in blood on the sand of a 2,000-year-old athletic coliseum.

The amphitheater was erected by Caesar Augustus for his gladiators in what is now the city of Nîmes, in southern France, but today's local sports fans deify the site as the cathedral of French bullfighting. More portentous for Jalabert, one of France's thirty-nine *manades*, or combat-bull breeders, it's here where the Spanish promoters, who select bulls for their country's 340 *corridas*, or bull rings, travel to scout the performance of the French competition.

"I'm a farmer who makes great athletes," says Jalabert. "When the Spanish arrive, I must show that my bulls have received reverent theatrical instruction." He points to an 800-pound bull thundering across the wild scrub of his 1,200-acre ranch south of the city. "Look at that one," sighs the trainer, whom experts say is the most promising bull coach in France. "Not enough run. With him, I must be a psychologist, too."

Jalabert's ranch, set along the eerie lagoons and salt marshes of the Camargue, is a place where champions are made. And bullfight experts say Jalabert has the best chance of winning France's 143-year campaign to give the bulls of the Camargue a shot against the Spanish heavyweights.

Known as *bious*, more than 1,200 of these ferocious French athletes, some weighing 1,100 pounds, are slain each year by matadors in the 240

French bullrings between Nîmes and Bayonne. An additional five thousand combat bulls, all of them Spanish or Portuguese, will face the sword in Spain's rings.

Over the past decade, Jalabert's fighters have grown in popularity with French crowds who sing "La Marseillaise" but whose passion for this ancient blood sport is distinctly Spanish in flavor. Two thirds of the bulls that do battle in France are imported from the Iberian Peninsula. "Our patriotic idea of France being the best in all things ends at the arena gate in Nîmes," huffs Jalabert.

Compounding this perceived smear against the graceful *biou*, say local government officials privately, was some Spanish politicking during the 1992 World's Fair in Seville, Spain. For the first (and the last) time in history, the Spanish summoned a card of six *bious* to appear in the Seville arena, the World Cup for combat bulls. But the Camarguaise and the Andalusians both spurned the exhibition as a diplomatic, not athletic, one. Jalabert wants to be the first manade to enter Seville without any politicians attached. "Everywhere else the crowd whistles when they don't like the bull. In Seville, poorly raised bulls are greeted with silence. Seville is the temple, and I'm ready."

But to enter the temple, the *manade* must first show the Spanish gathered in Nîmes that the Jalabert brand has the stuff of Seville. The municipal government, which organizes the bullfight card, has elected six of his bulls to open the 1995 season. It's Jalabert's maiden outing in the Nîmes ring, a culmination of twelve years of breeding and, he hopes, the penultimate stop on "my journey to Andalusia."

The ritual of the bullfight in France began in 1852, when the country's first fight was staged in Bayonne to celebrate the marriage of Emperor Napoleon III to the Spanish noblewoman Eugenie de Montijo. "The wife of the emperor liked the blood," explains Daniel Valade, a senior aide to Nîmes mayor Jean Bousquet and the director of the municipality's bullfight office. "The business grew from there."

Now the business of bullfighting, officials say, has become a vital element in the economy of southern France, notwithstanding dicey economic times and frequent protests by animal-rights activists. The bounty of the ebony *biou* is such that the Ministry of Finance allows local authorities to exempt the 18.6% value-added tax levied on ticket sales if a town holds more than four bullfights during a season, which runs from February through October. According to a market study commissioned by the mayor's office, the spectacle attracts over four hundred thousand tourists each year, pumping $26.6 million into the downtown economy. Some fifty-seven percent of those visitors come to Nîmes specifically for the bullfights.

"Marc is our star and ready for Seville," boasts Valade. "His cow selection is excellent. The mother gives the bull a combative nature, the father provides the shape, and everybody in Nîmes will tonight cheer and profit from that union."

But according to Valade, the *manade* doesn't necessarily share in the windfall. "The bull is like a dancer," he muses. "The manade falls in love with her, but she gives him absolutely nothing back in return."

Well, not exactly nothing, The French government provides cattlemen with a yearly subsidy of a few hundred dollars for each head of livestock: since both combat bulls and beef cattle are slaughtered for the table, no distinction is made between the two breeds. Jalabert says he can easily sell a head of two-year-old beef cattle for more than $1,500, but he prefers to wait until his cows and *bious* reach maturity, when he can evaluate them as breeders or for combat. But a good fighting bull can fetch between $3,000 and $40,000. On average, only forty-two out of about four hundred of Jalabert's bulls are good enough for the arena.

"A 700-pound *biou* is not ready to fight until he's three years old," explains Jalabert. "The 1,100-pound heavyweights favored by the Spanish aren't ready until they're four or five years old. An exceptional *biou* might not be ready until six."

To help pay for his passion, Jalabert farms rice, raises horses, and invites tourists to ride across his ranch and watch the *bious* ripen into fighters. He also rents bulls. For $400 to $4,000, he supplies arenas with ordinary *bious* for the Course Camarguaise, a nonlethal sport in which players attempt to place garlands on the horns of a charging bull.

"I lose money on my *bious*," says Jalabert. "The Spanish breeders use genetic science. Manades cannot afford such witchcraft." But many fans claim that Spanish bulls have grown lethargic from the fancy breeding techniques designed to make them look beautiful. A *biou* might not look as good as a Spanish bull, they contend, but the beast will provide more exciting moves.

"Spanish fans want mobility in a bull," says Jalabert, who sings to his bious as part of their training program. "But Spanish bulls suffer from interbreeding and overeating. They can't move."

Of course, the thinking is different on the other side of the Pyrenees. Felipe Lafita, the president of the Spanish Bull-Breeding Association during the 1990s, will only concede that the *bious* have "shown improvement." And he dismisses the contention that Spanish bulls have lost a step.

But whatever Jalabert's opinions of the Spanish bullfighting establishment, the final judges of him and his bulls are the Spanish. This is even true on the floor of the arena in Nîmes in late February, as the sixth and last bull of the evening awaits the matador's sword. Jalabert watches the action intently, his hands flecked with the blood of a bull killed earlier that night.

Five of his *bious* have already given the crowd energetic performances. As before, Jalabert looks away as the evening's final sword draws its blood.

Nearly ten thousand spectators rise from their seats to loudly praise the Jalabert brand. Jalabert takes this as a powerful omen, and he scans a nearby Spanish delegation for a further clue to his fate. But the Spanish remain seated, scribbling notes in silence.

"This is a tough sport," confesses Jalabert, "but I vow to bring the *biou* to Seville."

He's still waiting.

THE LONELINESS

OF THE LONG-DISTANCE

DRINKER

MARATHONERS RUN FOR THE GLORY, and certainly for the money, but only here in the heart of Burgundy do they sprint to the finish for a bottle of Hospice de Beaune Grand Cru Corton.

There are approximately two hundred marathons and semi-marathons officially sanctioned around the world by the International Amateur Athletic Federation, and the Semi-Marathon de la Vente des Vins isn't one of them. Nonetheless, over two thousand runners from eight countries lace up each year in the spectacular glow of the Hôtel-Dieu's multicolored gables to run through Burgundy in the annual November wine charity auction semi-marathon.

Nicholas Rolin, the chancellor to the duke of Burgundy, a man more familiar with the sword than the shoe, founded the Hôtel-Dieu and its renowned Hospice de Beaune wine auction in 1443 as a way to raise money for the poor. Town officials started the semi-marathon in 1985 to further herald the region's famed wines, and the course takes runners through many of the fifty-seven independent hectares of privately owned Grand and Premier Cru Côte de Beaune vineyards set aside to grow the coveted Hospice wine.

And the run covers such unique ground that Microsoft Corp. founder Bill Gates hopes to preserve its glory for the next five hundred years. Gates dispatched *National Geographic* magazine photographer Charles O'Rear to chronicle the many curious ceremonies surrounding the Hospice auction for Corbis, the software magnate's privately owned online photo archive, which includes the electronic rights to the *Mona Lisa*.

But is this sport?

"It's impossible for marathon runners to effectively condition themselves by just running marathons," explains Jean Luc Lheraud, Beaune's director of sports and athletic coach at the local Lycée Viticole, the wine-growing school. "Half-marathons are necessary for training because they are not as grueling on a runner's body."

Nor perhaps as stimulating. Marathon runners here have a huge incentive to lose. Although the top male finisher gets $1,440 and a none-too-shabby magnum of Louis Latour Beaune Premier Cru (the first woman to complete the race takes home a magnum and $600), race officials suggest that the richest rewards await those who finish below tenth place.

"We reserve some excellent bottles of Corton and Pommard for the losers," says Lheraud. "If put into the cave and properly guarded for twenty years, the wine might be worth more than the first-prize money."

And there's an overflowing temptation for runners to hold back along the 21-kilometer course. Stretching through some of the richest domains in the Côte d'Or, umpires along the way do little to dissuade the participants from slowing down to sample the likes of a Savigny-les-Beaune or Pernand-Vergelesses.

"The race is good for the sport and good for the wine," says Fabrice Jacquet, a city official and the administrative director of Maison Louis Latour, sitting in the wine school's locker room, surrounded by old socks and more than $25,000 worth of wine donated by the domains.

"Yet I doubt the marathon will help the Burgundy wine business," chuckles Marc Marechall, an executive at Ippa Bank in Belgium who monitors the wine industry throughout the Côte d'Or. "The course goes through land where one twenty-fourth of a hectare sells for a few million dollars. Back in the 1970s, for instance, a bottle of wine from those lands sold for less than one dollar. Today's harvest sells for around $100 and much more. That's enormous inflation for the same bottle of wine." Indeed, sources here indicate that ten percent of Burgundy's best domains are discreetly put up for sale to outside parties who know nothing about the region's specialized viticultural techniques. The offerings are in great part a result of a controversial French inheritance tax system that has forced the new generation of wine growers to sell off parcels to pay out-standing government death duties.

"It's a tough business," Marechall says. "You have an inflation of the land price, a deflation of the wine price, and a decreasing number of growers able to make it under the current circumstances."

And town officials add that Beaune's ability to use the semi-marathon as a marketing vehicle to promote the region's less-expensive wines is hampered by the *Loi Evin*, a French law that prohibits alcoholic-beverage companies from directly promoting their wares through sporting events. Instead, the runners head for the hills in logo-less shirts—but carrying index cards that describe the spirits of Chorey, Savigny, and Aloxe-Corton.

Over at the starting line, French sports minister Guy Drut, the gold medalist in the 110-meter hurdles at the 1976 Summer Olympics in Montreal, is looking for someone to pour him a refreshing drink. *"Bien sûr*, I prefer a glass of wine over a Coke," Drut says. "Many American athletes are very surprised to find this out."

But even those marathoners here seeking a cheaper and less provocative pick-me-up are never far from the lure of the Burgundy grape: instead of a medal, a silver tasting cup is draped around the neck of each finisher. After the race, many runners jog past the wine-tasting booths on the way to the ancient town square to participate in the auction's other premier athletic event, the Concours de Débouchage de Bouteilles, a century-old competition designed to see who can uncork thirty bottles of wine in the shortest amount of time.

And the winner is . . .

"Pouilly-Fuissé, Françoise Poisard," says Marc Bene, the cave keeper at Marches du Vin SA, one of the twenty *negociant-eleveurs* licensed to bid for and market the thirty-nine Hospice-grown wines. "This is the first time in history a Pouilly-Fuissé has been given the Hospice seal—and from only four hectares of land!"

Says François Ganoux, a Pommard grower who is president of the Côte d'Or Viticulture Committee, "I don't believe anyone is really sure who won the race."

PART THREE:
BEYOND CAVIAR

36

THE CHEESEMAN COMETH

THE CHEESES ROLL INTO TOWN as dawn breaks over the Gironde River in Bordeaux. Pencil in hand, Jean d'Alos tracks their movement across the marble pavement tiles on Rue Montesquieu and into the fifteenth-century monastic caves beneath his shop. One of a handful of master cheese cultivators in France, d'Alos nods approvingly at the fat pies of Roquefort and hexagons of Tommette des Corbières that farmers from around Europe have entrusted to his care. Scratching his gray beard, he ogles his young cheeses as beefy deliverymen lug wet rags dripping with Basque Greuilh and great lumps of freshly churned butter oozing with cholesterol.

"I can almost look a cow in the eye and tell what kind of cheese she's going to make," says d'Alos, who can rightfully claim to be the biggest cheese in France.

Emperor Napoleon III may have larded margarine on his toast, but don't dream of asking for the non-dairy spread here in the court of the cream king. For it is to this small shop, crusts of bread in hand, that cheese lovers come seeking a smear of d'Alos's handiwork. He is the master of a growing global market in exotically curdled delights, tongue-twisting mounds of raw milk; cheeses with names like Ammeai di Vic-Bilth—a rare goat cheese that smells like it's been blended inside a diaper pail. Despite the stench, d'Alos says there are no mad diseases lurking in any of his cheeses. "Our animals eat only natural grains," he tells customers worried that his cheeses might come from herds infected with bovine spongiform encephalopathy. "My rules are even stricter than those of the European Union. It's the only way we can continue as a business."

D'Alos has survived much since he left the finance department at Airbus Industrie in 1972 for a life of cheese. His curds have withstood the scrutiny of fussy French bureaucrats and weathered storms of imported Cheez Whiz. Though d'Alos says it's tough to wean young people away from processed cheese, he annually exports some thirty tons of European raw-milk cheeses around the globe. "I could do better if America allowed all my cheese into the country," he adds. For the moment, however, U.S. authorities refuse raw-milk cheeses that have been matured for less than sixty days. The rule has turned many of d'Alos's most delicious creations into outlaws. He calls the U.S. taboo "ridiculous."

Meanwhile, some 1,100 pounds of hard cheese maturing in the caverns of the old monastery will legally fill American tables. Many more crockpots of illegal Gastanberra and criminally drooping slabs of Tome au Gene de Marc, he suspects, will be smuggled past U.S. inspectors.

Such quibbling has hardly diminished d'Alos. "Anyone can sell cheese," he huffs. "I am an affineur." This nom-de-cheese, thought to have been used originally to describe alchemists out to transform base metals into gold, remains revered in France, and now is commonly reserved to honor the dwindling class of those who have raised to an art the process of turning milk into cheese. Depending on the type of animal milk, it can take d'Alos anywhere from three days to three years to mature the cheeses delivered to his caves from around the Continent. No one knows how many affineurs are left, d'Alos says, nor how many types of cheese are made in France. "We say there are as many cheeses as there are days in the year," he says over a weeping wheel of Époisses, the pungent cheese of Bourgogne. His dedication to the cheese-maker's art, which includes frequent cheese-hunting trips into remote regions of the Pyrenees on a donkey, has made him a popular figure in French cheese magazines.

His most daunting quest is sniffing out the great lost cheeses: Vacherin des Bauges, Vacherin d'Abondance, and Bleu de Termignon. These cheeses of the Savoie region, d'Alos sadly explains, are extremely uncommon because the small farmers who once cultured them now find it too expensive to follow EU cheese regulations. "I try to save and promote the small farmers who make rare cheese," he says. At the same time, few people are willing to pay $30 to $40 for a kilogram of Bleu de Termignon. Though the price might not sound exorbitant, d'Alos says even the wealthy expect their cheese to be inexpensive. "I have customers who gladly spend two thousand francs on a bottle of wine not willing to pay two hundred francs for a kilo of cheese," he says.

But for those eager to travel beyond the supermarket cheese counter, the stone caverns beneath his shop are a holy place. Slipping blue surgical slippers over their shoes and dodging pumpkin-sized Italian provolones hanging from the rafters, it is here that experts and amateurs alike come to learn the proper care and eating of cheese. In the goat-cheese cave, for instance, a temperature of nine to eleven degrees Celsius (forty-eight to fifty-two degrees Fahrenheit) is constantly maintained, and the cheeses are turned daily to ensure perfect ripening. Further down the labyrinth is the hard-cheese room, a humid chamber splashed frequently with water. The temperature here in the home of such big wheels as Comté de Jura hovers between twelve and fourteen degrees Celsius, the air heavy with the stink of ammonia.

Using piano wire, d'Alos slits a forty-kilogram Comté into spokes. The cuts unleash a foul smell. "Hold your nose," he instructs. "The most important thing about cheese is the difference between *odeurs* and *aromes*," he adds quickly. Handing over a thick cut of the moist cow cheese, d'Alos says to roll the morsel between the fingers and eat it while holding the nose. "Now let go of your nose," he commands. The horrid odor of ammonia is gone, replaced by the deliciously earthy aroma of a vintage 1997 Comté.

"Comté is a fascinating cheese," d'Alos says. "It provides eighty-three separate aromas, depending on where and how the cheese is made."

But all is not curds and whey in the cheese dungeon. Danger lurks in the specter of the explosive Emmental, the Swiss cheese. "The odd thing about Emmental is people want it with more holes," says export manager Patricia DuBourg. And that, d'Alos says, is where the problem pops up. All of d'Alos's cheese-bearing cows, along with his sheep and goats, are fed unfermented grasses. But if an Emmental-producing cow strays into a feed bin containing more widely used fermented feed stock, its cream can become a bovine time bomb. "Acids help create the holes in Emmental," d'Alos says. "But if the cow eats fermented grasses, then incorrect acids develop, more holes are created, and the cheese often explodes."

Cheeses also can be deceiving. Elegantly displayed near water-filled tubs of buffalo mozzarella and simple cottage cheese from England is what, in one sense, is d'Alos's most volatile *fromage:* La Tome de José Bové de Larzac, from the sheep of the fiery José Bové, who became a French folk hero for smashing up McDonald's restaurants. But gastronomically it is, well, distinctly sheepish. "It's a very mild cheese," d'Alos says. "Quite unlike José."

37

FRENCH FROG RANCHERS
BATTLE BUREAUCRATS FOR
FREE-RANGE AMPHIBIANS

LONG AGO, WHEN FRENCH FROG RANCHING WAS LEGAL, the plump beetles and therapeutic waters around the spa town of Vittel produced the tastiest amphibians in the world. When the government outlawed the trade in 1978, imported frogs jumped in, frozen and packaged in cellophane.

Now, Josette Pouchucq wants to put the slime back in the frog businesss. Along with the sixty other ruling members of the Brotherhood of Frog Thigh Tasters, Pouchucq leads the struggle to restore *la grenouille* to glory by persuading the government to put fresh French frogs back on the table. Resplendent in the green robe and yellow sash of the Thigh Tasters, Pouchucq flourishes a broiled frog leg of unknown origin and says, "We prefer the frogs we eat to be French."

It's a gastropolitical affair fraught with economic dilemmas, environmental bugs, and frog rustlers. The domestic population, whose members feed on insects and are important for pest control, had been dwindling since the French first started to sauté the critters in the eleventh century. Because frogs talk only in fairy tales, it was left to the Ministry of Agriculture and Fishing to speak on their behalf before they all were eaten. In 1977, it banned commercial harvesting of frogs.

The argument boils down to a battle between hopping-mad environmentalists, who like their frogs wallowed in mud, and diners, who prefer them slathered in white wine. The European Union annually imports over six thousand tons of frog legs. France consumes forty-two percent of the production, while the kitchens of Belgium and Luxembourg cook a further forty-four percent of the total. French frogs can be hunted only for personal consumption, and the laws against poaching are strictly enforced—so the government says.

According to government figures, the French now eat a mere seventy tons of domestic frog legs. Herpetologist Andrew R. Blaustein, the frog man at Oregon State University, greets that appetizing statistic with a soupçon of suspicion. A leading expert on global amphibian populations, Blaustein says it's impossible to gather reliable figures on the sale and consumption of frogs. "People in the frog trade don't want to talk," he explains. "Our most up-to-date research shows that Asia exported over two hundred million metric tons in 1995."

Pouchucq sniffs at the numbers. "If we could eat only French frogs," she argues, "we would not be buying foreign frogs."

Depending on their size, it takes between twenty-four and forty pounds of frogs to turn out one pound of stripped frog legs. A plate of twenty or so foreign frog legs costs around $14 at your average amphibian bistro. Some say frog tastes like chicken; in fact, Indonesian and French frogs alike taste like frog. And all dissolve in the mouth like soft rubber.

But not all frogs are created equal, particularly for the twenty thousand people and six tons of Asian frogs scheduled to swarm into Vittel during the last weekend of April for the Brotherhood's Annual Frog-Eating Festival, the world's largest frog-eating jamboree. Pouchucq says that frog-eaters from Belgrade to Quebec arrive most eager to grill, poach, or schnitzel the 450 pounds of free-range French frogs caught for the event in René Clément's lake.

In these parts, the late restaurateur Clément is known as the last of the great Lorraine frog ranchers. Back in 1952, Clément moved into a storehouse on the banks of the Saône River, looking to raise crayfish. The water was too brackish for shellfish, so he turned to frogs. "The frog is like a woman," Clément told the local newspaper in 1983. "Only their thighs are good."

In 1971, Clément founded the Brotherhood. He supplied Vittel with three hundred pounds of legs for the first festival. The bash grew at such leaps and bounds that the ban forced the Brotherhood to recruit emigré frogs to meet the demand. The chef for years told all who would listen of his anger over French politicians forcing him to eat foreign frogs.

"It's all true and embarrassing," rues eighty-year-old Pierrette Gillet, a brotherhood member and daughter of an Ourche Valley frog rancher. "Frogs became a business for poachers."

Vincent Bentata, a frog investigator at the Ministry of Environment, says the Thigh Tasters are "dreaming" to think France will legalize commercial frogging. "The government is dedicated to protecting frogs," Bentata says. "You get caught, you get fined €10,000 and we confiscate your vehicle."

Licking the sauce off her thumbs over a dinner of apparently Indonesian frogs at the Hotel d'Angleterre, Gillet wistfully remembers the ponderosa days. She would track herds of so-called green and mute frogs as they hopped across the mountain streams and misty prairies that stretch south from Lorraine and into the rich hunting grounds of the Loire Valley. Sometimes she ventured forth at night and, blinding her prey with a flashlight, whacked them over the head with a club. "The mute frogs are harder to catch because they have no larynx," Gillet explains.

The only croaking in Jakky Ferdinand's nearby frog and butcher shop comes from the crows perched atop the trees outside. For Ferdinand, the black market is the one place to find a sustainable supply of French frogs, yet he won't deal with rustlers because it's against the law. "All of my frogs are Indonesian," he grouses. "I'm waiting for 220 pounds to arrive for the festival, and I can't tell you how much the shipment will cost. The Indonesians know the French will pay anything for a frog."

"We French love our frogs," adds Elizabeth Simonin, who insists she will sell only French frogs at her Le Comptoir delicatessen when the tadpoles of Lorraine turn into frogs this season. A kilogram of French legs will retail for about $45. Are they skillet-legal? It's best not to ask.

Frogging is a bleak business. Unlike, say, a "bouquet" of pheasants, frogs are collectively referred to as "armies." Old Testament scribes tell of God raining a pestilence of frogs upon Egypt; the Book of Revelations warns that the world will end with the appearance of "spirits like frogs."

Pouchucq says that plagues and paucities fail to intimidate the Brotherhood. As she tells it, the French were the first to protest conventional wisdom and plop a frog in a saucepan. History seems to support her. Food historian John Mariani says French peasants ate frogs as a means of jumping through a loophole in Catholic Church law: "Meat was forbidden during Lent, and the church didn't view frogs as meat."

While the frogs were slapped down on the dinner plates of the poor, though, the French royalty living at Versailles began referring to those who lived in Swampy Paris as "frogs." Outside France, frogs lacked the international respectability afforded other French delicacies.

Then the legendary French chef George Auguste Escoffier delighted the Prince of Wales with a plate of chilled bullfrog legs in London's Carlton Hotel. Escoffier called his creation *Les Cuisses de Nymphes*, or The Thighs of the Dawn Nymphs. The year was 1908. French frogs were now sexy and in trouble.

The 1977 crackdown on commercial harvesting forced French buyers to travel behind the Iron Curtain, where a motivated huntsman twitching for hard currency could bag eight hundred Communist frogs a day. One by one, the frog-producing countries began imposing export quotas, finally leaving unregulated slicing and dicing in the hands of Vietnam, China, Taiwan, and Indonesia.

Back at the table, Gillet comes clean and says it's darn hard for a first-time frog eater to taste any difference between a fresh French mute and a frozen Bengali bull. "The secret of perfect preparation is the sauce, even if a few toads end up on your plate," she says.

THESE NOT-SO-LITTLE
PIGGIES WENT TO MARKET

THERE'S NO BALONEY IN GUIJUELO. Proletarian pork is unwelcome in the capital city of Spain's luxury ham industry.

Stretched across a range of wild acorn trees in Salamanca Province two hours by car west of Madrid, the pastoral outpost of Guijuelo boasts five thousand people, 182 ham packers, and almost three million Jamón Ibérico de Bellota pigs with fatty rear legs that the government says annuaully fetch $50 million on the world ham market.

And then there are the fifty-six thousand pigs of Joselito, the director general of privately held Cárnicas Joselito SA, the world's largest producer of customized, acorn-eating Iberian pigs. Call them bespoke hams. And call him Joselito. Just Joselito.

"I am thirty-eight years old, eighty-eight pounds overweight, and I don't have any cholesterol," says Joselito, snapping on a pair of surgical gloves and cutting into a vintage long-legged 1999 Joselito Gran Reserva Ham. "I am the poster boy."

The growing taste for acorn ham has made Joselito and his purebred beasts the objects of cult-like devotion among global gastronomes. It has reduced the roughly thirty-three million hoi polloi pigs Spain annually produces to hobnobbing as lunchmeat, while providing traveling ham carvers like Sergio Gomez with work at parties hosted by Alitalia SpA, Iberia Lineas Aereas de España SA, and the Spanish energy company Endesa SA.

"All of my clients prefer Joselitos," says Gomez, a former actor who now spends his time hamming it up at corporate gatherings in France,

Germany, and England. Gomez says the precision of his craft can be seen suspended from Joselito's warehouse ceiling: some hundred thousand raw pig legs with spiraled, royal red and blue cotton ropes lashed to their cloven hooves.

And the danger of his craft can be seen with his left arm wrapped in an elastic bandage, the result, he says, of a ham-slicing injury. "Slicing Iberian ham is dangerous work," Gomez says. "They have lots of fat, and if you cut yourself, the fat on the knife seeps beneath the skin and the wound is nearly impossible to close."

Joselito says his critters dangle for two to five years in the five-story curing warehouse, called a *secadero*.

"All of my pigs are professional athletes and they don't take steroids," explains Joselito, a fifth-generation Iberian *jamónero*, whose free-range pigs spend eighteen months wandering across 264,000 acres of oak trees, each animal consuming twenty-two pounds of acorns a day during the March-to-October acorn season. The pigs spend the winter chowing down on wild vegetation.

The freshly cut legs are first slathered in sea salt to prevent spoilage, then hosed down with water, and then hung to sweat and dry in the mountain air. Each level in the *secadero* has large shuttered walls that are adjusted according to wind direction and outside temperature. The drippings congeal on the rubber floor in the winter and flow like warm tallow during the summer. Individual hams are decorated with nametags pinned into the deep fat so Joselito's three hundred employees can identify the buyers.

In one corner are the vintage hams of Alain Senderens, the chef of the Parisian restaurant Senderens. The future meals served by French chef Joël Robuchon are in the basement, and workers on the third floor are inspecting a recently slaughtered brace of hams owned by the Spanish department store chain El Corte Ingles SA.

Weight determines the cost, from $800 to $1,500 per ham, with a minimum purchase of fifty. There's a five-year waiting list and no secondary market.

"Bespoke ham is either already eaten or spoken for," says Gonzalo Verdera, a former investment banking analyst at McKinsey & Co. and now director of TodoVino SA, a wine-and-gourmet food-consulting firm and distributorship.

Each of Spain's three Iberian pig-rearing regions—Guijuelo, Huelva, and Extremadura—produces a slightly different-tasting aromatic ham.

What all the pigs have in common is an acorn diet and a government certificate that alerts connoisseurs to what the animals have eaten outside acorn season. Top hams are marked with a red band that identifies them as coming from Jamón Ibérico de Bellota—pigs that dine on nothing but acorns and organic plants and grains. Yellow tags denote Jamón Ibérico pigs allowed to snack on commercially processed feed.

"There is no such thing as bad Spanish ham," says José Sanchez, curator at the Ham Museum in Madrid. Sanchez cares for a hanging display of three thousand hams, an edible exhibit that attracts hundreds of hungry people a day. Doubling as the museum's senior slicer, Sanchez each week cuts and sells 2,600 pounds of ham.

Back on the party circuit, at a recent private ham gathering hosted by officials from the Organization for Economic Cooperation and Development in Paris, Gomez and his assistant arrive with two Joselitos wrapped in gunnysacks and a Samsonite suitcase filled with knives, a selection of sausages, and first-aid gear. Guests quickly surround the operating stand and eagerly wait for Gomez to shear slices of ham into their palms.

"The anarchy starts when the ham comes into view," Gomez warns. "It's every man for himself once I start slicing."

Jockeying for position, Maria Martinez, administrator at the Cervantes Institute in Paris, which promotes Spanish culture and specializes in teaching the executive corps how to speak Spanish, elbows her way to the table. She intercepts a slice intended for McKinsey & Co. "He's an artist," Martinez marvels after downing her ham. "Sergio cuts fast and thin."

Gomez has contracts with Iberian pig farmers, who arrange for his clients to purchase their party meat as a piglet and watch it mature into a 400-pound hog with two 12- to 22-pound hams. "I call the business the 'liturgy of the ham'," Gomez says.

Joselito hams evoke Biblical testimonials. "The taste of a slice of Joselito Gran Reserva is like a stroll through paradise—a heavenly, insuperable taste," says Spanish culinary analyst Rafael García Santos, author of *The Best of Spanish Food.*

No such devotion is sparked by American abattoirs, where pigs get fat, hogs get slaughtered, and the 2007 pork-belly volume on the Chicago Mercantile Exchange was 68,409 contracts, down from 107,564 contracts in 2006. Each contract represents forty thousand pounds of bacon, with the rest of the hundred million pigs butchered annually sold off as cuts that are tagged ham, picnic, loin, trimmings, and Boston butt.

"There are no niche hogs on the Chicago Mercantile Exchange," says Chuck Levitt, senior livestock analyst for Alaron Trading Corp. "American pigs are a standardized risk-hedging and speculative device."

Spanish ham analysts in Madrid say the riskiest part of their business is lunch at Casa Patas, a restaurant with flamenco dancers on stage and master slicer Oscar Ceballos on the knives. "I learned the craft under Professor Miquel Diez, a legend," Ceballos says, sharpening each of the eleven blades he will use to debone and serve one of the hundred hams hanging from hooks above the beer kegs and guarded by an ultraviolet-light insect-zapper.

"You need a firm hand," Ceballos explains. "This is not work for the meek."

Ceballos suggests that most high-quality ham buyers destroy the meat because they don't know how to properly wield the knife through the fat-marbled flesh. "Amateurs try to rid the final cut of fat," the slicer says. "That ruins the taste of the ham. You must not be afraid of the grease."

The taste also can be affected by "what your ham ate as a pig," cautions Verdera of TodoVino over a plate of loin served up by Joselito himself at a "research and development" meeting in his test kitchen in Guijuelo.

Yet accidents do happen. Joselito says a chain of unlikely circumstances in 2000 created the world's first-known cantaloupe ham, a hazardous lapse in the Iberian pig quality-control process that Verdera says threatened melon-and-ham appetizers, a culinary mainstay.

Recalling the calamity, Joselito says a ham absorbs the taste of the last thing the pig eats before slaughter. "We had a few hundred pigs who had eaten the leftover melons our workers had for lunch," he says.

DINING **HABITS**

APRÈS SEPTEMBER **11TH**

O MAR GUERDA REMEMBERS when citizens of the West feared that the fluffy semolina grain of Algeria was an extremist threat.

The year was 1979, and Guerda had just plopped his first lamb chop on the grill at Chez Omar, one of the earliest North African couscous restaurants to open outside the Muslim neighborhoods that have been part of Paris life since the 1920s.

"The French and the tourists never came into my restaurant," Guerda recalls over the spicy aroma of merguez sausages. "In fact, they looked through the window, and then ran away."

No longer. Chez Omar and its multilingual owner over the past twenty years have become one of this city's culinary fixtures, a hundred-seat restaurant that caters to Christians, Muslims, Jews, and even those whose religion demands vegetarian couscous. "The best Muslim restaurants make all people feel at home," Guerda says. "Eating with strangers, making them your guest and introducing them to the other diners is the best way to get people to understand and appreciate different cultures."

Since the events of September 11, Guerda and other Muslim restaurant owners here with roots from the Maghreb to Iran say their ability to educate customers on the often-misunderstood traditions of Islam is now as critical as the quality of their food. Echoing an often-heard refrain, Guerda says, "Osama bin Laden has absolutely nothing to do with Islamic culture and religion."

Indeed, the table talk about Islamic terrorist assaults and the wars in Iraq and Afghanistan these days has placed Muslim restaurant owners here in the difficult position of explaining the realities of their religion against the growing backdrop of hate fueled by bin Laden and his Taliban allies. But for the Muslim chefs of Paris, a well-stocked kitchen of honey-rich tagines from Morocco and chilled stone jugs of vodka-laced *doughe* yogurt from Iran are their secret weapons against bigotry and the global war against terrorism. "They're also better for you," Guerda says of the kitchen armory. "Much less fat than in European cooking."

The role of food in Islamic culture goes far beyond physical well-being. According to Genesis 18, God gave Abraham his greatest reward because of the exceptional table the prophet prepared for his divine visitors. In fact, Old Testament scribes provide greater detail on Abraham's eating habits than on the conversation that took place between him and God. Since that time, the hospitality of Arabs—the modern-day heirs of Abraham—has been considered a noble trait, and the Koran says that refusal to offer hospitality to a stranger is an offense against God.

"The pleasure Muslims take in dining is not only sanctified and approved by the Koran, but is one of the most expressive ways that Muslims show their hospitality and essential goodness," explains food historian John Mariani, a former professor of English at City University of New York.

The tenets of gastrotheology are evident at Cheminée Royale, a family-owned Iranian restaurant that's a favorite among the locals here who line up for saffron ice cream alongside the visiting Gulf Arabs dispatched by the concierge at the Hotel de Crillon. Flat Persian *toftu* bread is prepared inside a large charcoal-pit oven and delivered to tables with plates of stuffed eggplants and *babaganouche*. It takes twenty-four hours to make the savory rice that accompanies the lamb, chicken, and fish served perfumed with herbs and grilled atop a simple barbecue. The result is no suburban backyard cookout, however. "It's extremely important for people to leave Cheminée Royale knowing about our culture," says Zare Arjomand, who gives each of her first-time customers a book on Iran.

At the same time, September 11 carries a bittersweet significance for the Arjomand family. The 46-seat restaurant opened on that date in 1987. "Our greatest thrill is to introduce people to Iranian cuisine for the first time," Arjomand says. But culinary explorers have been few and far between since the attacks. "We've lost thirty-five percent of our trade," she explains. "The customers who are most interesting for us, the first-timers, no longer come." Watching her small daughter roll *toftu* dough atop a table, Arjomand reckons that people are staying away because of politics. "People think: Iran, Islamic government, closed country," she says. "Americans, in particular, aren't really interested in any sort of Islamic style of cooking."

France's appreciation of North African cuisine was a direct result of the country's colonization of Algeria and Morocco. But Maghreb cuisine didn't materialize in Paris until 1927, when Algerian immigrants opened Le Hoggar, believed to be the city's first Muslim restaurant, near the Paris Mosque. Despite the popularity of dining out on couscous over the past thirty years, Islamic dishes are rarely prepared in French homes, says Paule Caillat, owner of the Promenades Gourmandes cooking school and in-house regional cuisine expert at La Librairie des Gourmets bookshop. The shop offers a rare copy of *The Lost Cuisine of Egypt*, but Caillat suggests that the book just gathers dust because people are much less curious about Islamic cuisine than they are about other regional cooking styles.

"Even before September 11, there was no interest in Muslim food," Caillat says. "Most Europeans don't even know where Algeria is, let alone the American tourists I teach in cooking classes." Still, "you are what you eat," said Jean-Anthelme Brillat-Savarin, nineteenth-century French magistrate and author of *The Physiology of Taste*, the first book to explore the rapport between the political and digestive systems. But even back then, the French weren't all that taken with Brillat-Savarin's opinions. The government of the time charged the gourmet lawyer with the crime of being "too moderate" in his political views and forced him into exile in Switzerland.

The stewpot of global cultures that blended to create America's eclectic style of cuisine also was void of Islamic influences, despite the boatloads of Turkish immigrants who arrived in the U.S. during the early twentieth century. The 1939 and 1949 editions of *Knife & Fork in New York,* one of the earliest fine-dining guidebooks, fail to mention any Muslim restaurants.

Mariani suggests that the lack of widespread interest in Islamic food is political—and unfortunate. "Food tells you a country's history," Caillat adds. "You learn the ways of others through the stomach." The famous French duck-and-bean stew known as *cassoulet,* she points out, would never have been invented had it not been for Islam. "The white beans in cassoulet came from the Moors who lived in Spain," Caillat says.

Even the sandwich, said to have been invented by an English Christian and years later refined by kosher Jewish delicatessen owners in New York, was pocketed from Islamic kitchens in the region today known as Lebanon. At least that's the story told behind the counter at Al Diwan, and the Lebanese restaurant's shwarma sandwich makers are sticking to it as they slather rolled chicken and lamb sandwiches with chickpea spread and tangy peppers. "Grand Lebanese cuisine is extremely refined," Caillat says. "The food is a mixture of Muslim and French styles of cooking."

Yet no matter the Muslim region, herbs and spices are the starting point for nearly every dish. Paper-thin pastries filled with fish or fowl also are constant. But at 404, one of this city's slicker Moroccan restaurants, the specialty of the house is a cocktail made from vodka, sugar, lemon, and sparkling water. Nonetheless, the red banner flapping from the hip eatery's wrought-iron grate proclaims 404 a *restaurant familial,* a place where romping children and adults love nothing better than a glass of sweet mint tea.

Back at Chez Omar, Guerda is slicing a crispy-skinned shoulder of lamb and scorning those Muslims whose actions have corrupted his culture and beliefs. "The few foreign tourists who are coming to Paris don't want to eat this kind of food," Guerda says. "It's a shame."

But at least Guerda still has customers to serve. Cheminée Royal closed its kitchen in 2005, leaving those in search of splendid dinner conversation and the most delightful Iranian meals west of Tehran to knock on Arjomand's apartment door.

THE COOKIES **OF BASRA**

ON THE FIRST FLOOR OF A BAKERY shattered by the shock wave of an exploding U.S. Tomahawk missile, Afran al-Saddi continues to make his cookies. Munch on one, two if you must, the baker tells visitors, and have a seat on a sack of wheat flour.

After tea is poured, the locals discuss the politics of *baksam*, the sand-colored, oval cookie that drew fans to Basra, Iraq's oil capital, long before the wildcatters in the 1930s drilled the region's first well.

"*Baksam* is the most famous cookie in the Muslim world," promises Muneasir Toma, the owner of the Layla-Layla nightclub and a lifelong aficionado. "I haven't eaten one since the start of the war," he adds, reaching across the cramped bakery toward a metal tray filled with steaming cookies. He bites through the crispy crust and into the soft interior.

Al-Saddi fiddles with a wooden spoon and awaits the verdict.

"Delicious," Toma says. "It tastes even better, now that Saddam is gone."

Iraq's ruler is gone, but so is al-Saddi's supply of flour, almost. The baker says he only has enough left to make a few more batches of his trademark cookies. Once the flour is gone, al-Saddi says he will be forced to find wheat on the black market. And with little money to pay his workers, al-Saddi has already been forced to lay off thirty-five of the bakery's fifty employees.

"The people want *baksam*, and I will run out of wheat at the end of the week," rues al-Saddi, who kept his ovens running throughout the coalition's siege of Basra. "I will not abuse my customers with raising the price because of the war."

Amid cursing and laughter, al-Saddi's loyal customers insist his *baksam* cookies can reunite the bickering children of Abraham, if not the taste buds of the world's Muslims, Jews, and Christians. The mildly sweet treat, explains mechanic Hameed Abdullah Rasheed, unified Iraq long before Hussein grabbed power in 1979. *"Baksam* united all of Iraq's cultures and religions," Rasheed says.

That would be no small feat for a lump of dough in a country of twenty-four million people that includes Arabs, Syrians, Armenians, Kurds, Turkomans, Iranians, Christians, and the Yazidis, a Muslim sect that refuses to wear blue. *"Baksam* is the best food to eat in Iraq right now," electrical engineer Radi al-Kabe says. "Peace through cookies is certainly possible. *Baksam* comes from Allah."

Actually, *baksam* was invented by al-Saddi's grandfather, a charcoal-maker and self-taught baker who in 1920 popped the first cookie from his oven as a breakfast and tea-time biscuit for British and French soldiers in the region. At the time, al-Saddi says, Shiite Muslim communities in southern Iraq and Iran were eating a similar cookie kneaded in corn oil and known in Arabic as *kaka*. It apparently wasn't very yummy, particularly among those Western customers who likely found the name unappetizing.

"My grandfather added a secret ingredient, improved the taste, and named the cookie 'baksam'," al-Saddi says. That ingredient was *baladi* oil. Skimmed from the fresh milk of sheep by Bedouin shepherds, *baladi* oil proved to be a hit among cookie-lovers at a time when Basra was a thriving vacation destination for thousands of Middle Eastern Muslims. "Collecting *baladi* oil from sheep milk is an art, and only the Bedouins know how to do it properly," Toma says. "Can you imagine? I ran a nightclub, and all my customers insisted I serve them *baksam*."

Gastronomically speaking, folks here say al-Saddi's prewar *baksam* was better. "I've been cheating for the past month," al-Saddi reveals. "The war has made it hard to find Bedouins with *baladi* oil. I must hurry up and find some. I don't want to lose my reputation."

Since the start of the war, Basra's *baksam* king has mixed his dough with Margo's Palm Oil, a replacement from India. The quality of the cookie can serve as an indicator of the resilience of the postwar Iraqi economy. "When the *baladi* oil is back in the *baksam*," al-Saddi reckons, "that will be an indication that Basra is back to normal life."

Baking *baksam* in Basra is a hazardous and stinking business. Saddi's three brick-wall ovens are fired by gasoline that gravity drips through a funnel, down a metal tube, and into the furnace. The home-made apparatus is a Rube Goldberg contraption that requires constant tweaking.

If the flow isn't regulated properly, al-Saddi says, the entire block could explode.

At the heart of the *baksam* baking system is a spent shell from Iraq's now-obliterated arsenal of Soviet T-52 tanks. The casings are capped, drilled with a handful of holes, and then filled with water. The gasoline-fed flames heat the water to create the steam that actually cooks the *baksam* and the shop's other cookies and breads. Al-Saddi says Saddam's regime wouldn't let him purchase modern ovens without first slipping a bribe to Baath Party officials.

"I refused to pay," says al-Saddi, who adds that his family for decades has used gasoline to bake its *baksam* without any casualties.

Dumping gasoline into a fuel tank above the oven, al-Saddi says that Iraqi tank shells aren't very good. "They only last a few days in the oven," he explains. "I hope to find some American and British shells. I'm sure they will last longer."

Al-Saddi says the gasoline fumes don't affect the taste. Moister than Kuwaiti *baksam*, it's a lip-smacking cookie and a deal at about twelve cents a pound. "Before the 1991 Gulf War, thousands of Kuwaitis, Saudis, Jordanians, Syrians, and Iranians came every Thursday and Friday from their countries to my family's shop to buy *baksam*," he says, leaping over a blown-out wall to pull a cookie sheet out of the octane-fed oven. "It was a ritual for eighty years."

To be able to meet that kind of demand again, al-Saddi says he needs to sell three months' worth of *baksam* to raise the $3,000 to repair his war-damaged bakery. That's a lot of cookies. Before the war began, al-Saddi baked a hundred pounds of *baksam* daily. The gunfire and food shortages that followed obliged him to cut production to twenty pounds a day.

"It's true that all Arab and Iranian Muslims love al-Saddi's *baksam*," explains Amani Mohammad, a Kuwaiti housewife in Kuwait City and the mother of two boys. "I'm sure he still makes the best *baksam*, and the children still love to dip them in hot milk."

Along Basra's main boulevard, the bakery is the only shop that has not been looted, and al-Saddi and his staff always happen to look the other way when little hands reach over the counters to snatch cookies.

"Americans like cookies, they will like *baksam*," al-Saddi says with soft-spoken pride. "Perhaps there's an American baker who would like to be my partner."

GOD AND EL CID GIVE
SPAIN AN "ALMIGHTY" RED

PADRE MARCOS IS A CHIEF EXECUTIVE OF FEW WORDS. "We are cloistered," the abbot of the San Pedro de Cardeña Monastery murmurs from beneath his white cowl, his words barely audible over the creaking hinges of a tenth-century cellar door that tosses rust to the stone floor.

A small white candle is lit. Padre Marcos tilts the flame toward his motive for discounting the Cistercian order's 905-year-old vow of silence: sixty thousand bottles of wine on a wall.

Today, more than thirty years after the monks corked their first bottle of Valdevegon wine, the once-impoverished Spanish monastery is thriving and busloads of visitors are lining up outside the monastic carryout atop a mesa 124 miles north of Madrid.

The monks have become so skilled in their craft of mixing wines and aging them that wine analysts in Madrid say Valdevegon has emerged as one of Spain's benchmark *Reserva* reds. That's no small miracle in a country that boasts six thousand wine manufacturers who annually make more than twenty thousand brands.

"Valdevegon is an artisan wine and one of the last to be created without modern technology," says Gonzalo Verdera, a director of the boutique Spanish wine distributor TodoVino. "It's a monk's wine with a strong character in the taste and spirit of a great French Burgundy."

As Padre Marcos tells it, he's only talking now because Padre Sergio, the monastery's late abbot, decided that discussion was essential to making money. In 1968, he tapped into a Vatican ruling that gave monks some wiggle room on their vow of silence, called a meeting, and developed a business strategy.

Abbot Sergio instructed Padre Marcos, Brother Emiliano, and Brother Jesus to scrape the grime off the monastery's empty and ancient oak casks, purchase a few vats of reasonably priced bulk wine from friendly producers in the nearby Rioja region, and pray for divine intervention.

All the talk came none too soon. About 150 years ago, the Cistercians had remained speechless when the government excavated the Spanish hero El Cid from his tomb and built a new money-making tourist attraction around the corpse about five miles down the mountain in the city of Burgos. They said nothing after the monastery's medieval roof burned in 1967, and kept their lips sealed when the once-flourishing pilgrimage business wandered elsewhere.

"Business cannot be done without talking," reasons Padre Jose, the closest thing the Valdevegon wine brand has to a marketing director—and spokesman.

"The monks realized that the rules for running a business are different from those of running a monastery," says vintner Petra Unger, who leases vineyards from Benedictine monks at the Goettweig Monastery in Austria.

Still, Padre Jose says silence among the monastery's twenty-two monks is "almost absolute," and the brothers who blend the wine beneath the stone church say nothing while in the cellar. "This is good, because I can tell you that wine doesn't like noise," Padre Jose explains.

Ambling through the musty San Pedro cellar with a plump smile on his face and blue sneakers on his feet, Padre Marcos says he knows absolutely nothing about business.

Still, Roman Catholic history overflows with commercial tales of monks tending vineyards and making wine to celebrate the Eucharist. In France, the Burgundian monks of Cluny were the original owner-operators of the wineries in Gevrey-Chambertin and Vosne-Romanée. The monks of Ither made Clos Vougeot, and Dom Pérignon was the monk who first gave champagne its bubbles. In the U.S., the Christian Brothers in 1882 started to make wine on Mt. Veeder in California's Napa Valley, later selling the brand and the production to Grand Metropolitan in 1989. Austrian monks at the Schloss Seggau and Stift Klosterneuburg monasteries years ago hired outsiders to manage their vineyards and make the wine.

Although Valdevegon's labels don't divulge the year of the vintage, the monks say that before being sold, their wine spends eighteen months in the cask and from three to five years in the bottle.

Some years, the monks don't make any wine at all.

"We work with quality, not quantity," Padre Jose says. "Most Valdevegon is sold to people who come to the monastery. Every year we make wine, every year it leaves."

As for capital investments in its wine operation, Padre Marcos proudly taps his foot on a swatch of green rubber tiling and says the monastic winery buys new equipment "every century or so."

Padre Jose says the rubber flooring was installed three years ago to keep the noise down.

"I really don't know how much wine we make each year," Padre Marcos says. "How many barrels in the cave? I have no idea."

Padre Jose throws up his hands. "I don't know, either," he adds. "Let's count them."

There are precisely one hundred barrels stacked throughout the long and cramped labyrinth; each barrel holds thirty-three gallons of wine.

"I must remember to write that down," Padre Marcos says.

Padre Marcos also isn't sure how the monastery arrived at a retail price of between $8 and $10 a bottle, depending on the vintage.

And for the monks of San Pedro, there is no tastier tipple. "It's the only wine we drink," Padre Marcos says.

Back in Madrid, the monks' nonchalant attitude toward running a business and the apparent simplicity of their operation give the folks at TodoVino a walloping headache.

"The monks do everything they can to protect themselves from the outside world," Verdera says. "Investment is not on their minds. Equating quality of wine with price is how an efficient market operates. That's not the case at the monastery."

Verdera says the monks nonetheless have helped spearhead a movement to isolate reasonably priced, traditionally vintified wines to replace the glut of expensive young wines (such as a $500 French bottle of 1999

Chateau Petrus or a $900 bottle of 1999 Screaming Eagle from California) that explode in the mouth like fruit bombs. Verdera annually samples six thousand Spanish wines for European corporate customers that include American Express Co., Credit Suisse Group, Westin Hotels, and Porsche AG. "Our client research shows that trendy wines are nearing their end," Verdera says. "Valdevegon is the kind of wine people are now looking for, but some years the monks refuse to make any wine at all and they never put the year on the label." He says that when TodoVino gets the word that Padre Marcos is making wine, "all of us run up there like mad to see what he's done. If it's good, Valdevegon is truly a benchmark wine and the best deal in Spain."

Draped over a chrome spittoon at TodoVino's headquarters overlooking the Spanish Parliament, French wine analyst Guillaume d'Arche says wine buffs have taken an interest in Valdevegon and other similar Spanish wines such as Tinto Pesquera Gran Reserva and La Rioja Alta Gran Reserva because French Grand and Premier Crus remain too expensive and can take a decade to ripen into perfection.

"That's left Spain as the center for rediscovering old production methods like the one used at San Pedro," says d'Arche, who three years ago left his job as a metal trader at Pechiney SA to help start TodoVino. "Great Spanish wines are ready to drink in a few years," he adds. "And with the deep nose and subtle taste that make a wine truly great."

Slicing a knob of sheep cheese on the counter of the San Pedro grocery, Brother Emiliano says he has yet to decide if the 2002 Rioja vintage is good enough to blend into a new batch of Valdevegon.

"I didn't like the 1997 and 2001 vintages, so I didn't make any wine," he says. Nearby, customers examine the store's non-alcoholic offerings: jars of honey, sacks of herbs, and car-dashboard statues of St. Peter.

"Brother Jesus and I use different combinations of Riojas," is all Padre Emiliano will say of his premier product. "There's no special formula, and God is with us."

Jose Luis Casado, TodoVino's chief wine taster, remains skeptical that the Almighty alone is responsible for the recipe. "Brother Emiliano just won't talk," Casado says. "The good years were 1989, 1991, 1994, and 1998. He is doing something special."

Brother Emiliano patiently grins at the suggestion that he's harboring a secret, swaddles his stinky cheese in a newspaper, and jerks his head toward the four vintages on display behind the broken cash register. Each bottle has a label that depicts the monastery's arched cellar, and only Brother Emiliano knows which bottles match which vintages.

The $9 1994 Reserva, he says, is the best of the lot. "If you're interested," Brother Emiliano adds. "I have thirty thousand bottles left, and they're good to drink through 2007." The rest of Casado's preferred vintages were snapped up long ago.

The winemaking monk says his French customers prefer the 1995 Valdevegon El Cid.

"But I don't," Brother Emiliano says, ripping a corner off his cheese paper to scribble a receipt for a customer. "I drink the 1994. Richer aroma. Delicious."

Padre Jose closes his eyes and doesn't offer any guidance. "I only drink water," he says.

CAESAR'S VINEYARD

THE BUSINESS OF THE ROMAN EMPIRE continues to ferment in Ugernum, Transalpine Gaul, but under new management.

Local vineyard owner Hervé Durand and a team of archaeologists invested $20,000 to reopen the largest distillery in Gaul, after a hiatus of 1,800 years. Now, a few aqueducts away from the town the French call Beaucaire, behind a sprawling pomegranate tree in the rebuilt ruin of a Roman farmhouse, Durand and his family are in their fifteenth year of resurrecting the recipes and engineering the machinery the Sixth Imperial Roman Legion used to produce wine when they controlled this territory.

"This was the biggest winemaking farm in France during Roman times," says Durand, kneeling over a clay vat to slosh up a goblet of antique refreshment labeled Carenum. "It's an interesting business."

That's putting it mildly. The whiskered winemaker of Provence claims to be the world's only remaining producer of the tipple favored by everyone from the Caesars to the priestesses who ruled the cult of the vestal virgins.

Although it's too early in this story to discuss the orgies associated with the winery's former proprietors, the writings of many long-dead experts in Roman bacchanalia insist that A.D. 121 will for smoothness remain the most prized and profitable vintage for wines produced at Les Mas Gallo-Roman des Tourelles. Durand discounts their portents with a laugh and reckons his current (that would be 2757, he says, counting the years from the founding of Rome) crop is exceptional and priced to conquer the market at $12 a bottle on the Internet.

With a callused hand, the cheerful farmer lowers a fresh glass into the clay caldron of Carenum, flutters his lips, and joins a visitor in a sip of history. The wine is brownish-red and sweet, with the taste of a peach and caramel candy bar. Durand says that the Romans loved the flavor; global thirst for Carenum and his other two Gallo-Roman wines, Turriculae and Mulsum, will exceed ten thousand bottles this year. That's an increase of about two percent from 2756, with thirty percent of his customers repeat buyers.

But don't get giddy, Pliny, not just yet. As you put it, "truth comes out in wine." To put it more bluntly, some modern wine critics suggest that merely one sip of sugary Carenum provides head-numbing evidence of why the Roman Empire fell. Still, as Xavier de Volontat, president of the Association of French Vintners, comments, it solved a mystery: how the wines of Gaul tasted. "There are thirty-eight thousand different brands of wine produced in France, and all of them can trace their heritage back to ancient times," Volontat says. "Durand's Gallo-Roman wine represents the soul of our association."

Downing a glass of Carenum at the association's annual exhibition in Paris, first-time Roman wine drinker Lilian Gerard pronounces the swallow a "curiosity" and quickly reaches for a lump of goat cheese. "It's not a dinner wine," Gerard says, buying a bottle. "I want to have some for friends to taste."

Confidence in the future of Gallo-Roman wine hardly runs high. "It's difficult for the modern mouth to access," says Cedric Durand, who helps his father manage the 210-acre contemporary vineyard that also produces red, white, and rosé wines under the Costières de Nîmes label. "Gallo-Roman wine has a very small but loyal following," he adds. "You must eat a lot of cheese and nuts when you drink them."

Or take a page from the illustrated history books Durand sells alongside his wine: the photographs of naughty tile frescoes offer a clear picture of the orgies many in the Empire enjoyed as a complement to their Gallo-Roman wine.

In terms of volume, Durand's sales figures are a dribble compared with the hundred thousand modern-sized bottles that flowed out of Ugernum each day during the reign of the Caesars. The ancient Romans paid two sesterce (around $1.60) for a bottle of wine from Gaul. Andre Tchernia, an archaeologist at the French National Center for Scientific Research, says Rome conquered Gaul between 125 B.C. and 51 B.C. specifically to take control of its vines, grains, and olives. Some twenty-seven million liters of the region's wine annually filled two million clay amphorae for shipment by oxen and galley throughout the Mediterranean, with Rome's one million citizens and slaves drinking an average of three liters of wine a day.

That volume might be too much ballast for today's drinkers. "It's not on many wine lists," says Gerard Margeron, chief wine steward for French restaurateur Alain Ducasse.

Yet the nascent contemporary market hasn't damped Durand's enthusiasm. Some twenty thousand tourists from France, Japan, and the U.S. visit the winery each year, and Durand says most head home with a few bottles. His most devoted customers are archaeology professors and museum directors.

"Businessmen need to reflect on the history of their industry, and that's why we continue to make the wine," he explains. "Roman agriculture faced the same problems we have today: sales, distribution, subsidies, marketing. You learn a lot."

Like how to spike the wine into tolerable taste. Pliny the Elder, for instance, advised adding "seawater to enliven the smoothness" of Gallo-Roman wine. Cato preferred his cup seasoned with a dollop of pig's blood and a pinch of marble dust. "The soldiers didn't care if it turned to vinegar," says Durand the Younger. "It gave them energy."

Hervé Durand says sales are particularly brisk over the Christmas season. "Great amounts of oysters and foie gras are consumed during the winter months," he explains. "Our 2752 Turriculae is the dry white wine the Romans liked with such foods." Yellow in color and laced with seawater, Turriculae tastes of prunes and is based on the recipe of the Roman agronomist Lucius Columelle.

Looking for a festive wine with the production value of a Cecil B. DeMille epic? Durand flips on a movie projector and suggests that his 2757 Mulsum is the way Ben Hur would usher in the New Year. To the sound of flutes, the film shows white Villard grapes first crushed beneath the feet of children wearing Roman slave costumes, and then further mushed by a stone weight lowered by a 2.5-ton oak trunk. From there, the juice flows into a stone wading pool and is scooped out to fill dozens of 400-liter clay pots packed with honey, cinnamon, thyme, and pepper.

Archaeologists dressed in burlap togas whisk the brew with broomsticks wrapped in fennel. After six days to three weeks in the clay fermentation tub, the concoction escalates into a lathery crimson liquid with a twelve-percent alcoholic kick. An opened bottle keeps for ten days in the refrigerator. After that, all Gallo-Roman brands turn into a lubricant that only a legionnaire or a lettuce could love.

As Durand tells it, Mulsum was the "Coca-Cola" of the Roman Empire. "It was Rome's most popular wine and what the spectators most likely drank while watching the gladiators," he explains. Nowadays, he adds, Mulsum tastes best with Roquefort cheese. According to Pliny, it also makes an effective disinfectant for use in treating sword wounds.

ON THE **TRAIL**
WITH THE
RAIDERS **OF THE**
LOST **VINE**

BERNARD MOLLARD is nursing a 720-year-old hangover. The barrel-chested proprietor of winemaker Domaine Marc Morey & Fils can trace his headache to 1286, when a local knight bequeathed land on the slope of Mont Raschat to a group of Cistercian monks. The soil was lousy, a mixture of bathonian limestone veined with silica, chalk, and iron oxide whose output, one French wine scholar wrote, "would interest only a goat."

So the monks chose to grow grapes, and the chardonnay vines they cultivated on these hillocks—land that today sells for more than $6 million an acre—poured forth with Montrachet, the most expensive and exalted white Burgundy wine in the world. Bottles now sell for $60 to $10,000 and higher.

Mollard, on the other hand, is condemned to sell his Montrachet-grown wine for $8 a bottle. Critical fame, fancy restaurants, and the superlatives heaped on Montrachet have eluded the 2,500 bottles he produces each year, all because a government grape inspector in the 1930s decreed that the wine wasn't Montrachet.

"It was a bad decision," is Mollard's verdict.

Villagers say Mollard would be clearing $60 a bottle if his uncle had given the inspector a drink instead of punching him in the snoot, but that's getting ahead of ourselves.

The Mollard family troubles began shortly before World War II, when in 1935 the Ministry of Agriculture was called in to juice up the watered-down French wine business and bring clarity to an industry that had been roiling in corruption and counterfeit labels. The solution was a state-managed system called the *Appellation d'Origine Contrôlée*, which ranks Montrachet's wines, like others in France, in a complex hierarchy whose top three designations are *Grand Cru, Premier Cru,* and *Village.* The idea was to ensure quality—and maintain price.

At the time of the A.O.C. inspection, Mollard's twenty-two rows of vines were tended by a relative, a penniless farmer with a strong right jab, no political clout, and a head full of steam over the inspector's demand for a few cases of wine in return for a pedigreed appellation.

"The wine is exceptionally round and full and should have at least received a Montrachet Village Appellation," says Jean-François Rateau, who manages the village cooperative that sells the region's wines. "But there was a fight."

Walking his puddled vineyard and flicking bugs off grape blossoms, Mollard claims that the A.O.C. inspector was fully aware of the "good history of this land" and the paternity of its wine. Nonetheless, locals say, the assessor exacted revenge by jinxing the place with the crummy tag *Bourgogne Contrôlée,* one notch above grape syrup.

Mollard for years used his half-acre patch to produce reds. Then, in the late 1980s, he returned the land to its white-wine roots, bottling the first vintage in 1990. Rateau offered it up as a bargain-basement alternative to the princely Montrachets on display in the village wine cellar. The wine was an instant sensation. "Its value for money is unique," Rateau says. "The buyers are the same people every year. We could sell more, but we always run out."

Some French officials and stalwart drinkers over the years have grown sympathetic to the plight of Mollard's grapes, confident that their taste of honey-grilled almonds and aroma of wildflower petals belong among the other liquid bonanzas produced in this Burgundy village.

Bertrand Devillard, president and general director of the winery Antonin Rodet SA, the largest owner of Grand Cru Montrachet acreage in Burgundy, says about one percent of the approximately sixty-four million bottles of Burgundy wines produced each year deserve an upgrade. Still, "Montrachet is a magic place, a world of mysticism," he muses. "Nobody would dare mess with a thousand years of tradition."

Except the Raiders of the Lost Vine, an irregular party of American and European bankers and businessmen who travel with a psychiatrist and since 1998 have left few bottles corked in their quest to track down the fabled and forgotten wines of Burgundy. While Mollard says he's powerless to push for promotion and that it's a crime to advertise his product as anything other than ordinary white table wine, the Raiders warmly refer to the ersatz Montrachet as *Chateau Crapaud* (Toad Castle) and niggle the professional critics by calling it the best deal in France.

Crapaud enthusiast Juan-Rene Geada says Mollard's wine is without question a Montrachet. "It's gorgeous and stupendous," Geada insists. "The man is a genius." Praise a bit too lavish for an $8 bottle of wine?

"Nonsense," the Miami psychiatrist says. "I'm a professional. Montrachet drinkers don't have any psychiatric problems, but we should start examining those who spend $1,000 for a bottle because it comes with the appellation."

Catherine Laporte, an agro-economist at the Ministry of Agriculture who helps oversee A.O.C. classifications in Burgundy, believes the story of Mollard's wine is sane and sober. "Of course it's true," she says. "The A.O.C.'s were strictly assigned on the prior reputation of the land and its wine. There was much funny business, and wealthy Montrachet growers didn't want their less-affluent neighbors sharing in any of the top three classifications."

For the Raiders, isolating rifts in the A.O.C. is thirsty work and begins, after lunch, in the antiquarian bookshop of Alphonse Chavroche, who's spent decades in the nearby town of Beaune acquiring unusual maps and vineyard histories after realizing that few others were preserving them.

Chavroche refers to the volumes as ciphers. The most expensive costs $15,000.

"*Dissertation on the Situation in Burgundy*, Abbe Arnoux, 1721," the 67-year-old Chavroche says, reeling off the title of the earliest guide to the area's wines. "It's a sixty-page pamphlet written in Old French, and it comes with a map. Very expensive, extremely rare. Eight known copies exist. There are no sellers."

The antique manual describes another small vineyard within walking distance of Chateau Crapaud that produces the red wine of Clos St. Jean. At around $15 a bottle, it's one of the cheapest Premier Cru pinot noirs in a market famed for the world's priciest red wines.

"If I had to purchase a wine for the king," Arnoux wrote. "I would go to this land."

The thirty-four acres of grapes described by Arnoux grow on the old nunnery of St. Jean le Grand d'Autun, which isn't world-famous and hardly even France-famous. The soil was first tilled by sixth-century Benedictine ascetics. Peter Wasserman, the 41-year-old manager of Beaune-based wine exporter Le Serbet, reckons St. Jean's pinot noir was banished from the Grand Cru kingdom along with Morey's chardonnay when the government instituted the divisive A.O.C. system.

The anonymous buyer who, in 2006, splurged $170,375 on six magnums of 1985 Domaine de la Romanee-Conti on auction in New York likely never visited the convent. Clos St. Jean's provenance doesn't even rate a bawdy yarn in the taverns frequented by the eight thousand wine-growers who tend the region's 13,585 acres of vineyards.

Sitting on the meadow above the field that annually fills some thirty thousand bottles of Clos St. Jean, John Lonardo, international vice president of Kerdyk Real Estate Inc. in Coral Gables, Florida, inhales the perfumed breeze that floats up from the village.

"If gold had a smell," the 57-year-old vine raider exhales, "this would be it."

Take a deep breath the next time a wine broker offers a Grand Cru bottle of 1985 DRC Richebourg for $3,500 or a 2005 DRC Romanee-Conti with a $17,000-and-rising retail price tag. Raider David Cogan is an authority on grape inflation and spends his days analyzing these sorts of bar tabs. A former director of business development at Pfizer AG, Cogan left the pharmaceutical company in 2001 to complete a master's degree in wine at the University of Dijon.

"The decline of the dollar against the euro has forced Burgundy wine-makers to increase their prices for the U.S. market by ten to twenty percent," Cogan says. "That's all the growers worry about, because America is traditionally their most important market."

A lock snaps open on the 400-year-old private cavern of Caroline Lestime, proprietor of Domaine Jean-Noel Gagnard and one of the few makers of Clos St. Jean red. Lestime guides the wine hunters past scampering clusters of spiders and into a limestone passage twenty feet (6 meters) beneath Chassagne-Montrachet.

Lestime's wines are fledglings, born in 1997 and 2005 and loaded with grape tannin, which is contained in the grape skin or peel. Tannins help to structure a wine's taste but may leave an astringent metallic flavor on the palate and further collapse the price of bargain-basement vintages among drinkers weaned on popular fruity young wines.

Lonardo puts down a glass and points to his shoes. "The footprint of greatness is here," he says.

The group presses deeper into the labyrinth, arriving in Rateau's subterranean lair. Nine bottles of Clos St. Jean from Domaine Ramonet are struck from a musty stone ledge. The earliest vintage is 1947, and Rateau says he already has sold it to a U.S. client for 250 euros. Back in New York, Domaine Ramonet's 2004 Clos St. Jean is selling for $47 retail.

"A restaurant could sell the 1947 for $1,000, easy," Wasserman says, holding the bottle up to the light. "Look at this. Just like Arnoux says: *The color of a partridge's eye.*"

Rateau fills glasses with the 1971 and 1986 Premier Cru vintages priced at 150 and 65 euros, respectively. He uncorks the other exceptional years ready for drinking: 1923, 1947, 1949, 1953, 1959, 1972, and 1976. The prices range from 75 to 250 euros a bottle.

"The wine doesn't have an image outside the village," Rateau says.

"People drink what the critics think they should be drinking, and Clos St. Jean is unfashionable," adds Clive Coates, author of *The Wines of Burgundy* and founder of the Wine Society, a mail-order wine distributor in the United Kingdom. "But let's forget about modern marketing. Clos St. Jean is where X marks the spot. There was a time when every great cellar in France was considered incomplete without an ample stock of its red wine."

Back at Chavroche's library, accounts of Clos St. Jean assembled by the early twentieth-century wine grower Camille Rodier in *Le Vin de Bourgogne* state that a bottle of Chassagne-Montrachet's red Premier Cru was worth two bottles of the local Premier Cru white. Those whites would be Le Montrachet and Batard-Montrachet, the wines the A.O.C. elevated to Grand Cru status and, according to Dr. Gedea's clinical diagnosis, the source of Chateau Crapaud's inferiority complex.

After a few glasses of Morey's white and Ramonet's red, the Raiders of the Lost Vine say both are long overdue for promotion.

Wine historian John Mariani, author of *The Dictionary of American Food and Drink*, says that kind of talk is heresy in the wine world. "The wine elite consistently overrates Montrachets," he charges. "Are these wines worth that kind of money? Of course not, but they sell because of the chic appellation and the limited amount of production. If the French give an $8 bottle of wine a Montrachet A.O.C., the rat is out of the bag." Mariani says that speculators and wealthy wine collectors aren't interested in cornering the Crapaud or Clos St. Jean market to push up the price. Without a well-groomed appellation on the label, he says, any pursuit of higher status is doomed to failure.

Up the road in the regional capital, Dijon, the discriminating taste buds of Pascal Durand have been auditioning local wines for thirty years. A former director of the Institute of Burgundy Wine and now an economist at the Ministry of Agriculture, Durand says the A.O.C. is reluctant to tempt fate and tinker with the codifications.

To do so, Mariani adds, "would within seconds trigger the interest of powerful U.S. and British critics who might not like the wine."

Indeed, Durand says that not one inch of Montrachet's officially recognized twenty hectares of Grand Cru, three hundred hectares of Premier Cru, and over seventy-five hectares of Village Vineyards ever has been kicked up or down the A.O.C. rankings. "Giving an unknown wine a ticket would immediately create new jealousies among the growers," he explains.

Mollard says he once lobbied for an upgrade. The other growers, who the law says must support any petition prior to initiating a formal A.O.C. investigation, refused to sign on. "There was a lot of resentment that I even asked, "Mollard says. "I could have doubled the price to $16 a bottle."

Durand believes Mollard is being modest. "It would have sold for at least $50," he says.

MAKING **WINE, NOT WAR,**

OLD LEGIONNAIRES

STORM THE VINE**YARDS**

W HILE THE FRENCH FOREIGN LEGION awaits its marching orders in the war against terrorism, elements of the legendary fighting force outside the village of Puyloubier charge into the fields with clippers drawn to engage the grapes of Provence.

"Don't use my first name," Sgt. Raymond Plesnik pleads, shuffling into the command bunker beneath Domaine Captain Danjou, the Legion's 550-acre retirement estate and wine-production headquarters. "My fiancée might see this and will be able to find me," laughs the seventy-something Slovak in charge of Legionnaire wine sales. "We can't let that happen."

Once better known for raising hell and leaving the girl behind, the soldiers at the Institution des Invalides de la Legion Étrangère near Aix-en-Provence these days play just as vital a role in Legion lore as Gary Cooper did in the 1939 movie *Beau Geste*. Old soldiers elsewhere may never die, but those here in Provence just fade away into the vineyards, or limp into the cellar to glue quaint French Foreign Legion labels on wine bottles. "The wine effort helps us pay for the retirement home," explains Commandant Gilbert Hensinger, an active member of the Legion's rugged parachute regiment and a veteran of Operation Desert Storm.

Now, with fewer conventional wars to fight and not so many troops to command, the world's original elite mercenary force lace up their boots and swarm into the vineyards. The harvest is usually so good that Comdt.

Hensinger requisitions platoons of young soldiers from Legion headquarters in Aubagne to help his unit of veterans with the intensive labor required to pluck 256 tons of grapes. It's enough to drown the sorrows of some 7,500 Legionnaires around the world and the five thousand tourists who visit the chateau each year.

"The men are respected for growing marvelous syrah grapes for rosé wine," says Karen Spinatto, who tends the vats at the Vinicole de Sainte Victoire wine cooperative. Each year, VSV winemakers use much of the Legion's hundred acres of grapes to produce Mont Sainte-Victoire Côtes de Provence. At about $8 a bottle, the splashy rosé won the gold medal at the 2001 Concours Agricole, a major wine competition sponsored by the French Ministry of Agriculture and Fish. "The *Michelin Guide* lists the chateau as an important heritage site worth visiting," Hensinger says proudly. "This is a place where we take care of our own."

Only 115 French Legionnaires remain at Domaine Captain Danjou and, rues their commandant from Alsace, the retirement castle first erected at the foot of Mt. Sainte Victoire by Roman legionnaires may soon vanish into memory. Over thirty-five thousand Legionnaires have died for France during the unit's nearly 200-year history, and many of their graves can be found in the cemetery of tombs and olive trees that abuts the vineyards. The Legion was founded by King Louis-Philippe in 1831 as a rapid reaction force to control French colonial possessions in North Africa.

Comdt. Hensinger says the contemporary blend of war and politics has resulted in fewer veterans interested in retiring to the chateau. There were forty-five thousand Legionnaires at the end of World War II. Today, the men who wear the group's trademark white kepi hat are a dying breed. "Modern Legionnaires are more intellectual and the selection process more rigorous," he says. "I wonder if the domaine will be here in ten years' time. Now those who retire from the Legion go on to other jobs or other lives," he explains. "When they leave the Legion, they don't want to come here."

At the same time, getting a bunk inside the chateau isn't easy, no matter your age. Though the only sentinel is a chirping green parrot named Coco, old soldiers require an honorable discharge to get past his perch outside the guardhouse. "We must be bachelors; that's the easy part," says Sgt. Plesnik, who participated in adorning the walls of the wine cellar with ribald cartoons of women drinking alongside gigantic Legionnaires. Comdt. Hensinger says the wine-making and other agricultural activities on the chateau's farm are a form of therapy geared to occupy the ancient combatants and help them cope with life after war. "There just used to be wounded men here," he says. "Those men served in the Algerian War of Independence and Indo-China. Most of them are long gone." Those who remain are mostly Legionnaires unable to survive the civilian world. "I command men wounded by life and not war," Comdt. Hensinger explains. "Unemployment, depression, and divorce. The Legion owes them a debt," he adds.

The language of the Legion is clearly tastier than the combat cabernet that carries its name, however. Pride is at stake in every bottle, but the Legion's red and white wines are bitter and worth raving about only inside a mess hall. And though Domaine Captain Danjou rosé is a splendid refresher for a summer bivouac in the Sahara, the Legion by law is prohibited from selling any of its annual branded production of roughly 280,000 bottles outside the estate. The remainder, about fifty-three million gallons, is poured in along with the production of 139 other local winemakers to create the Pagnol region's distinctive rosé wines.

Marching alongside the fields in a green camouflage uniform, Comdt. Hensinger pulls off his aviator glasses and says that twenty acres of grapes is enough to supply the Legion mess and any visitors interested in taking home a standard three-pack. "The tourists always go home with a case of wine," the commandant says. "It's never a problem to make them buy it."

Vintage Camerone at $7 a bottle is a particulary popular tipple and a big seller in the old stone stable that serves as the Legion's wine cellar. The label, which depicts a Legionnaire and his girlfriend, was created in the chateau's ceramic shop, where kepi coffee mugs are molded by a Greek Cypriot. Another retired Legionnaire from England used his pre-enlistment skills as an art director to create many of the designs on the wine labels and the other Legion souvenirs on offer. The wine's appellation pays homage to the doomed battle the Legion fought at the Camerone Hacienda in Mexico on April 30, 1863. Captain Danjou ordered a troop of sixty-five Legionnaires to defend their position at all costs against a sizable enemy force. The five Legionnaires who survived the first day of fighting fixed their bayonets and charged two thousand Mexican soldiers. Slaughtered along with everyone else in his command, Captain Danjou today lives on with a vintage red named after him, a two-day hangover at $2 a bottle.

Across the vale in the wine cooperative, Spinatto believes the marketing potential of Camerone and Captain Danjou would be spectacular if the government allowed the Legionnaires to sell their trademarked bottles alongside the other regional wines on display in the shop. An aide to the village mayor says the battered tin mailbox marked *ancien combatants* and screwed to the door outside the city hall is regularly filled with letters from folks hoping to have French Foreign Legion wine delivered to their doors and entrepreneurs looking to launch spiffy promotional gimmicks to sell the tax-exempt wine.

It's here the commandant draws a firm line in the sand with potential aggressors and greenmailers. He tells all those seeking a piece of Legionnaire action to get lost, including the Ministry of Finance. The strategy goes back to 1966, when the Legion first started making its own wine. "We are not wine marketers and don't want to be," Comdt. Hensinger says. "The French tax authorities look the other way on the wine we sell at the chateau," he adds with a wink. "They don't come around."

Sgt. Plesnik says he would be more than happy to "sell" the taxman a few bottles if he showed up in his wine cellar. Thumbing through the mildewed ledger book on his desk, Plesnik reckons the only thing more appealing than selling the public a bottle of history is fighting terrorists in the Middle East and the mountains of Central Asia. "Afghanistan is Legionnaire country," he says, while handing a customer a boxed three-pack. "This is Legionnaire wine."

THE CASINO DE MONTE-CARLO
ACCOMMODATES TO ÉGALITÉ

"ANOTHER STACK OF CHIPS, MR. BOND?" is what the visitor expects to hear upon flinging back the thick leather curtain to enter a "super-private" gambling salon in the Casino de Monte-Carlo.

But the celebrated secret agent—along with the ghost of Grace Kelly in the film *To Catch a Thief* and the aroma of Latakia tobacco wafting over the gilded mahogany baccarat and roulette tables—lives only in memory here at the 144-year-old Monaco casino owned by the Société des Bains de Mer & Cercle des Étrangers, or SBM.

"The casino had to change," sighs Jacques Dubost, the *charge de mission* at the most renowned gambling hall in Europe. "We now handle those who play the one-franc slot machines with the same elegance as we do the one-million-franc gambler."

Indeed, the casino, built by Paris Opera House architect Charles Garnier in Napoleon III style, is now little more than a throwback to the days when deep-pocketed tourists checked into the Hôtel de Paris, rubbed the bronze knee of Louis XIV's horse in the lobby for luck, and gamboled across the plaza in full dress to spin the wheel.

"The casino is now a museum," admits Christiane Cane, the public-relations director of SBM. "The times are different. During the day, we allow people to play wearing shorts and T-shirts."

Adds Dubost, "We once had people arrive with two million francs and spend three months at the tables. Now they're in and out."

So much for the days when Arthur de Rothschild played the 17 or the 0 for an hour if he was winning at the roulette table. Or when the Prince of

Nepal, whose religion allowed him to gamble only five days of the year, took over all the super-private rooms to get the most roar for his rupee. Or when the local Anglican minister, upon noticing unusually large Sunday congregations, stopped reading those psalms numbered below 36 because his flock was betting the numbers on the roulette table.

SBM calls its new and improved product "affordable glamour travel" and says the clink of the one-franc slots—and the pre-euro lure of hazarding three thousand francs on a three-million-franc super-slot jackpot—draws a million visitors through the casino's Renaissance Hall each year. Some fifteen percent of the traffic arrives on special SBM-arranged tours from Southeast Asia, which offer *pai gaw* poker. Most visitors prefer the slots and video blackjack machines that now fill the floor of the old baccarat room. Sadly, their mechanized drone more often than not drowns out the sound of the nearby roulette croupiers declaring *rien ne va plus*.

Chump change has always played a prominent role in the casino's history. The first slot machine was installed in 1934, and when Prince Charles III of Monaco opened the casino in 1863 on a square he dubbed "Monte Carlo," he erected gaming tables in the kitchen so employees could wager their salaries. Although those tables are long gone and Monegasques are now prohibited from gambling in their own country, the rooms that house the contemporary gambling gizmos are known collectively as "the kitchen."

As Prince Albert, the heir to the realm of Grimaldi, says in his pitch to potential tourists: "Come and visit Monaco. You don't have to be a millionaire."

But a cool million can help if you're a budding Charles Wells, the man who, as the song goes, "Beat the Bank at Monte Carlo." Wells, an Englishman with ten thousand gold francs in his steamer trunk, walked off the train here in August 1891 and spent a month at the tables. He left town with three million gold francs and returned to London a hero. But his exploits, says Dubost, gave the casino ten times the amount in publicity and turned the 190-hectare hillside metropolis into the most famous gambling attraction in the world. As for Wells, he was later convicted of fraud (unrelated to his Monte Carlo winnings) in Britain and sentenced to eight years in prison.

Nonetheless, beating the bank (each individual roulette table has a fixed reserve of money, and when this is paid out, the bank is said to be "broken") is nothing more than dumb luck. "The game is diabolic!" thunders Dubost. "You can win for a long time—and then never win again."

And he boasts that the only casino more popular than his is the New York Stock Exchange. "People come to the Casino de Monte-Carlo to enjoy themselves," he says. "People stay home and play the lottery to change their lives."

Dubost, who spent thirty-five years managing the Casino de Monte-Carlo's 1,200 croupiers and teaching thousands of visitors the mysteries of *chemin de fer*, says the three super-private rooms, where lives can still change in an instant, get their share of the action. And it's not uncommon for the stakes to reach $120,000 a hand. "References are required for the super-private rooms," explains the genteel Dubost. "We never let players into the supers with a brief-case full of cash. A letter from a banker is preferred, and if we don't know the player, I must first make sure he knows how to play."

Eyeing the new high-rolling talent also benefits the house because Dubost wants to ensure that he still knows all the nefarious tricks people use to cheat the house. "I'm sure I've seen them all," he says slyly, reciting a list that includes slugs, fake arguments among players to confuse croupiers, and fishing line tied to slot-machine coins. "Perhaps the best one I ever saw," he recalls, "was the man who applied glue to the palm of his hand. He would place a 500-franc chip on the roulette table, and use his palm to pick up a 50,000 franc chip."

But the casino does have a heart for those who lose the family fortune at the table. Employees still swear an oath never to reveal the losers' names. And should a player gamble away his train fare out of the Maritime Alps, casino tradition dictates a second-class ticket be given to get him home. Known as *la viatique*, the word comes from the Latin viaticum, the sacrament Roman Catholic priests give the dying to prepare them for heaven. Dubost, with a wink, insists that the practice is no longer observed.

And knocking on heaven's door can also help you beat the bank, according to one supposedly true "system" made famous by the writer Alexander Woollcott in his short story *Rien ne va Plus*. Decades ago, it was not uncommon for big losers to commit suicide inside the casino. And to avoid the death being blamed on the casino, croupiers were allegedly under instruction to quickly fill the dead man's pockets with a hundred thousand francs before the police discovered the corpse. In Woollcott's tale, a gambler splashes himself with ketchup, fires a pistol into the air, and collapses. The croupiers rush to stuff his pockets with a hundred thousand francs and then leave to alert the police. The man gets up and goes back to the tables, where he wins another hundred thousand francs.

"Yes, there were suicides," concedes Dubost. "But they were the result of love affairs. Maybe that's why many of our players prefer the tables to sex."

MONA LISA'S

PAJAMAS

THE WORLD'S MOST FAMOUS

SMILE SELLS PAJAMAS

AFTER SOME FIVE HUNDRED YEARS at the Louvre, the *Mona Lisa* has finally met her match.

A woman with a deep tan stands before civilization's most famous smile and peers at her own reflection in the painting's bulletproof showcase. Her sunglasses are shoved up atop her blond hair. Ignoring the crowd milling around her, the rat-a-tat-tat of flash cameras, and the poking of a German tour guide's green umbrella, the Floridian pulls out a Revlon lipstick, puckers her lips, and slicks them with a fresh coat of red paint. "Okay, honey, I got to get something to eat now," she tells her husband before rushing from the room. Her time in front of the painting: less than thirty seconds.

Ever since Leonardo da Vinci painted *Lisa la Gioconda* on a pine board in the early sixteenth century, the portrait has inspired envy, admiration, confusion, and anger. The oil has been studied, copied, and analyzed in minute detail. Picasso, Gauguin, Modigliani, and Leger all painted the famous Florentine in their own style. Historians, writers, and psychoanalysts have struggled to unlock the mystery of her enigmatic smile; the subject has spawned an untold number of books and Web sites. In 1956, a deranged Bolivian named Ugo Ungaza hurled a rock at the painting, wounding Mona's elbow. On one occasion, a ring of counterfeiters stole the masterpiece.

But for most tourists, the *Mona Lisa* is just one more item on the Paris checklist. So after they've done the Eiffel Tower and the Arc de Triomphe, they flock to the room where *Mona* hangs in the Louvre. By museum estimates, more than five million people visit the painting each year, sometimes at the rate of nearly five thousand an hour. They ignore the other Italian masterpieces in the room. They hum "Mona Lisa," a la Nat "King" Cole. Many pose by the painting to have their photos snapped. Makeup touchups aren't uncommon, curators say. Camera flashes ricochet off the glass, making the painting all the harder to see.

With the crowd so thick and the glass so reflective, what can one expect? Reverence? Appreciation? An aesthetic epiphany?

"I'm more worried about my sense of smell," gasps one American visitor, Rob Bushman. Standing in the sun outside the Louvre in a white sports shirt and an unblemished pair of sneakers, Bushman rubs his nose and reflects on his brush with artistic greatness. "The most powerful thing about my ten seconds with Mona was the olfactory confrontation with the mass of humanity there," says Bushman, the owner of RPB Investments Inc. in Houston, Texas.

Is this any way to display a masterpiece? Architect Eddie Prince of Charlotte, North Carolina, doesn't think so. He has waited years to see *La Gioconda*; "What I got was Las Vegas." And it's not just the bump-and-grind that bothers him; he's also disturbed by the ocherous wash of varnish that obscures the image. "I don't care what the experts say," he grouses. "*Mona* could use a bath."

The woman in charge of the Louvre's Department of Italian Paintings sympathizes. The global Mona craze has "victimized, vulgarized, and mocked" the painting, Cecilie Scaillierez says, drumming a pencil in her art book–cluttered office overlooking the Louvre courtyard and counting the hours until Republic of France artwork No. 779 is moved to an intimate glass chamber funded by a $4.2 million grant from a Japanese television station.

Scaillierez draws the line, though, at cleaning the oil. That, she says, "could change the image. Besides, it would likely cause a riot." Even the slightest rumor that the museum might clean it sets off irate calls from art experts, she says.

The Louvre's communication director can vouch for that. "We are always under suspicion that we are going to secretly clean the painting," says the director, Christophe Monin. Callers also fret that the Louvre plans to move *Mona* "into a horrible room or do something terrible to her." In fact, Monin spends more time dealing with *Mona* than he does with all of the Louvre's other art works (372,000 of them) put together. Right now, for example, he's fingering a British Midland brochure that uses a photo of the painting to entice air travelers.

Meanwhile, the Mona Lisa industry never sleeps. The Louvre alone sells more than 230,000 Mona Lisa postcards and more than five thousand Mona posters every year. Outside the museum, the image appears woven in neckties, printed on matchbooks, and glazed onto teapots. A "rare" set of Mona Lisa salt-and-pepper shakers recently went for $12.97 on eBay.

Back in 1915, the German composer Max von Schillings wrote an opera for Mona and, ninety years later, a bubblegum-song Britney Spears sang about her reached number 146 on the European charts. On screen, the Fillipina actress Gloria Yatco, star of *Sunset Over Corregidor* and *Tinangay ng Apoy*, calls herself Mona Lisa and should not be confused with the buxom salamander Mona Lisa, a physicist in the *Teenage Mutant Ninja Turtles* cartoon series.

On the sea, Scottish shipbuilders in 1965 christened an ocean liner in Mona's name and, in outer space, American astronomers on the Magellan Project named a nearly eighty-kilometer-long crater on Venus after her. Then there was *Moona Lisa,* a 2006 spray-paint-on-canvas of La Giocanda baring her bottom by British artist Nick Walker. The moon-shot sold for 54,000 £, more than ten times the upper sales estimate predicted by the London auction house Bonhams.

And let's not forget "Can't Be Wasting My Time," an R & B tune on the soundtrack of *Don't Be a Menace to South Central While Drinking Your Juice in the Hood,* by American songstress Mona Lisa.

"It's impossible to tally all the current commercial images of Mona," says Wendy Robinson, a North Carolina University doctoral candidate who is completing a dissertation on the painting titled "Simulated Property: Originality, Appropriation and Identity in a Digital Environment." The Mona Lisa parodies are endless, she suggests. "I've seen her in hair curlers and done up as Monica Lewinsky," Robinson says. "She's pushing beauty shops and pornography Web sites, and she's been ani-morphed to sell cats, dogs, monkeys, birds, and rabbits." Not to mention Miss Piggy, a.k.a. "Mona Moi."

All of this poses a dilemma for visitors to Paris, *Mona's* home ever since Francis I bought her in 1518. "A masterpiece," says noted art critic Robert

Hughes, "is an object whose aura and accumulated myth strike people blind." This isn't happening at the Louvre these days, and the Mona machine may explain why. Ask Shelly Page, an animation executive at the Hollywood studio Dreamworks SKG and one of the paintbrushes behind Roger Rabbit.

"It's hard for anyone to have a relationship with a painting that's used, like Bugs Bunny, to sell pajamas," Page says.

Back in the Mona mob, British portrait painter Anthony Palliser pushes through the throng and wags a finger at the old girl. The time has come, he says, to look at the painting with fresh eyes. "You know," he says, "Leonardo first looked at Mona like any portrait painter looks at a subject—as a piece of meat."

The mosh pit around *Mona* has no time for this disquisition. Never mind that Palliser has painted portraits of Graham Greene, Johnny Halliday, and the late U.S. ambassador to France, Pamela Harriman. Within seconds, a fresh wave of onlookers elbows him aside, until he's standing in front of Titian's *Le Mise au Tombeau.* Momentarily stunned by the flashing cameras, Palliser grows reflective. "Ah, the greatest thing one can wish is for *Mona* to become briefly forgotten, locked in a room and left to lose her commercial image," he says. "But it can't happen. Who would replace her?"

Putting the *Mona Lisa* on ice might make things worse, Scaillierez argues. "We put the *Mona Lisa* in storage for two years after Ungaza tried to deface her," she says. "It was precisely during that time when the modern commercial hype surrounding her image began."

So, shortly after the lipstick incident in 2002, the Louvre did the next best thing and constructed a special glass showroom designed exclusively for the *Mona Lisa.* The new venue opened in 2003 and allows only a few people at a time to view the painting. The project's architect, Lorenzo Piqueras, says the site includes a new protective shield that won't reflect light and allow *Mona* to be used as a mirror. Piqueras declines to explain how. Details of the project, he explains, are a state secret.

"I had to be quiet and keep my head very cold to handle this assignment," Piqueras says. "It was a very important job, and everybody has an opinion on how the *Mona Lisa* should be displayed."

47

NAKED **WOMEN LOSE OUT**

TO A STUFFED **SHARK**

GREG WYATT FONDLY REMEMBERS when the corridors of corporate power bulged with statues of naked women that were displayed like 3-D pinups in art collections throughout the U.S. and Europe.

Today's financial titans, laments the artist-in-residence at St. John the Divine Cathedral in New York, are fed a contemporary-art diet of sushi, monkeys, and, for dessert, a horse named "Tiramisu."

For instance, Steven A. Cohen, the founder of Stratford, Connecticut–based hedge fund SAC Capital Advisors, spent $8 million for Damien Hirst's fourteen-foot-long tiger shark pickled in formaldehyde. An anonymous corporate collector dropped $5.6 million to possess Jeff Koons's porcelain sculpture of pop superstar Michael Jackson cuddling a chimpanzee named "Bubbles." And an anonymous investor paid $1.2 million to perhaps dangle Italian artist Maurizio Cattelan's stuffed racehorse in a harness, "La Ballata di Trotsky," from his kitchen ceiling.

Wyatt says he prefers nudes. He also makes an excellent living forging eagles and representational bronze sculptures that can cost $2.4 million on display in more than twenty public spaces from New York to Beijing. Wyatt's trouble is the term "representational." It comes with some mighty negative implications in a contemporary-art market prone to rewarding perplexing fads, such as a Cattelan sculpture of a stuffed squirrel named "Bidibidobidiboo" committing suicide with a pistol at a kitchen table.

"Representational art is denounced by the art establishment," says Robert Fishko, director of the Forum Gallery in New York. The veteran

Fifth Avenue gallery owner says the nasty breach between Wyatt's representationalists and the contemporary artists who command headlines results from an "art world that's narrow, difficult to navigate, and wants at all costs to keep passengers on their road."

"Contemporary artists require the art bureaucracy of critics, galleries, and museums to validate their existence and value because their work requires explanation," Fishko says. "So it behooves them to scorn representational artists whose work requires no explanation."

In his catacomb studio beneath St. John the Divine, the perfectly proportioned nude women Wyatt sculpts for clients such as hedge-fund guru Jim Rogers rarely require further clarification. Except for Helaine, the model who in 1972 sparked a chain reaction that ultimately resulted in the only known volcanic eruption in Yonkers, New York, leaving Wyatt sprawled on a garage floor, his left arm riddled with molten bronze buckshot wounds.

"It was an enormous risk, close to foolish, and it defined my career," Wyatt recalls of the day he poured 150 pounds of liquid bronze heated to 2,100 degrees Fahrenheit into a jury-rigged crucible that contained the wax mold of Helaine's upper torso. "The first thing was the smell of burning wax, then blue smoke spewed out and the street began to rumble," Wyatt says of the incident that solidified his allegiance to representational art. "The floor blew up in less than three seconds."

The force of the blast sent a fountain of white-hot bronze skyward. Pieces of Helaine bounced off the ceiling and, cooling into thousands of red-hot pellets as the droplets hit the floor, ricocheted off the walls. After dousing the fires with blankets and spending three days recovering from the wounds, Wyatt hammered his way through the obliterated foundry mold. He named Helaine's poignant, greenish remains *Volcanus* and continues to decline offers to buy what's perhaps his signature masterpiece.

"It was a painful experience," Wyatt says. "So I must ask myself, did Damien Hirst actually go one-on-one with that $8 million shark?"

Walking down a frosty alley in the center of Florence, squeezed by both big-ticket galleries and the relentless marketing of what he calls "stunt art" on the auction-house block, is enough to make Wyatt laugh. He explores the Renaissance splendor that cascades up from the Arno River and into the Italian city whose wealthy merchant and banking families wrote the playbook on corporate investment in the arts. "Look at the elegance," Wyatt marvels, stroking his white whiskers and pointing to Giambologna's *Rape of the Sabines,* a series of sixteenth-century Renaissance marble statues and a bronze relief of Roman legionnaires with buxom women slung over their shoulders.

It's centuries removed from *The Virgin Mother,* Hirst's 35-foot-high bronze of a pregnant dancer, skin ripped back, with her fetus bared and on display in the courtyard of the Lever House in New York. Wyatt's world is more serene, a place where in 2003 real-estate tycoon Alex Parker came to commission a 500-pound bronze angel called *The Price of Freedom* for display at Arlington National Cemetery outside Washington. Stanley Wells, the celebrated Shakespearean scholar and chairman of the Shakespeare Birthplace Trust, also came to Wyatt's subterranean studio to spend more than $1.5 million for eight statues based on the Bard's plays for permanent display in the gardens of Shakespeare's home in Stratford-upon-Avon.

"I compare Wyatt to Rodin," Wells says. "He's that good."

"There's a historic argument over what's old-fashioned and what's modern," explains Wyatt, whose corporate commissions have included casting a Renaissance-inspired $350,000 nude woman for Andrea Jung, chief executive of Avon Products Inc.; a 14,000-pound bronze American eagle for the U.S. State Department; and a three-ton, $250,000 bronze statue of J.C. Penney Co. founder James Penney.

"I'm quite keen on Wyatt," says Rogers, who owns three of the artist's sculptures, including a 350-pound bronze nude named *Bathsheba.* "I consider myself a simple lad who buys things that he likes. If it happens to turn out to be an investment, then so be it. I don't follow the New York art market."

Wyatt says the contemporary-art market has erected an artificial wall against a growing number of young painters and sculptors who he says have been critically penalized and left struggling to gain notoriety for abandoning ephemera in favor of renewing the skillful techniques of the representational masters. Indeed, Ivan Massow, chairman of London's Institute of Contemporary Arts, has referred to much of today's high-priced exotica as "pretentious, self-indulgent, craftless art."

According to Artnet—a Frankfurt-based analytics firm that tracks the trade in everything from $10 Elvis Presley portraits on felt to Hirst's *The Elusive Truth* exhibition of $2 million works that included paintings of pharmaceuticals and a sliced brain on display at the Gagosian Gallery in New York—the global art industry is a $20-billion-a-year business. Wyatt says it's a market that has mostly jettisoned craftsmanship for gimmickry.

"Run your fingers along the gracefully detailed lines Giambologna brought to this sculpture," Wyatt urges. "Could it just be that abstraction in art has become so abstract that there's no longer any shock or long-term investment value to it?"

Perhaps. Yet broaching those sorts of questions won't win an artist many patrons in a contemporary-art market dominated by painters and sculptors who leverage their hip downtown reputations to charge the uptown crowd $2.7 million for the likes of *The Ninth Hour,* Cattelan's statue of Pope John Paul II getting whacked in the head with a meteor.

"Contemporary art is a reflection of the thoughts and ideas of the time, now, the twenty-first century, and nobody wants to build or buy another bronze eagle," says Frances Dittmer, the former curator of the corporate Refco Collection and now a private consultant for wealthy businessmen and corporations seeking art investments. "Representational art is great for a corporation that wants to commission a piece of commemorative art, but that's about stability and it's not about art, and it certainly has nothing to do with investment potential."

During the 1990s, the collection owned by the privately held global trading firm Refco Inc. featured the works of 280 artists, including the highly valued "retinal art" of Belgian artist Marcel Broodthaers, whose seminal piece is a sculpture of a giant casserole stuffed with mussels. The anthology also contained a Garnett Puett sculpture in reality made by two thousand bees that he released into a glass box fitted with a steel armature in the shape of a male head. After the swarm fashioned its honeycomb around the brace, Puett sucked the bees out with a vacuum cleaner.

"Art is about the idea, and once an artist has the idea, it can be painted or sculpted by anybody," Dittmer says. "Bottom line: Greg Wyatt is not a hot artist, no one in the contemporary-art market has ever heard of him, and my guess is that he's a retrograde figurative artist who finds support through sufficient contacts to show his work in places like government buildings."

Max Miller, a 24-year-old art student and representational sculptor from South Carolina now encamped in a Tuscan apartment block outside Florence, bristles at the contemporary buzz on Wyatt's work. Dressed in black and sporting a stud in each earlobe, Miller says, "The artists I know are sick of Koons and Jackson Pollock clones."

Along with some three hundred students from around the world who attend Florence's three main Renaissance-art training grounds—the

Charles H. Cecil Studio, the Florence Academy of Art, and the Michael John Angel Studios—Miller is part of a fresh coterie of art-world rebels. Many of them say they see mostly vinegar in the works of artists like the celebrated British sculptor Gary Hume, whose *Carnival* exhibition at the Matthew Marks Gallery in New York featured enameled and faceless bronze spheres stacked atop one another to resemble snowmen.

"The big-money art crowd in London and New York rarely wants to hear about great representational artists like Odd Nerdrum and John Sonsini, because they think they're doing politically conservative art," Miller says. "*The Rape of the Sabines*—the story of a bunch of naked guys who run into town and run off with a bunch of naked women—is about the most politically incorrect artwork in history. It's sculpture's ground-zero and the hardest art form to master," he adds. "The problem we representationalists have is that political conservatives are more willing than others to admit that they don't see a big blue spike stuck in the ground as a monumental piece of investment art."

Huddled in a cold, dusty, and crumbling sixteenth-century church that doubles as their studio and ersatz gallery, Miller and his fellow artists argue that corporate art buyers have allowed hype to supplant talent. "Successful artists must be better at selling themselves than creating good work," says Chris Eastland, a 25-year-old representational painter and sculptor from Fairfield, Connecticut. "The art critics and analysts who define taste are all in their forties, fifties, and sixties. They were brought up to believe that modernism is the norm and guys like Wyatt are useless throwbacks." The avatars of contemporary art, Eastland suggests, can concoct a rationale for anything.

"Learning how to draw and master the brush, the chisel, and the crucible like the Renaissance masters teaches accountability," Miller says. "Besides," he adds with a laugh, "we'll always have work. Someone has to fix those statues once they've been eaten away by pigeon droppings."

Wyatt says he doesn't mind being part of an art underworld that includes animal sculptor Kent Ullberg, human figurist Anthony Padovano, and Fred Hart, the representationalist who designed and cast the bronze soldiers that stand alongside the Vietnam Veterans Memorial in Washington. "We representationalists were overground for five hundred years," Wyatt says. "It's okay to be underground."

David Heleniak, a senior partner at Shearman & Sterling, a New York–based law firm with offices in nineteen cities around the globe, owns a commissioned Wyatt watercolor and says the view from below looks pretty good to him.

"Wyatt is an artist of the time when artists were master craftsmen," Heleniak says. "I'm not an art investor, but if I was, I would be buying Wyatts. His studio beneath St. John the Divine is enthralling and reminds me of the castle scene from the movie *Young Frankenstein.*"

Still, after more than thirty years of fulfilling dozens of corporate commissions and twenty-five years chiseling lumps of marble into angels and demons and peacocks beneath the foundations of the largest cathedral in the U.S., Wyatt's work has failed to cultivate the interest of any a la mode gallery or museum.

At the same time, public gardens in New York and Washington are awash with Wyatt statues that can weigh as much as thirty thousand pounds. He's also made long-term loans to former U.S. Senate majority leader Bill Frist, former New York governor George Pataki, and the U.S. House of Representatives Intelligence Committee.

Fishko says Wyatt's lack of marquee gallery glamour is hardly surprising in a secretive and clubby market defined by extremes and populated by trendy folks who would pay no attention to the "Bill of Rights Eagle" sculpture Wyatt has planted outside President John F. Kennedy's dormitory at Harvard University or to his exhibition of naked ladies at the U.S. consulate in Florence. "Honorific art is not traded on any market," he explains. "What galleries display is created at risk by the artist, and a corporation would never come speak with me to commission any of the artists I represent because the executives who want honorific work don't want to take any risk at all. Wyatt knows his work is sold before he starts."

Wyatt says all of that is about to change. One example that stands out is the *Socrates Urn,* a series of haunting and colorful bronze vessels inspired by ancient Mayan imagery set to sell privately for between $4,000 and $7,500.

"There's now a swing back toward representational and figurative art," says Anthony Grant, the former head of the contemporary-art department at the auction house Sotheby's Holdings Inc. and now owner of the Anthony Grant Gallery in New York. "At the end of the day, people like looking at recognized images."

RUNNING **SILENT**

AND

PARTYING DEEP

"IF YOU CAN FIND MY SUBMARINE, IT'S YOURS," teases Russian oil billionaire Roman Abramovich. And that's all the reclusive owner of the Chelsea Football Club has to offer on the yacht-club scuttlebutt about his life beneath the waves.

The ocean floor is the final spending frontier for the world's richest people. Journeying to see what's on the bottom aboard a personal submersible is perhaps the ultimate wretched excess, guaranteed to trump the average mogul's stable of vintage Bugattis or a $38 million round-trip ticket to the International Space Station aboard a Russian rocket. Luxury-submarine makers and salesmen from the Pacific Ocean to the Persian Gulf say fantasy and secrecy are the foundations of this nautical niche industry built on madcap multibillionaires.

"Everyone down there is a wealthy eccentric," says Jean-Claude Carme, vice president of marketing for U.S. Submarines Inc., a Portland, Oregon–based bespoke submarine builder. "They're all intensely secretive."

Who owns the estimated one hundred luxury subs carousing the Seven Seas mostly remains a mystery. Paul Allen, co-founder of Microsoft Corp., warned his boatbuilder that loose lips sink ships. "Not really supposed to talk about the sub, but it's a fancy one, a mighty nice piece of work," says Fred Rodie, one of the engineers who designed Allen's undersea yacht at Olympic Tool & Engineering Inc. in Shelton, Washington.

"If I told you, I'd have to shoot you," says Bruce Jones, president and founder of U.S. Submarines, about the names in his client book. Jones, the son of a marine-construction engineer, built his first diesel-and-battery-powered sub in 1993. Every sales contract since then has included a confidentiality clause to protect the buyer's identity. "This is a nasty, cutthroat business," Jones says.

Hervé Jaubert, a former French Navy commando, swapped his cutlass for a screwdriver in 1995 to build his first luxury submarine. Now chief executive officer of Exomos, a Dubai-based custom-sub maker, Jaubert takes a more romantic view of the work: "I'm a poet who builds submersible yachts for rich people."

"Spending $80 million for a boat that goes underwater in a market where one that doesn't costs $150 million is a deal," Jones reasons. "Our Phoenix 1000 is four stories tall, a sixty-five-meter-long blend of a tourist and military sub."

The ultimate war submarine, the U.S. Navy's *Virginia*-class New Attack Submarine, costs $2.4 billion and carries sixteen Tomahawk cruise missiles. Jones says the most dangerous projectile aboard the Phoenix 1000 is a champagne cork. "Navies want weapons-delivery systems," Jones explains, walking in a forest near Idaho's Lake Pend Oreille, site of the U.S. Navy's Farragut Naval Submarine Training Station. "I build luxury-delivery systems for people who have more money than they know what to do with."

***

It isn't cheap to run silent and sleep deep.

Jaubert's ten-passenger sub costs $15 million. A gymnasium is optional. U.S. Submarines' mid-size model is the $25 million Seattle 1000, a three-story-tall vessel with five staterooms, five bathrooms, two kitchens, a gym, a wine cellar, and a thirty-foot-long by fifteen-foot-wide (9 by 4.5 meter) observation portal. It has a range of three thousand nautical miles (5,556 kilometers).

"The one thing I won't make for anyone is a yellow submarine," Jones insists. The forty-foot- (12-meter-) long sub owned by Microsoft's Allen came with a $12 million sticker price and enough extras to remain submerged for a week. Its color: yellow.

Inside the Exomos showroom at Dubai's Jebel Ali Free Zone, customers choose from fourteen luxury models. Since 2005, Jaubert's 170 workers have launched eighteen vessels. In 2007, Jaubert had twenty-six clients awaiting delivery on subs such as the trendy Stingray runabout and the fashionable 65-foot- (19.8-meter-) long Proteus luxury liner. "The Proteus is an underwater bus," Jaubert says. "It's more fun in the Stingray, drives like a Ferrari."

Jaubert says one of the dangers shared by members of this underwater fraternity of the super-rich is being blown to smithereens by depth charges. "Side sonar scanners are always mistaken for torpedo tubes," he warns, slapping the blue hull of a three-seat, $350,000 "sport luxury model" under construction in his factory. "Government agencies make visits to see if there are torpedoes aboard our boats. Owners are supposed to let authorities know when they're in the area. They often don't, and it causes problems."

"What we might do gets into classified Tactics, Techniques, and Procedures," says U.S. Coast Guard spokesman Steve Blando. "TTP is not something we talk about."

As for the chance of Allen's sub being reduced to flotsam, "We don't comment on personal matters that involve the Allen family," says his spokesman, Michael Nank. Meanwhile, in Tahiti, Tetuahau Temaru, son and chief economic-development adviser to president Oscar Temaru, says the Pacific island territory is pursuing luxury-submarine skippers to sail into French Polynesia's warm, crystal waters. "Luxury submarines are the future vision for Tahiti," Temaru says. "We call it our 'life-saving plan.' Developing a luxury-submarine market and the tourism that would come from it is on target with visitors enjoying our beaches and marine life."

As for that marine life, the local dolphin population can be a problem for some submariners. Jaubert says he has clients who wrestle with how to conduct a deep-sea love affair in front of an observation window without creating an underwater paparazzi. "Dolphins are easily excited when they sense people making love," Jones says. "They get jealous and bang their noses against the window."

The best solution? Curtains, says Jones.

49

STEALING THE POPE'S

SECRET BOOKS

T HE BOOM OF A SOLITARY BELL spills through an open window
and into the office of Father Sergio Pagano inside the Secret Archives
of the Vatican. For an instant, the Italian priest charged with managing the
"paper assets" of the Roman Catholic Church turns his smile from the peals
toward a sentinel tower of six closed-circuit television screens. These
ensure that the 53 miles of historical documents buried in the labyrinth
beneath Pagano's desk remains safe from looters and sheltered from the
emerging market for paleographic investments.

"I'm a buyer, not a seller, but it's always the pope's call," says Pagano,
explaining the Vatican's rules for playing the market in rare correspondence, antediluvian books, and illuminated manuscripts. It's a quiet trade
that has been conducted for millennia between popes and potentates.
Modern pursuers of ancient tomes include investors such as British Land
Co. Chairman and Managing Director John Ritblat and Jean Paul Getty II,
the philanthropist and heir to the Getty oil fortune. "The dealers and collectors frequently offer to sell us items," says Pagano, arching his fingers
into a spire. "There's much foolery among them, but it's very difficult to fool
the Vatican," he cautions. "It's rare that we pay attention to market forces."

Yet book brokers say Pagano and institutional buyers such as the curators of
the sixty illuminated manuscripts on display in the Sir John Ritblat Gallery of the
British Library find themselves on guard against thieves. They also have to riffle
through rare-book bins in competition with private buyers, as some investors
increasingly see rare books as a haven from sliding stock and bond markets.

It's a blue-chip business driven by dealers who can spend years tracking down a clay tablet on which Mesopotamian grain prices were recorded by the priestesses of the Red Temple of Inanna in 3100 B.C. Other singular investments include a 500-year-old copy of *Summa de Aritmetica, Geometria, Proportioni et Proportionalita.* Rare-book hunters such as Emilio d'Aniello at the Ex Libris bookshop in Rome say they have businessmen eager to find an original copy of the tome, written by Luca Pacioli. "Pacioli's book is extremely important, the first known text that incorporates accounting rules," d'Aniello says.

"Ancient and medieval writings on business and economics are very rare, very difficult to obtain, and very much in demand," adds Claudio Cascianelli, whose family has spent the past seventy-five years sleuthing for rare books on business and economics for U.S., Canadian, and Italian executives. "Passion moves this market," the owner of the Antica Liberia bookshop insists. "Money is not an issue."

Standing on a cracked tile floor flecked with black marble a few minutes' walk from Vatican City, d'Aniello says an Italian businessman he declines to name has him on the hunt for a copy of *Mirabila,* a fifteenth-century guidebook for foreign merchants visiting Rome. "It's thirty pages and fits in the palm of your hand," Cascianelli marvels. "There are perhaps no more than six copies—a lot, by ancient standards. One of them is in the Vatican, and they will not sell," he adds with a grin. "I once had a copy, years and years ago. I sold it for $11,000. Nothing."

In New York, Mary Ann Folter, who has spent four decades scouring private libraries for published arcana to tempt her clients at the H.P. Kraus rare-book store, says an increasing number of investors are cashing out of the stock market and plowing the money into books. "There's no doubt people are leaving the market to find books," Folter says. "It's a safe-haven investment they can put their hands on."

That's a dilemma for Lynne Brindley, chief executive of the British Library. "The past ten years have seen a sharp increase in books as an investment. The prices become inflated and public institutions can't compete in that marketplace," Brindley says.

Kristian Jensen, head of the British Library's Early Printed Collections unit, says the rivalry is brisk. "When the stock market slumps, the price of rare books jumps," he says. "I've seen prices go up about thirty percent over the past five years." In 1997, for instance, Jensen says he went to an auction planning to bid on a 36-page fifteenth-century book titled *Properties and*

Medicines of the Horse. However, H.P. Kraus outbid the British Library and bought the folio at a gallop for $319,520. The book remains locked away, its $595,000 retail price tag beyond the acquisition budget of the library. "For collectors, books are nothing like paintings," Jensen explains. "Most buyers of fine art like to say how much they paid and display the painting. Reading is a private affair. Being secretive about the price and what's in your collection is part of the book game."

No matter the bankroll, tracking exotic investments like Sigismundo Scaccia's *Treatise on Trade and Exchange*, a 500-page essay on how to calculate seventeenth-century interest rates, may take years and much intrigue. Arturo Perez-Reverte, author of *The Club Dumas*, a novel on the rare-book trade that Roman Polanski used as the template for his 1999 film *The Ninth Gate*, mocks the industry as populated by "jackals, antique-fair sharks, and auction-room leeches who would sell their grandmothers for a first edition."

That sort of market activity has caught the attention of Interpol agent Vivianna Padilla, who says the global police agency's statistics show that book burglary is more widespread than fine-art theft. "The underground trade in rare books and manuscripts is more prevalent than people will ever know and a huge problem." Padilla, a Washington-based art historian who manages Interpol's cultural-property program, says Interpol gumshoes in 181 countries are currently seeking 1,693 stolen or missing books, including *De Revolutionibus Orbitum Coelestium* by Nicolaus Copernicus (published in 1543); a first-edition *Tres Epistolae de Maculis Solaribus* by Galileo Galilei (1612); and a 1538 volume of *Aesop's Fables*. "Stolen books are typically of interest to investors," Padilla says. "It's an easy type of theft. Robbers go into tombs for the clay tablets. With illuminated manuscripts, criminals razor out the pages and sell them as book art."

Across the Terrace of the Wild Orange Trees, a patio that connects the Secret Archives to the Vatican Library's separately managed collection of some 150,000 manuscripts illuminated with gold and other precious metals and gems, librarian Massimo Ceresa delicately opens a 624-page handpainted book titled *The Life of St. Benedict*. He suggests there are "dealers who would do anything" to possess this example of sacred calligraphy, written in A.D. 1000.

"The value of the entire Vatican collection is astronomical," says Vatican Library curator Father Duval Arnauld. "But how much is it worth? It's impossible to say."

Retired Ohio State University art history professor and former Vatican Library cardholder Anthony Melnikas knows something about the value of rare volumes. In 1997, Melnikas pleaded guilty to eight U.S. federal charges of possessing two illuminated pages he sliced from a fourteenth-century manuscript in the Vatican Library and attempted to sell for a total of $500,000. Both pages, one on the tactics of war and the other on the agriculture business, had been cut out of a treatise originally owned by the Italian poet Petrarch.

"The market in this type of investment is growing, and there are only a handful of us who specialize in the field," says Melnikas, out of prison after serving a fourteen-month sentence and paying a fine of $13,400 for attempting to sell smuggled and stolen foreign-origin artifacts under the provisions of the U.S. Archeological Resources Protection Act. "You must understand that Pope Julius II in the fifteenth century confiscated all the books from Europe's secular leaders and trucked them into the Vatican," he explains. "I was only reversing the situation."

Back in the Vatican Library, Ceresa describes the theft as naïve. "What Melnikas stole was not worth a lot," he huffs. Arnauld adds that he finds "nothing odd" about Melnikas's unrepentant motive. "Many of our books were stolen during the eighteenth and nineteenth centuries," he explains. "It remains a very valuable market."

One reason is gold. "A popular crime centuries ago was scraping the gold off illuminated manuscripts," says Michelle Brown, the curator of some ten thousand Western illuminated manuscripts at the British Library. "Around five pages of gold makes one wedding ring."

Antonio Cadei, a professor of medieval art at the University of Rome, says a rush of businessmen seeking to invest in ancient books on economics and commerce has modernized the market. "The difficult books to find are business books with art in them," Cadei says. "The new type of owners don't read the books, they just look at them as investments." He suggests that one codicil at the top of the investment wish list is *Biadaiuolo*. Written in the early thirteen hundreds, the 200-page illuminated text was commissioned by a commodity trader and tells the story of the grain trade in Florence. Only one copy is known to exist, and it's chained to a post at the Medici Library in Florence. "It's a unique book that happens to be a fiscal document and an absolutely splendid work of art," he says.

Michelle Brown at the Ritblat says Wall Street investors aren't the only ones looking for profit in the rare-book market. New readers appeared after the library acquired the 300-page *Splendor Solis* codicil, she says. "It's a sixteenth-century manuscript on alchemy that deals with turning base metal into gold," Brown says. "Witches and warlocks frequently show up asking me to take it out of the case so they can perform the magical incantations in the Ritblat Room."

50

DA VINCI CODE FANS
DIG UP THE DEAD

THERE'S PROFIT IN THINGS THAT GO BUMP IN THE NIGHT, but, for the mayor of this devil-infested hamlet, it's the dynamite going boom before dawn that has him tallying the mysteries evoked in Dan Brown's bestseller *The Da Vinci Code*.

"They set off explosions at all hours and climb over the cemetery wall to dig up the dead," gripes Rennes-le-Château mayor Jean-François L'Huilier, whose mountain village of 112 people atop the Valley of God in southwestern France has become a mecca for fans of novelist Brown's best seller.

"It's a remarkable book, but I'm afraid the world has entered a period of imperceptible folly," says the former French paratrooper turned politician. "And that's why I had to exhume the corpse of Bérenger Saunière."

Just who or what the devotees of the novel are trying to dig up in Rennes-le-Château remains a lucrative bone of contention.

Local innkeeper Andrew Usher, whose Hotel au Coeur de Rennes serves as the assembly ground for grave-diggers and ghost-busters from as far away as Japan and Argentina, says *The Da Vinci Code* is the most successful installment in a line of some five hundred books and numerous documentary films that orbit around a renegade Catholic priest named Bérenger Saunière.

The cleric arrived in the village in 1885 and spent the next twenty-six years resurrecting a ruined eleventh-century church dedicated to the Magdalene. Above the door, he chiseled the message "This Place Is Terrible," and then he erected a life-size statue of a devil wearing a green toga while balancing a holy-water font on his horns.

"It's right out of *The Rocky Horror Picture Show*," is how Usher explains the cobwebbed house of worship to his guests.

L'Huilier says the impoverished priest became inexplicably wealthy. Alongside the tiny church, Saunière, who died in 1917 at the age of sixty-five, built a luxurious villa and a lavishly appointed tower from which he corresponded with banks in Paris, received French financial newspapers, and surveyed the Valley of God below while sipping rum with his house-keeper and the priest from neighboring Rennes-les-Bains.

In 2004, L'Huilier moved Saunière's body from the village cemetery to a fortified mausoleum in the garden of the refurbished villa. It now costs €3 to visit the site, €1 to view the Valley of God through a telescope installed by the Rotary Club, and €5 for a bottle of Cuvée de Rennes-le-Château, a red wine with a photo of Saunière on the label.

"Saunière's devil and Brown's book have been marvelous for the economy," Usher says. "In 2003, we had eighty thousand visitors to the region. It's not yet Halloween [2004] and we've already topped a hundred thousand visitors this year."

Valley of God merchants such as Usher say the money-spinning mystery of Rennes-le-Château—now celebrating its second millennium—is a creepy yarn that *The Da Vinci Code* has detonated into a $20-million-a-year local industry. The novel is the gory tale of a Harvard University professor who discovers a Vatican conspiracy to cover up the marriage of Jesus Christ to Mary Magdalene and his fathering of an ancestral lineage observable on paintings that hang in the Louvre.

The Da Vinci Code has reigned supreme on forty-two fiction bestseller lists globally, selling more than nine million hardcover copies and generating an estimated $225 million in retail sales in the U.S. alone for its publisher, Doubleday, according to Constance Sayre, director of the publishing-industry consulting group Market Partners International in New York. "The book has a lock on the international market," Sayre says. "*The Da Vinci Code* is a huge business."

It has been a commercial phenomenon, L'Huilier says, transforming the crumbling village into a boomtown for those seeking, among other things, proof that Christ moved there with his family and that Saunière discovered and then hid the evidence.

*** *

"The South of France always has been popular for foreign visitors," says Marie Marselli, a broker who handles property transactions in the Valley of

God area at Cathare Immobilier, a real estate agency named after a heretical medieval sect.

Since *The Da Vinci Code* was published in the spring of 2003, Marselli says her agency has been inundated with international inquiries from people seeking to purchase land in the village. "But it's a small place and there's no property for sale," she says.

The surplus of supernatural resources in Rennes-le-Château for centuries has drawn paranormal tourists to the ancient Roman garrison outpost. There are precisely 19.5 million gold francs "spread on the mountain by the devil," according to an oral history assembled by villagers and transcribed in 1832 by French travel writer Labouisse-Rochefort.

The treasure story was rejuvenated in *Southwestern France*, an 1890 guidebook by Augustus Hare that recounts Vatican-backed French troops laying siege to a Templar stronghold in nearby Montsegur in 1244. Slaughtered along with the knights were fifty "perfects," Cathar priests who rejected sacraments and maintained that Christ hadn't died on the cross.

Medieval historians mostly agree that a handful of knights and perfects escaped the siege of Montsegur, and it's here where the mystery of Rennes-le-Château begins to ripen.

Usher says some of his guests maintain that the heretics fled with the mortal remains of Christ and the Magdalene. Others suggest they left with two coded scrolls that showed Christ siring the ancient French ruling family, the Merovingians. Still others believe the survivors absconded with the treasure of Solomon or found an underground passageway into Hell.

"Whatever it was," L'Huilier says, "people believe it ended up near Rennes-le-Château and the clues to finding it are in the Valley of God and inside Saunière's church."

The priest remained a popular local ghost character until 1967, when the French surrealist writer and prankster Gérard de Sède wrapped the entire package in an adventure novel titled *The Accursed Treasure of Rennes-le-Château*. In the book, de Sède uncoils a conspiracy protected for centuries by a group of fictional guardians called "The Priory of Sion."

In 1969, Henry Lincoln, a scriptwriter for the cult U.K. science-fiction television series *Dr. Who*, read de Sède's pulp fiction while on vacation in France. Three years later, Lincoln filmed the first of three documentaries on the mystery for the BBC history and archaelogy program *Chronicle*, interviewing art historians such as Anthony Blunt.

By the end of the decade, Lincoln hooked up with American short-story writer Richard Leigh and New Zealander photographer Michael Baigent to collaborate on their 1982 bestseller, *The Holy Blood and the Holy Grail*, originally published by Jonathan Cape in the U.K. The book is perhaps best described as a non-academic history that for many legitimized the Priory of Sion as an authentic institution.

London lawyer Paul Sutton suspects it's no coincidence that the opening page of *The Da Vinci Code* begins: "FACT: The Priory of Sion—a European secret society founded in 1099—is a real organization." Sutton, on behalf of Leigh and Baigent, filed a copyright infringement suit against Random House Group Ltd., the U.K. publisher of *The Da Vinci Code*. Sutton says that the suit seeks unspecified damages and an account of the book's profits. "My clients spent twenty years using all their skill and labor to do the historical research contained in Brown's book," Sutton argues. "That's the basis of the lawsuit."

However, a British court ultimately sided with Brown and his publisher.

Back in Rennes-le-Château, L'Huilier dismisses Lincoln, Leigh, and Baigent as peddlers of historical twaddle. At the same time, the mayor says the farrago has enhanced the Rennes-le-Château brand: "The various quests for ultimate truth already have paid for new public toilets and a parking lot for the tour buses." The economic growth also includes a tapas bar, a mystical bookshop, a hot-air-balloon magical-mystery tour, and a shop that sells plaster busts of Saunière's devil. "We have plans to extend the size of the village down the mountainside to accommodate the interest."

Much of the curiosity hinges on the four encrypted parchments Saunière purportedly found hidden in a pillar while rebuilding the church. Other aficionados say the area's sulfurous grottoes and crumbling castles are haunted by the wraiths of the Knights Templar protecting their treasure. Still other enthusiasts hold that flying saucers land atop Mt. Bugarach to pick up those pilgrims who have decoded the mystery.

"We also have a perfume shop run by a real, live alchemist," Usher says of the commercial development that has fed off the mystery. "Now there's a French fellow who makes €6,000 a day operating UFO expeditions. And please alert people that Christ is buried beneath Mt. Cardou and not under my hotel."

For Marcus Williamson, managing director of London-based software company Connectotel Ltd. and webmaster of a World Wide Web site (www.connectots.com/rennes) devoted to the village, each of the fictions contains wisps of truth.

"I've spent twenty years studying the history that Brown ultimately confected into *The Da Vinci Code*," Williamson says. "I bought a house here because I found the facts so compelling."

Williamson's Rennes-le-Château PowerPoint presentation, flashed to hotel conference rooms across Europe, says the two most important documents, genealogies of Christ written in 1244 and 1644, are locked in a safe-deposit box in an undisclosed bank in the City of London.

The other two scrolls mystery hunters say Saunière discovered can be seen on many of the 150,000 Web sites devoted to the whodunit, in a computer game called "Gabriel Knight 3," and in a series of French comic books.

Sipping soda in a café filled with the clang of bells from a "Medieval Madness" pinball machine, Williamson frets that the story has spiraled out of control. "It's like an Internet virus, with thousands of otherwise intelligent people convinced that *The Da Vinci Code* is a work of nonfiction," he says.

Indeed, Jacques Le Roux, director of tour company Paris Avec Vous-Culture, says many of his customers are "shattered" to discover otherwise. Le Roux's company and five other groups so far have ushered more than 180,000 people through the Louvre on "decrypting the thriller" tours that study the paintings cited in the novel.

"Rennes-le-Château doesn't appear in the book, so most people are unaware of the link until we mention the importance of the village," says Le Roux, an art historian. "Almost fifty percent of the people on the tours are disappointed to discover that the book is total fiction."

Dutchman Karel Van Hufflen says the story is factual. A chartered accountant and former auditor for his country's internal revenue service, he abandoned his job in 1996 and moved to the region to unravel the mystery. *The Da Vinci Code* brought new energy to his efforts, he says, insisting that "Brown's book is more than a novel. Oh, yes, he knows a lot more about the mystery than he tells the reader. The treasure is Templar gold, but there are more profound truths than where the money is. It's difficult for non-initiates to grasp."

That's putting it mildly.

Inside a stone house a few paces from the Church of the Magdalene, self-educated archaeologist Graham Simmans is wrapped in a tartan blanket and slumped in a leather armchair. The retired U.K. Royal Air Force squadron leader slices into a wedge of cheese and says he has devoted the past twenty years to the quest. To hear him tell the story, the popular delusions that have sprouted from *The Da Vinci Code* are the result of "the most powerful and enduring cover-up in Christendom."

Simmans, the author of monographs on the nuances Brown embroidered into *The Da Vinci Code*, also says he has discovered the Ark of the Covenant and isolated the burial chamber of Alexander the Great.

It's commercial folly not to take the spiritual slapstick seriously, says Will Cogan, proprietor of the Pizzeria de la Place in Rennes-les-Bains. "Over fifty percent of my customers are lost souls looking for something. I moved here in the summer of 2003, and land prices doubled because of *The Da Vinci Code*. The mystery wasn't originally part of my business strategy, but I'm looking to make Crusty Christ and Papal Pepperoni pizzas part of the menu."

AN OIL CRISIS FORCES
SHELL TO BANG
ITS DRUM QUIETLY

THE GLOBAL CORPORATE HEADQUARTERS of Royal Dutch Shell Plc in London has one word to offer on the subject of its musical oil barrels.

"What?" says Shell communications director Alexandra Wright.

"Oil-drum music is infectious," says Sepp Blatter, the president of the Federation Internationale de Football Association, soccer's global governing body and the man behind the World Cup.

For Blatter, the sound of oil cans filling stadiums as global soccer giants kick it out on the field means millions of happy customers. He envisions the rum poured and the conga line ensuing around the "panmen," particularly those who beat the drum for the Trinidad and Tobago Calypso Carnival Warriors team.

And therein lies the corporate dilemma of Gerard Mitchell, country head of Shell Trinidad Ltd.: more than a few thousand of Blatter's drummers are probably beating Shell oil barrels. "It's officially against corporate policy for us to hand out oil barrels," Mitchell frets. "We really don't know what to do about all this."

For many of the world's estimated thirty-five thousand panmen, the sweetest-sounding music comes from the fifty-five-gallon, twenty-gauge, red steel oil barrels made in Shell's lubricant mixing plant on Barracones Bay in Trinidad. A few miles up the road in Port-of-Spain, beneath the shade of the big breadfruit tree at 147 Tragarete Road, a future Shell executive in 1946 made history's first steel drum from an empty barrel of tractor lubricant bearing the company's distinctive clamshell insignia. According to American jazz musician Andy Narell, Shell oil-barrel pans and other big oil company musical drums made between 1946 and 1967 are as renowned and desirable as the Cremonese violins of Antonio Stradivari, Nicolo Amati, and Giuseppe Guarneri. Even the barrels made today are in high demand among pan players.

"We kind of have a reputation," Mitchell says.

William Rosales, Shell Trinidad's engineer charged with overseeing the manufacture of more than forty-two thousand Shell oil barrels annually, sticks to official corporate policy. "Let me state for the record that our used drums are disposed of properly and that Shell health and safety regulations prevent the use of empty drums for anything but Shell oil products."

That wasn't always the case. Sixty years ago, Shell in great part helped bankroll the development of the modern pan drum, the only new acoustic instrument to hit the music scene since Adolphe Sax came up with the saxophone in 1841.

***

Shell's archivists in London and The Hague have no record of the modern pan or its inventor, Ellie Mannette. Shell executives in Trinidad suspect that the company's documentation for both was lost when the government nationalized the oil industry in 1974 and Shell's presence was reduced from four thousand employees to its current 55-member operation.

Oldtimers on the island say Shell got into the music business in 1951, when a Shell Caribbean managing director they remember as "Mr. Alexis" put Mannette on the payroll with an annual salary of $2,000 to stop him and his pals—Birdie, Puddin', and Cobo Jack—from stealing the company's empty and toxic oil drums. Mannette remained with Shell until 1967, as a sales manager, steel-drum maker, and leader of the pan band The Shell Invaders.

"They called me 'Cairo,'" says Mannette, now in his eighties and an artist-in-residence and professor of music at West Virginia University in Morgantown. "We were teenage gang members, all viewed as social outcasts until Shell took an interest in us and our music. They gave us barrels and money and made the music happen."

Mannette named the world's first 55-gallon drum "Barracuda." It was last seen in August 1946, stuck in the high branches of the breadfruit tree.

"The big kids beat me up and stole Barracuda because it made a better sound than their drums," Mannette says. "They threw it up in that tree and I wasn't going up there for it."

By the early 1960s, Jeff Chandler, Shell Trinidad's British managing director, and fellow Englishman Michael Smallbone were spending their off hours as managers for the Shell Invaders. The group even played at New York's Madison Square Garden.

"They carried the beer and made sure it was cold," recalls George Martin, Shell's Caribbean public relations director from 1966 to 1996. "Chandler and Smallbone loved hanging out at the Shell pan yard. They arranged scholarships and helped all the musicians study abroad."

One of the early Shell Invaders, Malcolm Weekes, received an annual $2,000 scholarship to attend Howard University in Washington, D.C., where he played the double alto (two drums with sixteen notes on each pan) for the school's Trinidad Steel Band and graduated with a degree in chemical engineering. Now retired after a career as a chemist at Bechtel Group Inc., Weekes remembers when he and Mannette forged pans out of toxic barrels. "We built bonfires to burn out all the crap stuck inside the drums," Weekes says. "It was dangerous work. We all inhaled the fumes. But what the barrel had contained also helped define the sound of the drum."

Mannette now builds about a hundred pans annually from the unsoiled barrels that roll off the line at North Coast Container Corp. in Cleveland. "Weird thing is, nobody's really sure why a 55-gallon oil drum can be crafted into a musical instrument or why my early Shells have a distinctive sound," Mannette says. "I once made a drum out of a Shell barrel that had stored perfume. Now that was really exceptional."

Back in the lab at Shell Trinidad, chemist Saira Joseph claims that the sound is in the solvent. "A lighter oil would lend itself to higher notes and a heavier oil to lower notes," Joseph explains. "The gauge of the steel is the most critical factor. Shell stayed with the heavier twenty-gauge, while the other oil companies mostly went to fifteen- and eighteen-gauge steel."

Panman Chanler Bailey, who spent six years at Mannette's side studying steel-drum construction, says the oil companies no longer know how to make an oil barrel. "There's a lot of junk Japanese-made barrels out there," Bailey says. "They don't hold the sound, and the drumheads crack on impact."

Modern pan-makers, called "blenders" or "tuners," rigorously follow Mannette's system in constructing any of the nine drums that make up the pan family. The barrels are first sliced according to register, from soprano to bass. Then, using a selection of rubber and metal mallets, blenders stretch the thickness of the metal top to create a concave drumhead to produce anywhere from three to thirty notes. Before Mannette's first nine-note Barracuda, steel music makers could play only three notes on hubcaps and cookie-tin tops configured with convex drumheads. They went clunk.

In Trinidad, a blended barrel costs about $600. And should the oil drums tumble from this Shell factory—which they officially don't—add perhaps a few hundred dollars to the sticker price.

Majudell Raham is a master oil-barrel maker at the Shell plant. With a sheet of rolled Colombian steel in his gloved hands, Raham heaves the metal into the "drum rounder," the first of the assembler's four-step process. From there, the tubular sheet goes aboard the "beader flanger" to create the two rims that give an oil drum its industrial musculature and musical resonance. For panmen, what Raham does next is akin to the difference between a fiddle and a Stradivarius. He can either let a computer regulate the flow of the chalky substance that locks in the barrel lids, or he can tweak the stream to his taste. His choice is clear.

"I don't play any musical instruments," Raham says, fine-tuning the surge of sealant. "The barrel seam must fold together. For the sound, I think the solid seam is everything." To ensure that the finished product meets Shell's environmental standards, he checks for leaks and ruptures in the metal.

Back along the banks of the Monongahela River, in the workshop of Mannette Steel Drums Ltd., a set of the maestro's chrome-plated pans can fetch more than $10,000. The result can be heard accompanying the tunes of Harry Belafonte, Alison Krauss, Jimmy Buffett, and the National Symphony Orchestra at the John F. Kennedy Center for the Performing Arts in Washington.

"It's a lot different from the days when I'd go out every morning on my green bicycle to scout empty oil drums," Mannette says, pushing a finger through his crop of curly gray hair. "My gang, the Oval Boys, would go back at night to steal them. We took everything, including garbage cans, but those Shell barrels were gold." During his early years in Trinidad, Mannette estimates he tuned 512 Shell oil pans.

"The sound is completely different," says Narell, who counts a set of early 1960 Mannette pans among his collection. "You'll occasionally spot a vintage Mannette, but the drums are so old that it's hard to find one with the original Shell logo."

Mannette says part of his deal with Mr. Alexis was a promise that the Shell Invaders would always play with the Shell logo on their drums.

"Can't do that any more," Mitchell explains. "Corporate policy prohibits us from putting the logo on our barrels. We don't know where it might show up."

The Shell Invaders no longer exist. Once first among the 150 bands and three thousand drummers who practice in the pan yards along Tragarete Road in Port-of-Spain, Shell disbanded the group in 1974. They reappeared a few years ago as the BWIA Invaders, named for their new underwriter, British West Indian Airways Ltd.

Along the musical thoroughfare, the hippest band these days is the Excellent Stores Silver Stars, named after a supermarket chain. On a recent evening, a few BP Renegades were spotted playing alongside Tony's Ice Cold Coconut Truck in the center of town. They wouldn't say where their barrels came from.

Weekes, the retired Shell Invader, says he knows. "Cairo and I would blend the competition's pans on Shell barrels and then they'd paint BP, Texaco stars, and Mobil flying horses over the Shell clam."

"The panmen still prefer the Shell barrel," insists Miky Galera, Shell Trinidad's aviation fuel manager during the 1960s.

Suppressing a grin, Rosales, Shell's barrel superintendent, says, "I know we make the best musical oil drums in the world."

INDEX

ABOUT THE AUTHOR

A. Craig Copetas, a senior writer at *Bloomberg News* and former staff reporter of *The Wall Street Journal*, is also the author of *Bear Hunting with the Politburo* and of the best-selling *Metal Men*, the story of Marc Rich, at one time America's most-wanted white-collar criminal, prior to his pardon by President Clinton. In the early 1970s, Copetas was a correspondent for *Rolling Stone*'s London bureau and an editor at *Esquire* magazine. He has also been the Moscow correspondent for *Regardie's Magazine* and the *Village Voice*, a columnist at the *International Herald-Tribune*, and a contributing writer to Harper's, the op-ed pages of the *New York Times*, and the *New York Times Magazine*. He has lived and worked in Russia, China, Europe, Latin America, and the Middle East.